Sport's Perfect Storm

AN INDUSTRY NOW TOTALLY ADRIFT

ROGER PAUL MITCHELL

November 2023, Milano

Copyright - Roger Paul Mitchell
Print - Fontegrafica Lab
Layout - Claudia Pagnozzi
Illustrations - Jacopo Ziliotto
Research - Etienne Dussartre

Editor - Albachiara International Srl

FOR ETIENNE

A couple of years ago, a young man from France called Etienne Dussartre came to see me in Como, to offer to help me with this book. An ex pro rugby player, having just finished a Masters in Finance, with fresh eyes on both sport, and the murky world of finance. He has been a true companion on this journey in assisting me. We have challenged each other, argued, and his contribution to the book is all through it. He will have an outstanding career.

FOR TOBY

I'd like to thank Tobias Jones, award-winning author, and my splendid Evertonian in Parma, for showing me how a book should be edited.

FOR MY FAMILY

This book wouldn't have been possible without the encouragement, support and patience of my family, Raffaella, Luca and Valentina.

This book is dedicated to them.

I'm very thankful to Giulia Pagnozzi and Claudia Pagnozzi, whose creativity and dedication went above and beyond what is normal in designing and formatting a self-published edition.

I'd also like to thank Letizia Marazzi for her huge contribution on communication and marketing at 360 degrees.

CONTENTS OF THE BOOK

THE ARTIST'S WAVE

Things just happen.

I spent this summer by the sea, sketching various versions of the powerful undulating motion of the water. Waiting for inspiration for the cover of a book they had commissioned me to draw. I knew that I had an idea for "*Barbarians at the Turnstiles*". But it was being very stubborn in not yet presenting itself to me. I drew more waves.

My pencil sometimes knows things before me. I'm now told the new title of the book is to be Sport's Perfect Storm! Taken by enthusiasm and almost with a mocking sense of cheating, I leaf through my notes and see clearly what was always the meaning of the whole book, with its inevitable proper title... a moment of reset and rebalance. Nature always finds its new balance, sometimes with violence.

I sense all this needed the Perfect Wave, as too many things were out of harmony, too many things were not right. "*This wave MUST be perfect*", I think to myself. Immediately, "*The Great Wave of Kanagawa*" by master Hokusai comes to mind. I look at my own sketches, almost with compassion, I look at Hokusai's wave...and in an instant I see that the perfect wave that will represent the book has to be his. I draw it, unashamedly close to the original, but from there it undergoes a process of adjustment, changes, as the client reacts. The 3 initial boats, which were supposed to represent the industrial sectors (sport, media, finance) about to be overwhelmed, are eliminated. Roger in the water, and then Roger in the background with cocktails in hand, are also eliminated. "*Less is More!*" He keeps repeating to me and I, more annoyed than convinced, just remove. Now only a single boat, without even the name (I had trivially written 'Sport' on the hull), and no longer in Hokusai's pastel "*Eastern sunset*". In a gloomy, dark, distressing sky. And then I add rain ("*not enough*"), I add wind ("*darker!*"), I add lightning. And more rain. And finally, the author is happy. That is, he finds himself in the image that will give shape to his book.

So I look at my perfect storm, satisfied. And I find myself drawn to this handful of men and women, in that boat, dwarfed by the fury of the sea. I desperately hope they will make it. I know, in my heart, that if this happens, it will also be thanks to this book, to which I wish every luck.

JACoPo ZILIoTTo

ETIENNE'S JOURNEY

If the AYNE podcast stood out in the vast sea of sport business content available to me, it's probably because of Roger. His Scottish accent, his unconventional opinions, and his uncanny ability to back them up intrigued me. He would often question what most consider obvious, immutable or even sacred. If the podcast was a must listen, he seemed to be someone I should start following more closely. So when I saw he was looking for someone to help him "break the inertia" with this book, I immediately thought that was for me. Perhaps it was a little naïve coming from a random non-native English speaker, with no corporate experience. Besides, since when do retired athletes write books that neither talk about themselves nor about personal development? Regardless, I had nothing to lose and so much to gain. I had the intuition it could be special.

I reached out to Roger, and he replied by asking me the one thing that mattered: "Do you have a finance background?" I had never thought reading 500 pages of Brealey & Myers during my Masters would finally pay off. I was credible, but to show I was serious, I broke my own inertia and went to meet the man himself in Como. When he eventually told me we would do this book together, I felt incredibly excited. But, similar to what I felt as a young player about to have his baptism of fire with the first team, with excitement also came heavy pressure. Considering Roger's high standards and his audience, I felt the need to excel. The further we progressed into the writing, the more it became apparent that it would be my most significant intellectual challenge. As I reflect on all of this, I believe I responded to the challenge and I am immensely proud to see some of my thoughts disseminated across this book. Invigorating at times and humbling at others, this 18 month journey had a profound impact on me. I learnt far more than I could ever have imagined, which inevitably made me realise how little I initially knew. It is also incredible how everything new suddenly seemed to appear everywhere. In reality, it had always been there, but I just wasn't paying attention. I now see the world, not just the world of sport, with very different eyes.

I would like to sincerely thank Roger for giving me such an opportunity and trusting me to deliver. If anything, a rugby career teaches you how valuable that is. But more importantly I would like to thank him for giving me a goal. Transitioning away from professional sport is not easy as life can suddenly seem painfully boring. Having something tangible and meaningful that you can work towards and get excited about, is essential. For this, I am especially grateful.

One of our goals was to write the book I would have loved to have read as a young student. We wanted it to be as insightful as entertaining. I think we succeeded and I hope many of you will enjoy the reading.

ETIENNE DUSSARTRE

Sport's Perfect Storm

INTRODUCTION

"The fog's just lifting. Throw off your bow line; throw off your stern. You head out to South channel, past Rocky Neck, Ten Pound Island. Past Niles Pond where I skated as a kid. Blow your air-horn and throw a wave to the lighthouse keeper's kid on Thatcher Island. Then the birds show up: black backs, herring gulls, big dumb ducks. The sun hits ya – head North. Open up to 12 – steamin' now. The guys are busy; you're in charge. Ya know what? You're a goddamn sword-boat captain. Is there anything better in the world?"
George Clooney (Captain Billy Tyne) in "The Perfect Storm"

It is often the most calm and tranquil just before the biggest storm. This book is about three very interconnected industries, sport, media, and finance, now all facing hurricane headwinds, where many of the passengers on their boats have no real idea of the impending doom coming their way. And even if they did, they wouldn't be ready.

Sport is something I really care about. It is passion, loyalty, and irrationality, it provides us our tribe, our generational bonding, our diary of memories, and the film score of our lives. It is something bigger than us. I'm a classic hard finance guy who has personally seen, from the inside, both the publishing and music businesses utterly disrupted; and now watches with dread as the sequel unfolds in my current sector of sport. This book will try to explain to that industry from where the multiple storm clouds will come, and what we can perhaps do to prepare ourselves.

In their book The Fourth Turning, Strauss and Howe put forward a thesis that our world is cyclical and changes every *"saeculum"* (a long human life, which usually spans between 80 and 100 years), when new thinking attacks and weakens institutions. It is 78 years since the end of WW2 and the start of the Boomer generation. This book will argue that sport itself is at its own Fourth Turning and is losing what is called its *"product market fit"* with younger generations.

In the early 50s, a strikingly handsome young man called Elvis Aaron Presley walked into his first recording studio in Memphis and changed the world of popular culture forever. His generation instantly knew something different had arrived. John Lennon commented *"nothing really affected me until Elvis."* On hearing him, Bob Dylan said *"it was like busting out of jail"*. Elvis spoke to a moment in time, to a new generation who knew nothing of the Depression and war. The *"adults"* and the incumbent powers at the time missed the point completely, calling Elvis a *"threat to moral wellbeing… personification of evil, n**** music, a savage."* Even the sainted Frank Sinatra called him *"deplorable, rancid, destructive to young people".*

As with Elvis then, there is today a vehemence of denial, and a violence of attack, towards new versions of sport as entertainment, from what generously are called *"legacy fans".*

Substitute the crooner and jazz devotees back then, outraged by the new Rock'n'Roll, with today's traditional golf aficionado, or the lower league football fan, and you can see history, if not repeating, certainly rhyming. Sport would do well to take note of the fate of popular music from the moment the King arrived. In simple language, the risk is that the new audiences of today may not be as into it as Boomers were, and, if so, that has major implications.

This industry has enjoyed two generations of riches, from a florid and competitive media sector buying its rights, to a massive influx of low-cost easy capital from Big Finance. These two macro trends have pushed the valuation of sports assets everywhere through the roof, but that boat is now taking on water, with the media sector itself needing to re-invent its business model, and capital suddenly getting very expensive. If its funders and bankers are sneezing, sport is going to catch a very bad cold.

Without doubt, the future of the creative industries is now extrinsically linked to Big Finance. But banking, debt, and the capital markets are not well understood by my colleagues, as in many ways they are polar opposites. Sport for example is about tradition, emotion, loyalty, unscripted drama, victory and tragedy, heroes and redemption stories, and the fabric of society. Finance instead is cold, about numbers in spreadsheets, and return on capital. Crucially, one of them loves uncertainty and risk, the other despises it. This book will explain the general principles of finance to our sector of sport and entertainment, badly in need of fresh capital, but terrified that taking it will damn its soul. It will explain the intelligent use of finance techniques to reduce risk profiles and make for better operational management, decision-making, and real sustainability. Equally, I'd like to offer established providers of capital the context and insight into the cultural differences in sport, that can derail even the most robust due diligence, and modelling of return. Where is there hidden risk that needs to be factored in?

In my own personal journey, from a young Scottish Chartered Accountant, an auditor, to an investment banker, a corporate CFO, and finally a venture capitalist, it is only now that I truly realise what finance actually is, and what it is trying to achieve. The eyes of the newly qualified accountant in 1983 have very little in common with those of today's experienced corporate financier. One of the aims of this book is to help students and newcomers to understand these differences. Because the type of career you will have is dependent on how quickly you understand that.

On the bookshelf of anyone who has studied finance, hidden away in some top corner, there will be a very particular textbook called Principles of Corporate Finance, by Brealey and Myers. This book was first published in 1980, by coincidence my own first year of university, and remains to this day the cornerstone of any finance profession. We all must pass through that particular lecture room and the material is neither the easiest nor the most entertaining. To add to the challenge, finance often gets confused by the lay person with accounting and economics (both micro and macro). We hope to break down some of the barriers to entry of the old book, to make it accessible and understandable to as many people as possible. That is not simple, because much of finance is a hard, maths-based *"science"*, whereas the best and most valuable bits, around capital structuring, creative accounting and intellectual property (IP) are arguably *"art"*. This book wants to bring that out via examples in our industry, and with the right context.

Many think the world of finance is also living its own Fourth Turning, the end of years of cheap money. The old demon of inflation is again rearing its head, bank *"runs"* are back in the headlines, all undermining people's faith in the role of money. This book will explain how, in the 40-year period since Brealey and Myers, the world has entered a parallel universe of voodoo-finance, that those authors themselves would struggle to recognise. They would look around for a couple of days, as if on the Yellow Brick Road, and stutter *"we aren't in Kansas now"*. Many of the basic tenets of our monetary system have been turned upside down, and we are now entering a world of finance that anyone younger than 50 probably hasn't yet experienced. They are a generation that has only known a bull market of ever-increasing valuation and share prices, where a rising tide has made a genius of everyone. This book will seek to help them understand the old principles of *"return"* and traditional *"value investing"*, known to many as The Warren Buffet Way.

Being an investor in early-stage sport technology companies, I have lived the incredible growth of the Palo Alto venture capital industry and its attitude to finance called the Silicon Valley Playbook. More and more people, and indeed athletes, are now investing into such start-ups, so the playbook needs explaining. It has developed its own way to value companies and quantify intangible assets and IP; things called *"per user unit economics."* Given that the world's biggest companies come from this culture, the book wants to explain what has dominated value-creation in this new millennium to date. If we are now seeing a return to a more traditional *"value"* based mentality, where does that leave us, and where does it leave sport?

This book hopes to be both an SOS call, and a compass for an entire sector. Always asking if you are entertained.

Foreword

SYMPATHY FOR THE DEVIL

"Please allow me to introduce myself I'm a man of wealth and taste. I've been around for a long, long year. Stole million man's soul an faith"

As I finished this book, what I concluded is that this is really a story of temptation, and what the dark forces of Mammon may reap upon the purity of our world of sport, if left untethered. The author, my fellow Glaswegian, has a penchant for the theological and the eternal struggle between the forces of good and evil. For him, Lucifer exists.

So Sympathy for the Devil seemed so apposite for his Foreword.

In what is considered one of that band's most iconic songs, Jagger seemingly is sneering at us, as if with some kind of inside knowledge on the subject at hand. The lyrics of Sir Mick, rock music's greatest frontman, and member of the Marleybone Cricket Club, suggest a seductive and sinister empathy with Beelzebub that is, in my opinion, thoroughly influenced by Soviet author Mikhail Bulgakov, and his novel Master And Margarita. This book has been so profound also for Charlie and I. In it the Russian playwrite imagines a most charming, socialite version of the devil in Moscow, dispensing lessons on truth and morality, raining down all manner of chaos and calamity on that city's most gilded and stultifyingly hypocritical class.

Roger's book reeks of similar metaphors. The finance guys always look good don't they? And sport isn't such a stranger to hyprocrisy.

Jagger himself has always side-stepped enquiries as to the Satan-centric lyrics of Sympathy.

"Naaah! It's so much more about the darker nature of man - than celebrating the devil."

One wonders though. Too many dots seem to join up perhaps. The Stones idolised Robert Johnson, otherwise known as *"The King of The Delta Blues,"* and *"The Father of Rock 'n Roll."* Legend has it that he willingly sold his soul to the devil at the crossroads of Highways 49 and 61 in Clarksdale, Mississippi. The Faustian pact made that day bestowed on Johnson a talent and technique so good that the world wholeheartedly bought into the notion that he had to be operating from another wholly much darker realm.

Much in the same way I myself have always felt watching Diego Maradona, leaving me still, all these years later, to question whether I actually saw those things in that football stadium in the shadow of a volcano in Napoli. Or, had I been hallucinating?

Jagger's co-composer Keith Richards, someone always rather more relaxed about, well, just about everything, doesn't diminish any of this intrigue.

"Aw, come on Man! 'Sympathy' is quite an uplifting song really. It's just a matter of looking the devil in the face isn't it? Cat's there all the time. But if you confront Lucifer, he's out of a job. It's all about how you deal with him. Right?"

This book's soul to me is about sport needing to confront and deal with him, with the source of all evil; money! Undoubtedly this industry is set to enter an entirely new age, approaching its very own crossroads; its Perfect Storm. Temptations all around ominously threaten the health and purity of its existence as we have come to know it.

So I would suggest that it's worth your time to *"batten down the hatches"* and meditate a while on all that this book has to offer.

You may find it good for the soul!

JIM KERR
Taormina, Sicily. September 2023.

Part One:
Sport Isn't A Normal Asset

Chapter One

AN EPHEMERAL AND ECLECTIC ASSET

The history of our civilisations has been a story of Gods and Heroes, and perhaps there is something very deep in the human psyche that makes us look for someone to put on a pedestal.

Today, our hero fixation, our need for someone in whom to believe, is now perhaps directed solely to sport, and the elite athlete. Its origin story, from Greece, to Rome, via Victorian codification, absolutely matters to us all on a human, emotional and societal level. Any attempt to describe it narrowly, in the words of Mammon, as a product or a business, is received by many as heresy.

Sport matters, and always has.

But can that still be taken for granted? And is its importance still the same for everyone?

Evidence would suggest that younger generations today consider sport and its protagonists merely comparable to other modern forms of entertainment and leisure pastime, as simply content, actors, talent, influencers. It is so much more.

For many boys of my generation, it has been a rare place of male bonding, where each week people visit nondescript stadia of minor teams, up and down every country, and enter some kind of metaphysical trance, in memory of the long-dead man who first took them to this magical place. Their tears and regret for those relationships are, in all truth, stronger in these bleachers than at his graveside. This was their place, talking of their hopes and dreams, their joys and disappointments, also in life itself. These green fields in fact broke down, more than anywhere else, the eternal awkwardness of male bonding, and endless father-and-son silences. As the industry now finally opens its doors to the other half of the population it has to date ignored, a whole army of young girls will soon feel the same. They will find their own belonging and meaning as a participant and a fan.

All of this is the very definition of an intangible asset. The French football philosopher king, Eric Cantona, puts this best:

"You can change your wife, politics & religion. But never, never can you change your favourite football team."

True, but things can change. They can evolve. We are now living in a world of increasing *"cross-over"* in entertainment, where genres of content, taste, and audience are proactively encouraged to blend into each other. There is no longer any real collective noun for *"sport"* or *"the fan"*, and this fragmentation has now delivered us a tapestry of a thousand segments and definitions.

This notwithstanding, anyone who disrespects sport, underestimates the depth of its emotional roots, or tries to apply some other set of corporate standards to it, will get a very sore face. The best example of this would be the 24-hour implosion of the proposed European Football Super League, where a very credible *"business"* case for new structures and formats was utterly torched in less than a day, in a frenzy of outrage from politicians to postmen.

Sport is never going to passively accept its role as mere entertainment and content, battling gamely for attention in a time-poor world. It's too proud for that. And rightly so. It exists in a complex minestrone of what modern marketers call *"purpose"*, with a capital P.

At the time of writing, I, like many fans, have our *"product"* on in the background, in this case the Ashes series. At Lords, the home of English cricket, we saw unprecedented scenes of very mature and distinguished men spitting fury at the Australian players in the historic Long Room, for what they saw as a ruthless act of gamesmanship, that was *"not in the spirit of the game"*. This wasn't a *"debate"* about sport as content, sport as a business; this was about its true meaning. Pure philosophy, about how one wins, and what lines one should or shouldn't cross, in the endeavour. As in the old days of duelling, this was a deadly serious matter around honour.

The American Jack Nicklaus is the most successful golfer of all time. He has won more of the big prizes than anyone, and is a true icon. Yet, arguably he is remembered most (fondly) not for winning all these pots and medals, but for his amazing generosity to his rival in the decisive Ryder Cup tie in 1969. The Concession, where he doesn't ask his rival Tony Jacklin to hole his very missable last putt, is burned in every golf fan's brain. Its glory is boundless.

"I don't believe you would have missed that, but I'd never give you the opportunity, in these circumstances."
Jack Nicklaus

The *"circus"* in Juvenal's *"bread and circuses"* is a Roman poet's attempt to explain all these intangibles around the role of sport. Sometimes it's not just about the winning; indeed, simple arithmetic will always remind us that most of sport is de facto populated by losers, and their fans. The circus works because it has the clown as well as the lion tamer. Heroes and villains, winners and losers. Triumph and defeat. Perhaps, in fact, not winning is the very essence of sport, its real truth?

All this is complex and nuanced, full of different perspectives, that some of the more recent investors into the sector may find rather quaint, but it is the key to understanding sport as an asset class.

The fact remains that the fan(atic) is not the simple, easily classified, beast he/she may appear. Talk to them during the passions of the actual event, and then the day after, and you could be speaking to two entirely different people. So, trying to manage and control that, especially when money and finance is introduced, is exceptionally difficult, requiring, at minimum, dollops of emotional quotient (EQ). In fact, to labour the point with a personal example, let's visit Juvenal's Rome itself, the capital city of EQ, to show why sport, achievement and business can never be a one-dimensional, linear economic relationship. And can't ever be adequately represented with an excel model.

I lived in Rome for some years. Life there is not easy: terrible traffic; inefficiencies; rubbish and dirt on the streets; charlatans and bureaucrats galore; problems on every corner. And yet, none of all that matters. When you least expect it, that city will take you aside and whisper in your ear:

"Stop, look around at where you are, just smile, laugh, love!"

It is a city of sfumature (nuances) where there is a premium on the intangible; of relationships, beauty, life and art. Simply think of the best Roman films from the likes of Federico Fellini, or Sorrentino's La Grande Bellezza. It's not the plot that captures you, it's all the colour. Unsurprisingly, then, that football there is difficult to describe, but means everything. There is no clear plot to follow, only a million colours and emotions, the understanding of which is central to everything we will say in this book about investing, and managing, in this industry.

When Jim Pallotta, a very successful Bostonian financier, bought AS Roma in 2012, it was reported that he felt that he had done the business deal of the century. A proper club with the enormous competitive advantage of a huge catchment area of talent, a world-class city brand, and the most passionate of loyal fans, also with a low bar of expectations. Perfect. He was getting an underperforming asset with significant potential, at a distressed valuation (of perhaps less than $100m to start). In business and finance terms, Pallotta was right to smell a great deal. The due diligence stood up.

That's not however how it played out, with him neither achieving sporting honours, nor building the new stadium, nor finding a cultural empathy with the local heroes of Francesco Totti and Daniele De Rossi. And definitely not making any financial return. In fact, he cashed in his chips after 10 years of grind, likely just breaking even. Milano Finanza, the financial journal of some weight, calculated that Pallotta barely got back the total €260m he invested. Not good business after 10 years. He'd have been better buying a widget factory.

Does that make the Bostonian a bad investor? If Jim Pallotta has any fault, it's maybe in trying to manage a sports franchise like any other business asset, when it is better described as an emotional state of mind.

The key to understanding football clubs like AS Roma is to feel their particular and unique history and context; in this case the Eternal City itself. The Romans ruled the world with unchallenged superiority for such a long time, in combat, culture, society, rule of law, that they found themselves with no real rivals. They were so far ahead that they started to get bored, and began killing each other in jealousy, getting lost in depravity and excess. Never since, therefore, has this ancient and glorious city aspired to rule the world, or even been focussed solely on competing hard for excellence. They've done that empire dominance thing, and perhaps life for them now is simply for living. Maybe it is a post-modern mindset, where success is defined differently; where winning, for many of them, is overrated and not essential. So, every September, AS Roma supporters will sup at a tavern of hope and glory, knowing deep down it will be futile. They will almost certainly lose. They know this, the club knows it, the players know it, the city knows it. Only the "*how*" is uncertain. This tavern is however a magical place of irresistible seduction in late summer. Evenings full of bella gente, people with perfect tans and handsome white shirts, all walking the cobbled stones of Trastevere, to an impossibly charming trattoria of incredible food. Overly intense discussions of new signings are interrupted only for the passerella of stunning girls that Rome offers with unnerving frequency. It's a brief pause, with nodded heads, before returning to the serious matter of fullbacks and wingers. Early weeks of the season can be thrilling, and side-splitting humour will fill the air on the back of the regular promising starts to the campaign. Winter, however, usually brings harsh reality back to the city and the team, whose hopes are turned off, like the central heating in February.

The insight and added value in allocating capital well in this industry is always in seeing and feeling this kind of context.

"Better to lose, with our identity, rather than winning with outsiders and mercenaries".

I don't think Pallotta fully got this about that city. I know I didn't when I arrived. Would he have behaved in any way differently if he had heard it before?

As an "*asset*", sport is ephemeral and eclectic, certainly fragile, and a businessperson has no chance of managing it, for return, without understanding all of this. You can't judge AS Roma, or the Packers in Green Bay, or the Lakers in Inglewood, in a normal business school way. Sport operates on different metrics, with different key performance indicators (KPIs). It is, in the language of finance, the ultimate example of the Balanced Scorecard. A scorecard that in any city will read with the local version of these intangibles. Sport matters, yes, but one always needs to understand why. It's never going to be the same everywhere.

This is the exact opposite of a homogenous asset class.

I'm from Glasgow, another one of those crazy cities of intense football passion, where the actual sport, the match itself, pales into insignificance compared to this wider meaning. The insights are again around *"passion"* but for very different reasons. In Scotland, politics, society, the establishment, business, and the professions, have never really gotten over the trauma of the Reformation. Scotland is a country that doesn't just have memories from all that; it still has open wounds. Scottish football is therefore a story of two tribes, Catholics and Protestants, fighting an ongoing proxy religious war, via two football teams, Celtic and Rangers. There is really nothing that can describe the emotions that are felt in Glasgow when these two play each other, in what is called the Old Firm derby. And if you are in some way a protagonist in all this drama, as I was when I ran Scottish football as CEO/Commissioner, it tests you in ways that will mark you for life.

As a corporate financier, I can quickly and easily deliver a very decent financial analyst report on the listed asset called Celtic PLC, and its forecasts, strategies and valuation. But I would need days to explain to you what that club really means, and why.

Roma and Celtic are merely two personal examples that make the point that every fresh investor into sport should digest.

Understanding these examples, and this industry in general, is a real test of your IQ and EQ at the best of times, but now it's even harder, as we enter a moment of changing tastes, volatile financial markets, rampant corporate raiders, and a generational passing of the baton.

When I reflect on this over a cigarette and Prosecco here in Como, I see sport as a tiny fragile sailing boat of intense beauty that has lost its compass, adrift in very uncertain and dangerous waters. We all want this boat to get to shore safely, and survive this perfect storm, but to do that we need to know the direction to port, what needs to be done to get there; and especially what must and can be thrown overboard to save us.

To achieve all this, we need to understand sport's context and from where it comes. In everything, the past is always prologue.

Chapter Two

CREATIVE INDUSTRIES: A QUESTION OF BALANCE

Sport is part of what are called *"the creative industries"*.

Many of the people in these sectors have a troubled relationship with the business side of their profession.

My own experience in advertising agencies, publishing houses, the music business, and sport, has a clear fil rouge, a common thread running through everything. Whether it is the moody and difficult creative director in advertising, or the arty book-publishing editor fed up with his imprint investing in celebrity recipe books, or even Martin Scorsese lamenting about the lack of courage and imagination in Hollywood, these *"special product"* sectors, these creative industries, have always had philosophical and practical issues with making money.

Notably, in recent years, Scorsese has lamented how much of today's movie production investment goes only towards established franchise movies like Marvel and DC Comics, leaving the long tail of quirky arthouse offerings, that appeal to niche audiences, scrambling for pennies:

"That's not cinema. Honestly, the closest I can think of these films, as well made as they are, with actors doing the best they can under the circumstances, is as theme parks. It isn't the cinema of human beings trying to convey emotional, psychological experiences to another human being".

Artistically, one can certainly have sympathy with Scorsese, but the reply always just follows the money.

Matt Damon was recently asked why certain niche audience films don't get made anymore:

"I talked to a studio executive who explained the economics of a $25m movie. They would then have to put that much again into print and advertising (P&A) to market it... so now they are in for $50m dollars. Anything they make needs shared with the exhibitor, the people who own the movie theatres, so they would now have to make $100m just to break even, and the idea of making that much on a story about this love affair between these two people...that's suddenly a massive gamble".

This is a wonderful example of how finance thinks, and business works. It balances risk and reward every single day, and creators have never been passive in accepting this. In my own experience, the complaints seldom come at the start of careers, when wide-eyed youngsters are looking for a break and a financial backer. They surface a bit later, when perhaps the conscience and soul of the *"artist"* starts to bother them, long after they have resolved their chronic *"being talented but broke"* problem.

Some then attack those same original backers, with resentful zeal. Understandable but a bit unfair, I've always felt. In 1975, EMI's Pink Floyd recorded the track *"Have a Cigar"*, as a fierce critique of what they saw as the rampant greed and cynicism of the music industry:

"And did we tell you the name of the game, boy? We call it riding the gravy train".

Perhaps not a track they would have written when gasping for a recording deal years before.

Many reject any comparisons between sport and the music industry, but they are wrong. Anyone who, like me, has inhabited both sectors knows the truth that is common to both.

At the end of the day, investors and owners are looking to earn a return on capital, to make money.

We can all fall in love with a very special product, but it is still a business.

Between 1994-98, I worked in the last great years of the music industry for Virgin, Richard Branson's iconic label, part of EMI. The music industry was and is dominated by the major labels, big companies like EMI, Universal, Sony and Bertelsmann, whose task, to be clear, is to make regular money from what is at its core a volatile product, created by unpredictable and emotional artists. It is not a stable industry, and makes for delicate management, especially if, like EMI PLC, the company is listed.

Earnings in any publicly quoted company should ideally be smoothed out, in a gentle yearly increase. In the creative industries, that is not a banal ask, especially when shareholders won't have a lot of sympathy if Mariah Carey has a nervous breakdown and doesn't release her scheduled new album that year. They will still want the usual growth in earnings, that the public markets demand.

For precisely this reason, of trying to create stability amongst inherent volatility, the CEOs of these music labels know exactly what makes money for them, what is likely to be a reliable blockbuster, and what instead is new and unproven. And they act to position their company accordingly, finding a strategic equilibrium, between exploiting established catalogue like Pink Floyd, and trying to break new acts, creating the catalogue of tomorrow. The former is on average a wonderful high-margin business, the latter is risky and uncertain.

That's one of the great skills of the music business; finding that balance between the two and knowing exactly the right moment you can take on more risk. In strategic consulting terms, it's the balance between monetising your *"cashcow"*, and investing in tomorrow's *"stars"*.

All of the creative industries and companies know this. A fashion house is clear on what product is for the runway and the brand, and what product makes the money, putting the logo on a wallet or perfume.

Every great music or fashion executive will try and find the right balance between the glory of proper art, and the need to make money for shareholders. The leaders at a label understand lucidly the difference between *"real deal"* artists, who often are not so commercial, and what is just bubble-gum music for hitting budget. Music CEOs accept that they don't just sell one product, but many, all with different profiles of risk and reward.

All that is very difficult to pull off, and needs cold clarity as to the role each different product plays, either as brand and authenticity, or as revenue-generating; and ideally sometimes both.

At EMI we had artists like old jazz guitarist John Lee Hooker, who certainly wasn't selling big numbers, but did wonders for our credibility and brand. We also had the golden catalogue of true music, from Beatles, Pink Floyd, Queen, to newer art like Radiohead and Smashing Pumpkins.

Authentic music, like authentic sport, isn't a normal product, and is always to be cherished. This special stuff is of course deliberately mixed in with less worthy, mass-market product; things like the Spice Girls or BackStreet Boys. The Girl Power band was a commercial *"product"*, with a label's manufactured vision on the concept, the personalities, the music, the audience, and the marketing. It wasn't art; but goodness did it make the EMI PLC numbers sing.

On Virgin, Scottish superstar band Simple Minds had exploded in 1985 in the States with *"Don't You Forget About Me"*, a song they didn't write, as a soundtrack for the zeitgeist movie of the era, *"The Breakfast Club"*. Unsurprisingly, the label and the money men wanted more of the same for the band's next album. Because the best de-risked benchmark you have, to make consistent money for your shareholders, especially in tough times, is just repeating what has worked before and has already proven its product/market mix.

Sadly, one could argue, artists don't think like that, at least not the real ones. They believe that there is a truth to their work; that they are expressing themselves and pouring out their soul on a recording. Often, they go into the studio and don't even know themselves what they are about to compose.

The Simple Minds artists, Jim Kerr and Charlie Burchill, didn't feel any real connection with the Breakfast Club *"pop"* music, and instead developed as artists, in that moment of their lives, in the completely different direction of *"Mandela Day"* and *"Belfast Child"*. As an executive, there is not much you can do about all that, and you can't tell real artists what to write.

But that doesn't stop the music industry from often trying, so it's no surprise that so many of the true artists of the 70s and 80s, like Pink Floyd, Prince, George Michael, all ended up rebelling.

In the creative industries you are not in the business of selling soap; you are commercialising passion and emotion. You can't create those to order the way an impatient *"suit"* would want. You most definitely cannot tell a real artist what to create next. Queen were told to do another *"Killer Queen"* type song for the radios; they ignored that and recorded the 9-minute-long *"Bohemian Rhapsody"*.

From all this it should be clear that the sports industry is, a generation later, facing so many of the same issues, around what is authentic. Trying to find a balance with the *"real-deal"* product; whilst making ends meet, by providing the media sector with what it wants.

Pink Floyd's gravy train, of following the money, will take sport fully in the direction of the Spice Girls, if untethered.

And when a recession comes, and monies to spend get ever tighter, the decision-makers will double-down on going safe and commercial in choosing the product in which to invest. They will see what has worked financially before, and for what audience.

That outcome would be unfortunate, as the essence, glory and art of sport is finding a way to stay pure at its core, and write:

"mama... just killed a man..."

That's the prize in all this debate. Protecting the authenticity of sport, whilst making the necessary return on capital. We as an industry must therefore challenge ourselves to strive for the right balance of product, categorised as Hollywood versus Arthouse, and try to make them live in harmony in a way that works for passionate fans and investors alike. In this fiendishly difficult mission, it would be a deadly mistake for this industry to have too many absolutes and sacred cows. Some of our *"darlings"* may need to go.

Sport, and its administrators, media and fans, still haven't fully grasped this need for balance, compromise and sacrifice, and all too often today we see them rage passionately against what they see as the dying of the light.

They have little understanding of what drives show-biz and media-biz thinking, a record label mentality, a publisher's model, any content business really. They are too stuck on creating siege barriers to protect what they see as the purity and truth of sport, misreading entirely where it now sits in the entertainment landscape. They don't understand that it is a business for a return. And if the business isn't working, the whole fairground will stop.

Unscripted drama might be the best product, but it is not necessarily the best business!

This is the nub of the problem. If Scorsese or sport doesn't want to act and make choices like a proper business, it shouldn't put itself in a position to need a businessperson's money.

But it does.

To make and promote a film, or to run a European sports club, requires a lot of money or risk capital. There is a huge upfront cost of talent and event delivery that needs to be recovered. Executives responsible for a Profit and Loss Account will more and more only do that with products that have proven brand stars and audience. Because taking the extra risk could be career-ending for them personally.

The media and finance sectors will therefore need to *"educate"* sport as to what works for capital; be that new leagues and formats, and/or a predominance of the biggest names. Combat sports between YouTubers or influencers has proven this point.

Overtime has built sports leagues from a media brand around high school basketball. Kings League indoor football is full of gimmicks to keep newer audiences engaged. New sports are now being created in the first instance as entertainment content, using people who already have an audience.

Indeed, it could be argued today that *"audience"* dictates and informs the offerings of sport, and not vice versa. That is a dramatic change, philosophically reminiscent of Plutarch's Essays and Miscellanies, asking whether it is the egg or the chicken that comes first.

Sadly, for the sector, it has in recent years stubbornly continued to prioritise the format, the product, the traditional way of things, over finding a balanced business model. It has only sought out new audiences around the edges, without any real belief or commitment. That tinkering hasn't really worked in traditional sports, with the average age of the fan continuing to get older and older.

Taking the examples of the US, the graph below illustrates the average age of fans of the 3 main sporting codes.

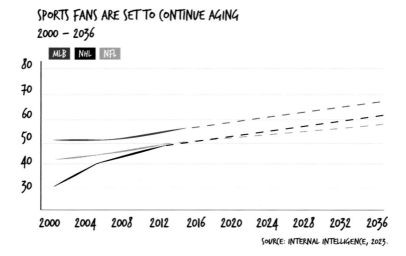

SPORTS FANS ARE SET TO CONTINUE AGING
2000 – 2036

SOURCE: INTERNAL INTELLIGENCE, 2023.

To date, the sports industry hasn't managed this polarisation and balance at all well. It has railed against innovation, looked down its nose on new ideas, and laughed at the imagination of new formats. Gen Z is as a consequence losing interest.

GEN ZERS ARE ABOUT HALF AS LIKELY AS MILLENIALS TO WATCH SPORTS OFTEN, TWICE AS LIKELY TO NEVER WATCH

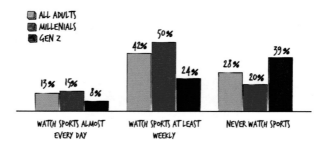

SOURCE: MORNING CONSULT, 2020.

The slugfest of T20 cricket is a financially successful product enjoying mass popularity; but the 5-day test match is the soul of this most historic of sports. An investor wants the former financially successful output; the real win for this industry is securing a future for the latter.

What our industry misses is the idea of finding a balance, where both Black Label Armani, and Emporio Armani, have a role to play. We need to find that future for the sports industry with product and brand differentiation, segmented strategic marketing, all driven by serious balanced risk management.

In the creative industries, it's always a question of that balance.

Chapter Three

THE SPIRIT OF THE GAME

During the Battle of Marathon in 490BC, the Greek messenger Philippides witnessed a Persian vessel changing its course towards Athens. It is said that he then ran the entire distance to that city without stopping, discarding his weapons and clothes, losing as much weight as possible, burst into the assembly with the news, before collapsing and dying. The modern race and its distance is his legacy.

The origin story of sport isn't banal or forced. Whether ancient Greece, Corinth, Roman chariots, or medieval tales of horses, archery, jousting, and swords, sport has always been central to the lore of our history, from that Greek messenger to Ben Hur; from Robin Hood to the musketeer D'Artagnan. Anyone today wanting to engage with this industry, especially in Europe, needs to know well its past.

Sport is, at its core, epic, and that ethos comes not just from intense competition, but from the idea of a rite of passage, the physical and mental testing of a man, (it was men back then), very much linked to his ancient role as protector, hunter-gather, soldier and head of the family. Sportsmanship as a consequence was, and is, a synonym of honour, endeavour, commitment, excellence, and especially never cheating. In the halls of one of the great theatres of sport, Wimbledon's All England Tennis Club, Rudyard Kipling sets out this credo best:

"If you can meet with Triumph and Disaster, and treat those two impostors just the same... yours is the Earth and everything that's in it, and - which is more - you'll be a Man, my son!"

To some, especially younger generations, all this may sound a bit *"cringe"*; but even to them, it must surely be very apparent that sport with this heritage can never be considered as simply throw-away, transient, snackable content. It's deep inside our soul as humans; perhaps much more than we realise. And, it has utterly informed the development of our modern societies.

During Victoria's Industrial Revolution, sport began its process of a more formal organisation and codification, basically via Britain's elite public schools. It's very important to appreciate that sport back then was born, and seen by society, as character building, to toughen up the young men, in preparation for them to rule Her Majesty's Empire. Most modern sports started exactly like this, as this pastime of the wealthy and middle class, on the playing fields of England's Jerusalem.

The best examples of all this, football and rugby in the late 19th century, come exactly from two such prominent English public schools, Rugby and Eton. At the former, their rules for progressing the ball upfield included the possibility of using hands, and the game we today know as rugby was born. At Eton, the ball was moved exclusively with the feet, and developed into modern association football. So, if Brits globally have always been known stereotypically for their stoicism, stiff upper lips, and sense of fair play, it's going to be fairly intuitive that so much of sport's character will reflect all that DNA, even to this day.

The traditional English spirit of the game therefore absolutely matters, with roots so profound, spreading far from its home village greens, to now every corner of the globe.

Britain's historic schools, their masters, their pupils, have always considered sport absolutely as Corinthian and amateur, and indeed rather elitist if truth be told. It's actually a very fair representation of England's class system of the time. One could debate with credibility that many of sport's flaws in 2023 come from a belief that this world still exists, or should. We all need to recognise that sport at this core comes from old money, old privilege, and will always tend to look down its nose at any nouveau riche trying to make a buck from what they created for more glorious reasons. They may not say it, but by God, they are thinking it. These 19th century sportsmen in the main never needed money from the sport itself, so they never have had any real imperative to make themselves profitable and attractive to providers of capital.

The old British pastimes of football, rugby, tennis, golf, cricket, horse racing/eventing, and even modern athletics, will never ever willingly see themselves as a business asset. Tennis and golf have remained to this day remarkably amateur in mentality and governance. Rugby Union didn't turn professional until 1995 and its rulers still haven't really changed in mentality.

Football however, whilst from the same stock, has taken a very different route, worthy of serious study in a business book. It is the biggest sport in the world, appealing today to an audience well well beyond its Downton Abbey origins. Almost immediately, it very quickly became the dominant leisure entertainment for the British working classes, who, crucially, were the beating heart of the Empire, delivering the labour and sweat in the industrial cities of the island.

Football soon became the property of the working man, soothing his pain after his week in a mine, a factory, a shipbuilding yard, becoming of truly vital importance for the social stability of Britain. The local football club offered a sense of belonging to a community, and something of which to be really proud, when precious little else lifted the monotony, grind and gloom of the factory smog. So as the steam engine heralded the start of the industrial revolution, football pioneered the industry of organised professional sport that took root 150 years ago. And, as always, products that gain mass popularity drag money into the picture pretty close behind. The elite players, very soon became assets to be acquired, and market forces made their first appearance.

ASSOCIATION FOOTBALL TURNS PROFESSIONAL

Blackburn Olympic, a team composed mainly of factory workers, won the 1883 FA Cup Final, as the first working-class team to claim the competition since its inception in 1870. Tellingly, although professionalism was actually not permitted, Blackburn had arranged jobs for their players in the town, supplementing their income with additional payments. This wheeze caught on and became immediately a gold-rush race to recruit footballing talents for cash, especially from Scotland where the players had adopted a much sought-after advanced passing version of the game. These *"Scotch Professors"* were the Barcelona Cantera talent factory of their day, and they all flooded south to make themselves a better life. Northern England, and especially Lancashire clubs like Bolton, went all-in on this *"shamateurism"*, and in the inaugural season of the Football League (1888–89), champions Preston North End fielded ten Scottish professionals. At the same time, in Sunderland, the wealthy mine owner Samuel Tyzack funded the professional advancement of the club, often pretending to be a priest while scouting for players in Scotland. The devastating power of football had started to make itself apparent, and that trend would, from there, never reverse. In panicked response, the self-appointed amateur governing body of football, the FA, tried unsuccessfully to put nationality restrictions in place. But, in a phrase oft-used in this book, *"you cannot buck the market"*. After Preston North End won an FA Cup match in 1884 against Upton Park, the Londoners protested, demanding the result be overturned due to the presence of paid players in the Preston ranks. Preston withdrew from the competition, and fellow Lancashire clubs Burnley and Great Lever followed suit. The protest gathered momentum to the point where more than 30 clubs, predominantly from the north, announced that they would set up a rival governing body, the British Football Association, if the FA did not permit professionalism.

The very governance of the game was coming under challenge, with clear differences between the amateur idealists from southern England and the increasingly professionalised teams from northern industrial towns. 18 months later the FA relented, and in July 1885 professionalism was formally legalised in England. The restrictions on Scottish players collapsed by 1889. This is the first and still best example of the economics of cold money dictating the future of what was set up as an amateur, Corinthian sport. The parallels with today's football are there for all to see. Players, earning their living from the game, will always go where the money is. Football took off, with unprecedented numbers of spectators, up to 80,000 in the late 19th century, and the world would never be the same again. It had arrived and was universal, with no barriers to entry. The game would soon expand overseas, carried from Britain to the Empire, and beyond. For example, many of the teams in Italy like Milan and Genoa, are steeped in English culture, and have the flag of St George in their crest, and English spelling of their names. They also, to this day, all call their coaches *"Mister"* because of a certain William Garbutt who became manager of Genoa in 1912. He was always to be called *"Mr Garbutt"*. This is not a here-today-gone-tomorrow product.

Professional sport, in this first guise of working-class industrial football, representing a factory town, was generally *"funded"* by a local businessman, often the owner of that same factory or mill, and was seen by him (or her) as a mix between a trophy asset, employee motivation, and a community popularity tool.

This on reflection makes abundant sense, as life on the factory line, building ships, down a mine, was barely tolerable, with workers prone to understandable strike actions of protest. In hindsight, it is clear that the owner's *"investment"* into the football team, his mens' leisure time and happiness, was in reality some kind of quid pro quo:

"I can't pay you what you want but I can invest to give you a splendid sports team to enjoy on a Saturday afternoon".

These assets were in this way never seen as a business investment for financial return. That was never the culture. And those old non-financial reasons for owning a football club are not so different to Arabia's current investments into the sector. Maybe the Arabs have understood the soul of sport, its power, more than Wall Street? At the end of the day, how many sins have been accepted, injustices swallowed, in exchange for a winning and conquering local sports team.

The most obvious and glamorous version of this, of sport as *"soft power"* and influence, again from my own direct experience, is in the Agnelli family's ownership of both Juventus and Ferrari. In times of recession or lay-offs in the motor industry, the distraction of world class sports teams certainly has helped their car business FIAT.

THE AGNELLI DYNASTY

FIAT was founded by the Agnelli family at the end of the 19th century, and it, and that family, have defined Italy in so many fundamental ways. They put mobility in the hands of the working class, post-war, with the legendary 500 utility car, unlocking the recently unified peninsula of Italy, devastated by WW2. That car, that company, that family, delivered a truly epochal cultural change, representing the engine of the Italian economic miracle of the 1950s and 60s. They acquired and funded the football club Juventus in 1923, and Ferrari in 1988, and those assets became part of their brand and popularity; the golden family giving work and enjoyment to so many. Their factories attracted the poor workers from the South of Italy, in search of a life. This is also why Juventus has such a wide diaspora of fans from that Mezzogiorno. It was *"the team of the man putting bread on our table."* The Agnellis became the de facto aristocracy, where their sports assets contributed hugely to their image and brand.

Investing in sport often generates this significant intangible return, not shown by the financial accountants, but always recognised by the best investors, even today.

In wanting to capture this return, to successfully manage in sport, one needs to understand this British and European past, know the history, and be comfortable in the company of these kind of old owners, and their traditional culture. In my own career in sport, I have spent many a day in the Boardroom or golf course with such characters.

In my experience, a Geoff Brown of St. Johnstone in Perth, or an Antonio Gozzi of Virtus Entella in Liguria, are outstanding people, self-made men, and women, with homespun wisdom around business and sport, from whom I have been lucky to personally learn so much.

Geoff Brown, for example, insisted on a self-financing football club, making ends meet by selling their best players. They did it by pulling off the impossible task of making their fanbase know and accept their reality as a selling club. Very difficult to deliver, and so much to observe about the management of people, customers, fans. Because, good business, at its core, is always about people and motivating them, to work for you; to buy from you, to follow you. Atalanta, Brighton and Hove Albion, are two clubs who have perfected this same art in recent years.

Gozzi, the owner of an amazing international energy conglomerate, Duferco, instead accepts that he is giving back to the community. His club Virtus Entella won't break even and drops maybe €5m+ a year to fund that local team of Chiavari (home also to his WyScout sports data business, and WyLab the sports accelerator). Sitting in his garden overlooking Portofino, discussing how to make his club in some way slightly more sustainable, but really knowing it can never be, is a sports MBA right there. And maybe also a philosophy degree. This is the Humanities, applied to our industry.

I have been very lucky that sport has allowed me to meet such people. But the lesson for this book is this; whilst in buying a soap factory or a chain of retail stores you don't really need to know in depth the history of the past owners and customers, in sport you absolutely do. The true culture and asset value lies entirely in the memories of people like Brown and Gozzi. Get them to speak about their passion and, crucially, about the challenges of management, control and governance in this industry. It will stand you in good stead. For example, the first time I met Gozzi, in a Milanese bistro, our wide-ranging conversation about Italian football started to focus on the key risk factors, and he tested me:

"You do know who controls Italian football don't you?"

When I replied *"Lotito from Lazio"*, I saw his mood change immediately, as if he felt released from the grinding chore of the next 90 minutes of conversation with a naive incredulous foreigner. He knew that I knew already, and so came straight to the point:

"Ok. Let's talk seriously; if I could get you elected to the Board of my league, Serie B, would you

be interested?"

In wanting to influence Italian football, in wanting to manage and control anything, one always needs to understand how it governs itself. Who is in charge, who calls the shots? In Italian football, to this day, the owner of Lazio, Claudio Lotito, has so much sway with the long tail of medium and small clubs in the country, that it is impossible to secure the votes to get anything done without him. This role was previously held by Luciano Moggi of Juventus.

To make this point as forcibly as possible; it would be extremely foolish to try and pass legislation in Washington if one didn't know the intangibles around power, popularity and votes of each congress person. It's the same in sport.

As it grew, sport became evermore political and started to organise itself around a self-regulating governance called local, national, and international Federations, like the Olympics (IOC) in 1894, and the governing body of football (FIFA) in 1904. Below them, league structures organised week-by-week fixtures, and the English Football league started in 1888, the Scottish counterpart two years later, with other European leagues soon after.

All these organisations, born often in the utmost good faith, have sought to run themselves in a kind of *"one man one vote"* self-regulating democracy, electing their members to various committees of power and decision-making. Thus, the voting power of a small club, or a small nation, carries equal weight to a much larger participant in the ecosystem. Sport has accepted that Macclesfield FC could decide things side-by-side with Manchester United; that the Israeli Football Association got heard as equally as their Italian brethren.

Exactly this set-up allows the Lotitos of this world to make significant hay, politically.

It doesn't take a genius to work out that the interests of all the different constituent members of the governing bodies of sport will not be aligned.

If sport is indeed this broad church, comprising grassroots to elite, amateur to professional, local community to global, then it's going to be hard to agree what hymns to sing at the Sunday service.

Sport is politics, but dealing with something people actually care about.

In European and world football, for example, there is an ongoing power struggle between FIFA, UEFA, big club lobbies like the European Club Association (ECA), national leagues like the EPL, the trade association of European leagues, and fiercely independent club brands like Real Madrid. All these bodies are working very clearly and fiercely to their own agenda, competing for game time in a cluttered football calendar. It is a *"Mors Tua Vita Mea"* (dog eat dog) culture and mentality, set up to deliver poor decision-making and strategy.

European football is a great illustration of the famous prisoner's dilemma, which describes a paradox in game theory, where two individuals, trying to maximise their own self-interests, generate in fact a sub-optimal situation for all concerned. The best outcome for all is only possible when both prisoners cooperate, but because their interests are not aligned, they betray each other instead. Consequently, they all end up losing.

Indeed, one could argue in 2023, as the capital-fuelled growth of football in America and Saudi Arabia becomes meaningful, that European football is losing the hegemony it has had since those public school boys in Eton. If it does, that will be a classic example of prisoners' dilemma. The various stakeholders of European football couldn't co-operate, and lost it all.

For many years, all this sub-optimal governance was fairly manageable; but in the last generation, it's become patently not so. As times change, what once could be seen as traditional, solid, stoic, resilient, all of a sudden, quickly, can become inflexibility, stubbornness, reluctance to listen. And one of the prickliest and most pressing issues for sport, and its investors, is resistance to change.

These governing bodies seem to be, and actually are, from another era.

They set themselves out, and pride themselves, as a full democracy, but any good democracy at very least should aspire to a robust constitution that has a very clear separation of powers.

The governance of sport is in this way set up to fail right from the starter's gun. There is no separation of powers at all. In thinking itself passionately independent and a special social product, sport has always resisted outside intervention from governments and common law. It has always believed to know better, and to act in some ways like an isolated mafioso family; being their own legislative, executive, marketing, and judiciary.

From direct personal experience, running a sports federation or league with this inherently flawed constitution is not easy. You feel a bit like Josh Lyman in the West Wing, rustling up consensus in Congress, dealing with big personalities, successful people of gravitas, and you need their votes. They have to like you; they have to admire you and trust you. And they've got to believe that you treat all clubs, big and small, with the same attention and respect, when in reality you are everyday just horse-trading votes.

You therefore need to spend a lot of time with the members, building a relationship, because ultimately you need their vote for your agenda. These cats must be herded in the right order, as some of your members will only say yes if they see others already agreeing. To run a sports league, you need to know your order of persuasion. You also must be the ultimate realist because some things you won't manage to make happen. Pick your battles, and your retreats. And as in American politics, you can only get things done at the start of the term/mandate. Once relegation becomes front and present for some clubs, your members' head is gone on any long-term stuff.

This *"original sin"* in the governance structure of sport is the source of so many of the challenges the industry now faces, and means that, in stormy waters, there is no clear commanding voice or rudder.

And that's a problem, made worse when the monies coming into sport have become noteworthy. Various people have come out of the woodwork, all wanting different things. The pie is now big enough to start fighting over. Players and their agents in primis; they know their worth in what is being generated. They have very successfully leveraged their value.

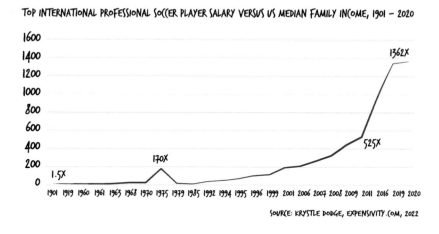

TOP INTERNATIONAL PROFESSIONAL SOCCER PLAYER SALARY VERSUS US MEDIAN FAMILY INCOME, 1901 – 2020

SOURCE: KRYSTLE DODGE, EXPENSIVITY.COM, 2022

Broadcasters and sponsors also want their pound of flesh for the monies they invest. Politicians and social causes want to use sport for their agendas, culture wars, and to gather votes. The Big Money Bear smells honey.

If the point being made is that sport truly is politics, it is perhaps a good idea for any person interested in this industry to understand the political philosophy of its birth, behind its mission, core beliefs and policies.

One of the biggest tenets of any good politician is in maximising opportunity and the chances of social mobility. Sport in Europe has embraced that, and is the ultimate meritocracy, perhaps the last one, in this world of nepotism. Being someone's son or daughter isn't going to give you an advantage on the field of play as that assassin centre-half crashes towards you.

European sport therefore has always believed in social mobility, in the form of a pyramid of achievement. All leagues and tournaments have always been open, available to anyone who could earn the right to participate on the field of play. You progressed through the pyramid, according to your abilities. Nothing was closed. Small clubs like Sampdoria, Leicester, Villareal, Aberdeen reached the very top by being good enough in that moment in time.

Most European sports fans adore this concept, indeed will protect it to the death. Nothing excites more than an underdog story.

Until very recently, this very culture and tradition of European sport has never thought of itself in any way as a business. One could describe European sport as more Aneurin Bevan socialist, than Adam Smith capitalist, and when we hear sport described so often as a *"family"*, a *"community"*, we aren't far away in mentality from Hillary Clinton's *"It takes a village"*.

That's doubly important, especially considering that the Olympics IOC organisation, and the governing bodies of Association Football (UEFA/FIFA), motorsport's FIA, all sit in Europe.

Sport is politics, and in Europe, its credo has been redistributive, and opportunity for all.

This isn't a natural match with Wall's Street's masters of the universe, and the power of market forces.

None of their animal-spirit capitalistic traits of the marketplace are in the traditional spirit of the game.

Chapter Four

SPORT IN AMERICA: ALL ABOUT THE BENJAMINS

Sport in the New World is a very successful contradiction.

It carries none of the political and social baggage of Europe, and is blessed with almost no knowledge of the class system that has so influenced sport in the Old World. The idea of elitist amateurism to them is likely seen as quite twee, in comparison to American sport, which has always been about *"the Benjamins"* (President Franklin's face adorns the $100 bill).

So, when, in recent years, sport, and its industry, has been utterly dominated by American media companies, American tech, American celebrity culture, and American capital, this difference is absolutely key.

If anything, the juxtaposition with Europe will become starker, and needs to be understood really well, if investing and managing in this sector.

Whilst sport in Europe comes from elite schools, it was probably introduced to America by English pilgrims, with their frontier spirit of hunting and horses. Rugby and rounders look rather like American Football and baseball. Lacrosse however is gloriously Native American, descending from, and resembling, games played by various tribal communities. The nature of slave plantations also played a significant role in the ways sports like boxing, wrestling, and running developed. White owners made black slaves compete for their entertainment, but, more honourably for sport, it could easily be argued that the emancipation of those same Afro-Americans was greatly helped by their role on the fields of play, with pioneers like Jackie Robinson, the first black man to play in modern-era pro baseball.

In America, sport has evolved over the decades simply and naturally into three clear levels of ability that are less about fluidity and social mobility, and more about talent and structure: pro sports, university and high school sports, recreational and amateur sports.

PROSPORTS

There have been, and are, three major professional sports in the United States.

Baseball is probably the oldest and most American, with its governing body, Major League Baseball (MLB), starting in 1876. The National Football League (NFL) was founded in 1920; the National Basketball Association (NBA) got going in 1949.

These are all private member leagues of franchise owners who self-regulate and run all aspects of the sport and its business. This includes negotiations with broadcasters and players unions. They are much simpler governance beasts than in Europe, with no confusion about who is running a sport, in that there aren't federations or governing bodies; there are just these all-powerful professional leagues run by fully empowered CEOs called Commissioners. Its constitutional culture is more like a private company, run for shareholders, by professional management. Stakeholders are fewer, so compromises are less.

In the United States, sport seems to have been imbued from the start with little of the romanticism and ambition of Corinth, and it is less about the glory of amateurism and the fabric of society. It could be argued that it has been conceived and born from day 1 as a professional business, an asset to be owned, a return to be earned, closed to any outsiders, regardless how much they deserved to be allowed in.

American culture is the home of the free market and dog-eat-dog capitalism. You work hard for yourself, and the American dream tells you that you can get to the very top and be fully rewarded for your talent and effort. For my own generation, growing up on a diet of Yankee culture and TV, Ellis Island was a North Star of ambition, and for a young boy from Glasgow, or Naples, this was the example we needed, to demonstrate what could be.

America is the home of competition, has little time for the loser, and absolutely has always been consistent in this credo. Europe, instead, likes to celebrate its humanity in, shall we say, a wider canvas of values. The dignity of the street sweeper, picking up that last wrapper, just wanting to do his or her job well; a miner still covered in dust, humbly drinking a pint with his pals, and knowing he is the most respected guy in the pub. The student finally scraping through an exam at the 4th attempt and being celebrated. And yet, remarkably, sport in America breaks all its cultural rules. The reality here is perhaps not as we would expect and is very important to ultimately understanding this global asset class.

American sports leagues and its owners cooperate more than they compete, also because they can. Their membership is fixed, and they are de facto closed shops, meaning there is no promotion or relegation. You are not getting in unless the other existing owners agree. There is no concept of entry through excellence or meritocracy; of *"anyone being able to be President if they work hard enough".* The central league *"grants"* a franchise to an owner to compete in their competition. The word franchise is therefore the correct one and that is fundamental. Sport is a business and clubs are operating under the permission, and by the rules, of the higher body, the league, the brand. Central leagues are set out to make the franchises profitable, and free of the relegation risk, and the owners are in the cool kid's club. Being allowed to buy a sports franchise is the ultimate trophy asset in America.

"... Sports franchises are how we knight people in this country...", "... and you're not royalty, you're a robber baron."
Billions ShowTime TV Series

In this way, franchises are working together for the long-term prosperity of their league and their value. There is an understanding that an equalised league is a more attractive product. The weakest teams, will be helped, and much effort is therefore put into attempting to give everyone similar revenues, allowing them to spend the same through a disciplined salary cap, and then rebalancing the sporting levels of the teams.

So, it is truly illuminating and fascinating to observe how in reality American sport has been so successful by secretly abandoning its nation's core competition philosophy, and actually rewarding the loser. The worst team is not punished, not relegated. Instead, it is handsomely rewarded with the choice of the best young players from university sport, to help them improve. This Draft System, which is the beauty parade of college athletes each year, allows pro teams to have their pick of the young talent, with the worst team having first pick. All in the name of making the weakest stronger, penalising the winner of today, to rebalance the league.

Ironically, Europe has the social mobility and reward of the pyramid, encouraging competition, whereas America has a mindset, not of achievement, but of the business monopolist, where there is no chance of entering the top tier in American sports on merit.

Their leagues are closed, sacrificing the idea of competitive capitalism at the altar of *"protected"* business. No-one in or out, and every effort made to balance the teams for maximum interest and uncertainty of result, to make the product they sell the most attractive.

This is sport organised to protect the incumbents, keep them equal in terms of quality, operating in a controlled, risk-free environment, with built in profitability through fixed salary caps. And there is no pathway to challenge or break into this through simple merit. It prioritises business structures and financial performance over the emotional ups and downs of the unscripted drama of sport.

That is a profound reality, very different from Europe, where clubs are formally together in a common league, but are actually and utterly in competition with one another. They compete to qualify or win titles, but more importantly, a lot of them fight for survival. Weak teams get penalised by relegation, rather than rewarded with next year's top rising star. As a result, there is an unholy, uncontrolled and unsustainable battle for playing talent, making the whole industry unprofitable. Especially as there is no effective cap of player salaries.

If the glorious story of Wrexham FC, bought by two Hollywood stars, and then promoted to a higher league, struck home so vividly with those Americans, one wonders what the ultimate endgame for sport is. The American pro model of today is the polar opposite in credo, outlook, and business structures, from Wrexham FC.

People investing, owning and managing sports assets need to fully grasp this fundamental and counter-intuitive reality, and wonder how it all will play out. When in doubt, look to the actual popularity of the product. What is now called product/market fit.

The NFL is the biggest sport (and business) in our industry, and probably the best illustration of the success of this American league model of pro sports. It's a brand that is now an intrinsic part of American culture, built on the teenage Wonder Years of high school and cheerleaders. It sets out to mirror and project the exact image of working America, of hard graft, progress up the field of life, often by slow grind, sometimes by vast leaps of progress, triumph over adversity, all with your teammates, sharing true grit and ambition. To quote Al Pacino's Coach D'Amato in Any Given Sunday, this really is the America we know, and admire:

"You find out life is this game of inches. So is football because in either game, life or football, the margin for error is so small. I mean, one half a step too late or too early and you don't quite make it. One half second, too slow, too fast, you don't quite catch it. The inches we need are everywhere around us. They're in every break of the game, every minute, every second. On this team, we fight for that inch. On this team, we tear ourselves and everyone else around us to pieces for that inch. We claw with our fingernails for that inch because we know when we add up all those inches, that's going to make the fucking difference between winning and losing, between living and dying."

Understanding sport is always about the culture that it mirrors.

Whilst very different from Rome or Glasgow, and certainly Eton, American life is dominated by *"the game"*, the NFL. For most Americans, Thanksgiving would not be complete without playing a game of football or watching the holiday broadcasts with your family. It is the language of familiarity across the nation. The famous conversation opener between any two guys:

"How about them Dolphins?"

The NFL has this perfect connection as a product because it is stable and long-term in its thinking. There are no prisoners, and no dilemma. It has moved with the cultural times and now is undoubtedly America's sport, the gorilla of the entire global sports ecosystem.

The NFL understands its product and audience perfectly. So much so that when you contemplate European sports, and its industry, they can all perhaps best be described as *"doing the exact opposite of what the NFL does."*

The NFL has embraced in economic terms, *"the Principle of Scarcity".* The regular season takes place over only 4 months, followed by 4 weeks of electric sudden death games. It is arguably the opposite of every other governing body in sport, throwing endless fixtures into the calendar. Unlike the NFL, most sports are full of non-jeopardy games that make the viewers ask themselves: *"why do I need to watch this?".* It instead is make or break every week, and there is very little drift in the game time. Every play is maximum intensity of hard hits, full sprints, and outlier athleticism. It's as if the entire football game is a highlight reel.

Leave aside for a second that the time between those plays is just perfect for ad breaks.

Other sports in comparison have their *"doze off"* moments. Golf over 4 days, cricket over 5, tennis over 6 hours on clay, F1 processions of cars, sterile ball possession in football.

The NFL is a sport that completely embraces the idea that true value comes from maximum unpredictability of outcome, from sporting balance between teams. No matter where you live in the country, your team has an equal chance of winning the Super Bowl. This has caused the game to grow in popularity throughout every corner of the USA, not just in New York, Boston, Chicago and Los Angeles. Every NFL team can aspire to ambition and success just around the corner. There are repeated instances of teams coming from obscurity, as laggards, to having a successful year. Fortunes change. A first-draft star going to a poor team can turn things around remarkably quickly. The number of teams who make Super Bowls is very varied, unlike most of sport. This unpredictability also works for the bookmaking industry, which prospers when uncertainty of result encourages increased volume of interest and betting.

Professional sport in America is a very successful business, with a world-class research and development facility, gifted to it by the talent factory of university sport.

UNIVERSITY SPORT IN AMERICA

University (or college) sport in America, is a truly extraordinary phenomenon, utterly unique. Promising athletes from high school are enticed by scholarship offers from universities around the country, to *"study"* with them whilst playing college sports. A good basketball player at high school will already have a queue of undergraduate destinations available to him or her.

This is the mechanism of talent scouting and player development in American sport. It is as traditional as mom's apple pie.

College sports in America is a big business, showcasing the stars of tomorrow, generating very sizeable crowds, with the deepest fan and alumni loyalty. It delivers huge TV audiences, and many say that this product is as big a part of the sport ecosystem in the States as the pro leagues. The record for the largest attendance for an American football game, 156,990 people, was for a National Collegiate Athletic Association (NCAA) game between the Tennessee Volunteers and the Virginia Tech Hokies. College sports to date have generated very material amounts of money for the universities, mainly from broadcast rights. In 2022 the total revenue generated by NCAA was $1.14billion. These numbers seem on an endless trend of growth.

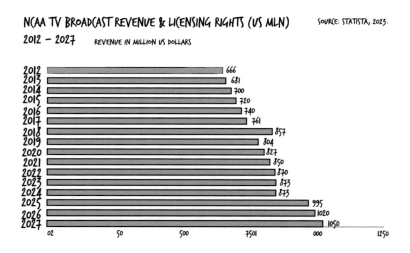

NCAA TV BROADCAST REVENUE & LICENSING RIGHTS (US MLN) SOURCE: STATISTA, 2023.
2012 – 2027 REVENUE IN MILLION US DOLLARS

Year	Revenue
2012	666
2013	681
2014	700
2015	720
2016	740
2017	761
2018	857
2019	804
2020	827
2021	850
2022	870
2023	873
2024	873
2025	995
2026	1020
2027	1050

Without witnessing it live, it is very difficult to understand the reality of all this. There are young kids, even teens, performing in front of 100,000 people, on national TV, as *"students"*, receiving popularity and adulation for themselves that they are expected to manage. Watching a documentary, like Netflix's Johnny Football, narrating the Beatles-esque frenzy around freshman quarterback Johnny Manziel, at university in Texas, gives some kind of idea of the madness.

Up until 2021, universities paid exactly zero of all this money to these young athletes, as they were considered merely as *"amateur"* students. But universities did and do pay their coaches very significant amounts of remuneration. In 2017, Alabama's head coach, Nick Saban, was offered an 8-year contract worth $94m!

In another example of how sport must evolve, albeit reluctantly, a recent Supreme Court judgement will now dramatically change this going forward and will have far-reaching implications for the entire industry.

In 2021, the U.S. Supreme Court issued a ruling agreeing that the NCAA has, in effect, been operating a system that is a classic restraint of competition. In short, a system that violates the nation's antitrust laws.

There's that *"monopoly"* word again.

Justice Neil Gorsuch said that the NCAA *"seeks immunity from the normal operation of the antitrust laws."* Justice Brett Kavanaugh added that the sports traditions, near and dear to alumni and others, *"cannot justify the NCAA's decision to build a massive money-raising enterprise on the backs of student athletes who are not fairly compensated. Nowhere else in America can businesses get away with agreeing not to pay their workers a fair market rate,"* he said, adding:

"The NCAA is not above the law."

University sport in America is truly a phenomenon and a vital part of the entire ecosystem. But it is changing right in front of our eyes now, and that matters. The ripples will affect everything, everywhere.

The rest of sport in the US *"the Recreational version"* is for everyone else in a park or gym, and merits no further comment in this book, more than to say that there is little if any pathway to serious sport in America from the local community.

• • •

At this point, even to the casual observer, the structures, governance, culture and mentality of sport in the US is very different from Europe.

All this has an enormous impact on how finance, mainly American, should approach investing in European sport, compared to their process in assessing similar American assets, as the risk profile, either side of the Atlantic, is completely different.

Risk changes everything in finance and makes capital much more expensive. One of the first ways to create financial value in sport is simply to remove *"risk"*. But to do that, many would argue, is to rip out the glory of the unscripted drama, the edge of the seat live-or-die uncertainty, to actually surgically remove sport's soul.

Perhaps so, and many say this is a hill of principles worth dying on. Sport, outside of the

US, doesn't think it is a business, and shouldn't have to corrupt itself to satisfy the needs of those now financing it. It still has a *"leave your credit card behind the bar"* attitude to financiers and investors.

But principles are expensive, and one could argue strongly that sport can no longer afford them.

It needs money, and the people with money think they can make great business investing in sport.

They are now being attracted to each other like a magnetic experiment, with to date very mixed results.

Big Finance thinks it understands the asset class of sport. It feels it has the emotional intelligence, empathy and experience to identify and manage the irrationality, tribalism and politics of sport. It really doesn't. Not in Europe, as Pallotta found in Rome, and the Glazers demonstrate in Manchester.

The consequences of this mismatch are likely to be very rocky.

As the old joke goes:

"How do you make a small fortune? Start with a large one and invest in a European football club".

Chapter Five

THE BOOMER BUSINESS MODEL OF SPORT

Sport has always had a simple model. Many would say too simple, even lazy and complacent.

The industry has made its money by selling access to its events, to its teams and its stars. Initially, physically at the stadia, where it sold tickets to fans, and concessions to people offering products to those same fans.

In the early days, tickets to sporting events were relatively cheap, and mainly for the *"Normal Joe"* type of fan. The average price to the Super Bowl in 1967 was $12. Even in 1980, the cost of entry to watch the Arsenal at Highbury was low, at £3. Fans could turn up on the day of the match, queue, buy a ticket and get in, as depicted in Lowry's famous Going to the Match.

You sweated your stadium asset the best you could, and, once every fortnight, you had a day to make money. Maybe you also sold some premium VIP seats, boxes, food and drink. And that was pretty much it, and true for most sports, football, rugby, tennis, cricket, baseball, basketball etc. So, this was a humble and uncomplicated industry, especially when many of its customer/fans bought upfront season-tickets. Consequently, there just wasn't a lot of money in sport, and players were not getting rich and becoming millionaires.

"Everton FC makes less money than the local supermarket in Goodison."

The classic career path for a loyal one-club British football player right up to the 1990s was to be given a loyalty benefit match when they hung up their boots. This *"testimonial"* put some decent money in their pocket with which they often bought a pub. Sportsmen and women never earned enough during, or after their career, to become too distant from the fans themselves. Even the top athletes were not excessively rich. Their incomes were bigger than the wages of their fans, for sure, but not excessively so. Graeme Souness, a top Scottish football star of the 70/80s earned ten times the wage of the average worker. Today it is 500 times or more. A top player or NBA star 40 years ago was still identifiable as *"one of us made good".* That was all before market forces started paying some attention to the business of sport.

Given that it was an accessible product, with intense social connection and fan loyalty, it was never going to remain simple for too long. In the 60s, the TV industry wanted to offer that very same access to the sports fans who were not just in the vicinity of the stadium. It was fairly clear that sport was popular entertainment and could generate big audiences of eyeballs, to be sold to, via adverts. So, broadcasters and media companies started to buy, very cheaply, small sports packages and round-up magazine content, the last 4 holes of a golf tournament, the final of Wimbledon, the English football cup final. Very few sporting events were covered live in their entirety. The inherent value of that product was still under appreciated, and programming budgets for sport were fairly modest. So national broadcasters like the BBC in the UK, or RAI in Italy, became a natural home for all of the country's great sporting moments.

And they got to do that, frankly, on the cheap. The sports industry was massively undervaluing its product, as, of course, they didn't even think that they were in business, or in the world of commerce, at all. New types of media entrepreneurs would educate them some years later.

Whilst still very limited, the rise of sport on TV is what lead to the birth of the sport sponsorship business. Sports clubs could generate income from offering brands the opportunity to be seen by stadium and TV audiences. It was all very embryonic, and many will remember advertising billboards at their local team promoting small local businesses, the town bakery or a domestic paint brand. That is because those adverts were still aimed mainly at the local fans.

As TV and sport really got going, reaching a global audience, it drew in more ambitious sponsors, like the Rolex clock at Wimbledon, a cigarette brand on a Formula 1 car, Adidas and CocaCola at World Cup billboards. But there were still no logos on player shirts.

Sponsorship value back then, and perhaps still today, was calculated around the equivalent TV media exposure. For example, if a 30 second ad during a soap opera, seen by 25m people, was worth £200k, then a billboard at a football ground could be benchmarked accordingly, from its audience. But it all would get more complex, as association with the heroes of sport became seen as very attractive for building a product's brand perception, not just its awareness.

Sponsorship grew very much on this basis out of America, as they fully grasped sport's popularity, with business eyes, and those big audiences were obviously very attractive to the Mad Men of their marketing industry.

A pioneer lawyer called Mark McCormack, who represented the commercial interests of golfer Arnold Palmer, created a symbiotic sports ecosystem, involving team owners, players, sponsors and broadcasters. His company, IMG, has in many ways defined the sports industry as a business, and survives to this day as the sector bellwether, now called Endeavor.

As in all successful and efficient businesses, the best operators seek to take *"rent"* out of all parts of the value chain, and in McCormack's case, he started as a talent agent for the stars, but from there created his own sports events, where those same stars would play. He produced these events for TV, sold the rights to a broadcaster, and attracted sponsors to them. Today IMG also sells the data rights to those events to bookmakers.

McCormack in many ways invented the sports industry and developed a playbook on how to make money from every one of its elements.

WHAT THEY DON'T TEACH YOU AT HARVARD BUSINESS SCHOOL

McCormack's book, of the same name, is essential reading for anyone wanting to work in sport, and to understand these strategies better. The book is divided into 3 parts: People, Sales & Negotiations, and Running a Business. Here are some of the key learnings from his book.

ON PEOPLE

The more you understand people, the better you can create a situation where they will respond favourably to your proposal. You learn about people by observation. One remembers Mr Brown and Sig. Gozzi. You need to understand what people want and find a way to deliver it and make profits. You also need to have a good understanding of how the game is played.

ON SALES & NEGOTIATIONS

You will not reach the top positions of your company unless you master the powers of persuasion. Sales situations are the best way to learn this skill. Silence is good; it keeps a seller from saying too much and makes a buyer say more than he or she should. It gives you an angle and also forces a decision. It's always harder to make someone want to buy than to set the terms under which they will buy.

ON RUNNING A BUSINESS

The challenges of starting and running a business are vastly different. Everything gets harder to change once you are established. The trick to get things done is to fit activities into your time, not find more time to accommodate activities.

Whilst IMG showed how you could make a very decent living around the fringes of sports, it was still an ancillary business, an agency, neither a league, nor a club/franchise, nor an athlete. Making money directly was still underdeveloped, but was starting to layer in a fair bit of complexity and conflict to the commercialisation of its rights beyond the match day revenues.

Sport wouldn't for long sell itself as a single event, but rather each match or race would be sold as part of a bigger and longer competition, a tournament, a league. These are called *"central rights"*, sold on behalf of all participants in a competition, whose revenues then are distributed back to the clubs/franchises (for team sports) and athletes (for individual sports like tennis and golf).

The competition organiser and owner are in theory not-for-profit marketeers, giving all revenues, net of running costs, back to the protagonists.

These Leagues and Tours, via their Commissioner or CEO, would market and commercialise the assets as best they could, normally by auctioning them off at tender. This could be the season-long MLB baseball World Series, a weekend of the PGA Ryder Cup, or a single WBO boxing match. Think tennis and golf tours, think Olympics and World Cups: the sports broadcaster ESPN buying NBA rights, Coca-Cola buying English Premier League (EPL) sponsorship rights, Fanatics buying the rights to the MLS league logo for merchandising, Genius Sports buying the data rights to the NFL.

Over the years, these central rights have represented more and more of the revenue mix of clubs and franchises, and this point is very important.

It's from where most of sports' money comes from, and from where derives inherent risk, volatility and instability. These are monies coming principally from the media sector, and not directly in the control of the individual clubs. A familiar lament from many franchise/club CROs would be:

"So much of my job here it out of my control, and that frustrates and scares me".

By auctioning off these central rights, sport has created the business model and mentality for the entire industry, developing mainly as a Business to Business (B2B) organisation. It has sold off its games and events to others; soliciting offers for a certain and safe amount of money up front, a rights bid, a minimum guarantee license, a sponsorship fee.

Once received, they have wanted very little to do with their fans, and today know precious little about them. In every aspect of its commercial activity outside direct ticketing, sport has outsourced and sold its community of fans to others.

Broadcasters and sponsors who bought the rights, by default, took the heavy lifting of marketing the entertainment. That has limitations, not matter how good they are.

How can you easily tell a really great story for your product or brand when the chapters are all told by different people? One could argue that even the flawless NFL is now exaggerating. This rights cycle, its games have been spread across days, nationally and locally, Black Friday games, Thursday, Monday. Traditional broadcasters, streaming platforms, Amazon, Google, Nickelodeon. The monetisation is great, but the narrative risks losing focus, told in different styles, to a confused fan, who also needs a variety of different and costly subscriptions to enjoy the whole story. Compare this to the laser-focus marketing and communications of wrestling's WWE, which has always tried to run a business with a much more direct relationship with its fans.

Maximising B2B money as a business model could be considered as sport's fault line. It should be the ultimate community business, the purest Business-To-Consumer (B2C) organisation and mentality, and yet, it's not. It has been run relatively sleepily, and sport's senior leaders haven't been asked to do much at all really on the business side. It's been staffed by rules and regs (regulations) guys, paperwork clerks, all pawns in the empire-building of the all-powerful manager like a Vince Lombardi, Bill Shankly, Matt Busby, Alex Ferguson or Brian Clough.

Whilst other fast-moving consumer goods (FMCG) industries from the 50s onwards got into the theory and practice of world class strategic marketing, to win market share, sport looked for a "*secretary*" who could read the rulebook.

In this way, with this attitude and model, sport has arguably poured its finest champagne and juicy margins into other people's flutes, be that broadcasters, social media platforms, merchandising companies.

In summary, in the old Boomer model of sport, a club or franchise in its revenue statement each year would have match day revenues from direct sales to fans, their own sponsorship efforts around their stadium, kit, and games, and then distribution of central rights back to them (actually coming from outside their direct control).

Here lies the risk and instability.

The sharp-eyed will notice one of the first inherent challenges about managing in this industry. A natural tension and competition between a league itself and its biggest club/

franchises, around capturing value from the bidders for assets (broadcasters, sponsors etc).

It is very possible for Manchester United to sell a club sponsorship to say MacDonalds and have the golden arches logos around their stadium and website. But what if Burger King goes to the EPL, the competition that contains the club Manchester United, to negotiate a league central sponsorship?

This happens all the time and requires disciplined protocols of behaviour to manage.

These rules and protocols never really work well, and resentment grows. You will hear conversations like this:

Big Club A:

"So, you want me to refuse a club sponsorship, to allow you a central league deal?"

League Commissioner:
"Think about the long-term benefit of the league. We all get stronger together, the league becomes more competitive, more valuable."

Big Club A:

"Even if I wanted to be that altruistic to my league colleagues, the numbers just don't add up. My share of a league deal is 100K, but if I sell directly to a brand, I can get 300K for those exact same sponsorship assets."

And here is the uncomfortable truth about the *"central rights"*, of an entire league, or a complete season. The product being sold is not homogenous, and hence makes the sharing of those revenues across unequal teams very difficult and politically fraught.

In media and entertainment terms, a sport league, tour, or competition is classically a bundle of hits and fillers. Big games, big teams, but also loads of less compelling matchups. When you buy the season's broadcast central rights of the EPL, you are buying a mixture of events and games. Some are absolutely box office, say Liverpool against Manchester City, and others that are more filler-type games, like Luton versus Bournemouth. Equally, when you buy the sponsorship rights to Serie A, you are getting branding at Juventus, but also Salernitana.

Every central league or competition in the world comes up with a *"distribution model"* to try and address all this. None of them are perfect in replicating the exact value generated by each club. One could argue that in almost every case, central leagues, and how they share the money, is always a redistributive model, where big clubs are actually subsidising small clubs. In the NFL, as we have said, this rebalancing philosophy is proactive, not a reluctant compromise.

But in a world of brutal financial market forces, leagues with this flaw are inherently unstable, especially when times get tough, and stormy waters hit. Big clubs and franchises are absolutely not deaf to the notion that they should be getting more of the pie.

The bundle concept is also sub-optimal on the buy side. When broadcasters and sponsors purchase *"the league"*, they can't cherry pick which games or teams they actually want to buy; they need to take the whole package, the whole bundle. And to date they have.

But this is bucking the market, and more importantly, vulnerable to technological and financial disintermediation and disruption.

And a set-up for piracy.

A sports league as a bundle is not a new concept. The music industry I inhabited in the 90s had a very similar product, called the long-playing (LP) record, also referred to simply as an album; a simple bundle of hits-and-filler.

We, the music-biz, sold albums for £20, on the back of usually 2 or 3 hit singles contained therein. People bought the bundle, often to get access to the hits. A wonderfully high margin business for EMI and all the other labels.

Enter the process of disintermediation, which means removing the bundler, the middleman. A market, via technology innovation, will always work hard to give a customer exactly what they want, at a fair price. Why pay £20 for a product when the actual hits you are interested in can be sold to you separately and for much less? When digital technology arrived (Napster, then iTunes, and ultimately Spotify), offering the music lover the chance to buy only those exact song tracks they wanted, the entire industry of recorded music suffered an existential earthquake. Technology empowered the forces of disintermediation and unbundling, to arrive at the ideal product/market fit.

I saw, from the front row, a sector, and its entire C-Suite senior management, taken entirely by surprise when its bundled product and business model was basically rendered obsolete overnight, from digital technology offering a new delivery method.

It is not a great leap to see similar parallels with the industry of sport. Why can't I just buy and watch the big games? Or just my own team's matches? Why can't I put my logo besides the sponsorship assets of the big clubs?

This book explores the importance of the bundle in sport, and questions its sustainability when exposed to the gale-force winds of disintermediation and financial arbitrage (market forces pushing to arrive at exactly the right price of everything).

The debate is not merely financial, but also philosophical. As a league Commissioner myself, I heard all angles of this conversation many times.

A small team will use 3 main arguments:
- the sports league bundle is not like an LP, because our games cannot exist in isolation. They are part of a league season, where every game contributes to the story of the tournament and final league standings. The single big game that is attractive for mass appeal means nothing on its own;
- if you let the broadcasters and sponsors cherry-pick, they will make the big clubs bigger, and destroy the competitive balance. The league has value when competitive and uncertain, not a foregone conclusion;
- sport is not a business, and these arguments are totally an anathema to the whole culture. If big clubs don't like that, they can go away and play in their own leagues. Yes, I heard that one many times in relation to Celtic and Rangers in Scotland.

Big teams will counter:
- why do you think broadcasters and sponsors are offering all this money? For your team? They are media businesses who are looking to sell products on the back of our fans. Subscriptions, advertising breaks, mobile phones, betting opportunities. You already get much more than you deserve, the central deals restrict me from selling my own stuff directly;
- subsidising you prevents me being fully competitive in international competitions;
- I agree with you on increasing lack of competition, it's not ideal but that's the way of business. It tends towards monopoly always. And regarding your decades-old threat of telling us to find a new league to play in, here is one I'm thinking about; it's called the Super League, in golf it's called LIV.

This is the epicentre of the storm front coming towards sport: market forces eroding the central league bundles and its redistributive model. In America, they understand all this better, and minimise the space for the arbitrage vultures to operate. In Europe, they are a sitting duck.

Understanding the bundle is key to investing well in sport. It has been the cornerstone of the Boomer sports industry to date and is a great business model, even if a good lawyer may even claim that the whole practice is nothing other than glorified *"conditional selling"*, which is usually illegal.

Today, the market forces of tech and finance by definition do not work like that, and won't accept this. Digital technology can track and show you exactly how an asset or a piece of content performed, which then offers full transparency on its value. Similarly, the skills of investing and finance work exactly in the same way, by finding assets that are not priced at their true value, and trading to address that. If it can be seen exactly what a particular team or star in sport is adding to *"value"*, let's say simply in sponsorship assets, that can be articulated in money. Modern tech may tell us that the value of Phil Mickelson to the sponsor value of the PGA Tour is say $2m. But he is only getting a fraction of that from the Tour. So, when a financial person goes to Mickelson and explains that he is being underpaid, he listens. When the financial person offers a new solution to pay him what he's worth, that is called arbitrage. What happened to Phil when he heard that pitch? LIV Golf.

The market forces of polarisation and financial arbitrage will not be easily stopped, and put enormous risk into this industry, its model and revenues.

As we know, sport sells its bundles. its rights, its IP, to others. Often, not directly to broadcasters, but to the sports agencies, called IMG, Octogon, Wassermann, Infront, Sport5 etc. Agencies are intermediaries.

The insiders' secret in the sports industry is the 3-card trick of these agencies, which has allowed them to make real margins at volume and capture a disproportionate slice of the value chain.

As with the entire entertainment industry, sport has been dominated by bundles of agency assets and, just as in Hollywood, the agent will try and manage a project by inserting as many of their assets as possible into a client sale; eg their own director, scriptwriter and actor clients into the same film. In order to secure a Brad Pitt on a film, you may need to accept the more *"commodity"* clients of mega agencies like William Morris and CAA. They sell you a bundle of talent.

In sport, if you want to buy the major rights like the NBA or the EPL, the sports agency that holds them may *"insist"* you also buy lesser assets like Italian women's volleyball, and English darts.

When I was a fresh naive CEO of Scottish football, I was very pleasantly surprised to receive significant bids for our overseas rights from these agencies. Whilst it looked a good deal for us, and it was, we were unaware that the agency could bundle Scottish football with other more attractive rights they had and sell the package to a broadcaster at a significant mark-up.

This is the business model of the sport intermediary agency. It is seldom spoken about with transparency. The agency makes their money from the non-stars, the non-Hollywood rights. Those assets cost them little, but if they can be bundled with the premium rights and talent, you can make excellent margins.

But business isn't just about revenues, and the other side of the equation is the cost line, vastly dominated in sports by the athlete player cost. Sport is like any industry, there are good businesses and bad businesses. The real difference between the US and Europe is not how they make money, but rather how they spend it.

In the States, with no relegation risk, strong salary caps, youth development in the hands of colleges and universities, and cities buying you a stadium, your costs are very controlled, predictable and fixed below your revenues. It's a business with an in-built and positive margin, which has reduced risk and volatility, and where a rise in top-line revenues flows down to the bottom line.

In Europe absolutely not so. There is always fan and media pressure to spend for short term sporting results. It's about glory or survival. The expenditure that can move the needle always goes on better playing talent. This market for *"natural resources"*, players, is very easily and negatively distorted by a bad actor owner of a competitor club, desperately overpaying to outdo his rivals and appease the fans. If there is no salary cap, it's a recipe for disaster.

Whilst American sports work successfully to a negotiated fixed salary cap with players unions, in Europe, and especially in football, it's been nearly impossible.

An anonymous Belgian footballer called Jean Marc Bosman in 1995 took a complaint to the European Court of Justice and won a landmark case that established the idea that football players, as employees, had absolute rights of freedom of movement at the end of their contracts. Their clubs could not demand a transfer fee from future employers if the player's contract had expired. Looking back, it's astonishing that it took so long, and Bosman had to fight so hard for what seems the most basic of workers' rights.

The governance of sport considers itself outside and above the law, fiercely independent, acting as parliament, government, judge and jury. But that European court judgement utterly changed the balance of power in football in favour of the talent, the players. And boy did they take advantage. Without a union deal and a salary cap, European football lost control of its cost line.

There are absolutely many parallels with the NCAA having the Supreme Court now force payments to their college athletes.

Without a hard salary cap, I call all this the volatility of contagious irrationality. One madman obliges everyone to enter the asylum.

European sport has thus always paid all of its revenues, and more, to players and is a negative margin business. Lord Sugar, briefly owner of Tottenham Hotspur Football Club, beautifully visualised the model as the prune juice effect. Whatever came in at the top, went out uncontrollably below.

This brings our story up to the 1990s. The management of sport was starting to get rather difficult. The old business model, of the Boomer generation, was at the end of the day a small industry, operating and making its money at stadia once a fortnight, and merely scratching the surface of the central revenues available from sponsorship and broadcasting. The valuations of sports assets were thus contained, and the entire asset class of sport was probably too small for anyone in cold finance to bother about. It was still in the control of the local entrepreneurs with decent wealth. The Agnellis, the Geoff Browns, the Antonio Gozzis.

There was no attempt by sport to nurture a true B2C community business and be valued as such. Sport has exceptional brand but, for 30 years, has lent it cheaply to other businesses.

One of those was the media broadcasting industry.

Chapter Six

LOVE AND THE MEDIA SECTOR WILL TEAR US APART

To quote a famous grocer's daughter:

"you can't buck the market, it will always have its way".

Margaret Thatcher was talking about, in her opinion, the futility of her Chancellor Nigel Lawson's attempt to keep a lid on a rising pound sterling by artificial intervention in the markets. He failed.

The sports industry started to really evolve in the go-go years of Thatcher and Reaganomics (the laissez-faire capitalism unleashed in the 80s).

Everything changed in these years through untethered economic market forces, including arguably, the collapse of the old Soviet Communist Bloc. The crumbling stones of a wall in Germany started a series of shock waves that would dominate the next decades. From the fall of the Berlin Wall in 1989 the world really started to spin differently, and so did media, broadcasting and communication.

The planet got smaller with globalisation, as Asia entered the World Trade Organisation (WTO). The rise of technology and the internet offered unlimited communications and distribution, with the digitalisation of everything, as mobile and software ate the world.

The globe may indeed have seemed tinier, but target markets for everything were all of a sudden exponentially bigger. In that kind of world, brand IP and popularity would be everything.

Technology enabled companies and products to reach an unlimited number of customers at a very low marginal cost. We had entered the age of Silicon Valley and technology start-ups, where, once you build a platform of delivery, it costs you very little extra to sell to a new customer. Content, especially in digital form, didn't need to be made again to sell to a new person, like a CD had needed to be. It had no additional *"on-cost"*.

The buzzword became *"scale"*, and new ways of looking at business came into vogue, labelled with fresh thinking like *"unit economics"*.

In all this, the sports industry at the start of the 90s would therefore no longer be just about the people who could physically get to the stadium; and club owners and marketeers could now aspire to reach new fans on the other side of the world. Once that became the thinking, the concept of marketing, and especially brand, wasn't going to be far behind.

"How do I get a boy in Jakarta to like my team over my rivals'?"

Sport has always been a universal language, and was now booming, global and omnipresent, with immense fan loyalty, delivered digitally with new technology products.

Sport 2.0 was no longer analogue, and no longer ambivalent to brand. Its Total Addressable Market (TAM) got a whole lot bigger.

This would increasingly attract all kinds of new people, interested in the asset class. The sector was now, to use a Wall Street term, *"in play"*, in the sights of Big Finance investors, especially in the middle of a bull market.

Sport's little Victorian sailing ship was going to start getting blown about, despite much of the old industry still wanting to remain quaint and pure. The truth is always that if you offer significant intrinsic value, someone, if not you yourself, will always grab it.

Sport in the 1990s didn't proactively change itself, and disruption was forced on it without pity or hesitation. The catalyst was the media sector, when a new form of broadcast model called cable or PayTV began to evolve. Broadcast entertainment delivered to the home would no longer be limited to traditional (free) TV, funded by the license payer or by advertising; it would be paid for by monthly subscriptions.

Media moguls like Rupert Murdoch (BSkyB Fox), Silvio Berlusconi (Mediaset) and John C Malone (TCI Liberty Media) realised a very simple fact: that to succeed, their new PayTV ventures needed very quick penetration and scale, and those fresh customers would only come for *"must have"* content.

They would only come for live sport.

"Sport will be used as a battering ram against all media rivals, because sport absolutely overpowers film and everything else in the entertainment genre."
Rupert Murdoch, News Corp annual general meeting in 1996

Almost overnight, it stopped being a small cottage industry, sleepily existing for the good of the game and a local parochial community. The Age of Innocence was over, as it became the killer content in what would be a global media and entertainment industry; cable and satellite PayTV.

Inevitably, Big Finance did what it always does. They smelt money, bought this vision from Big Media, and backed those mogul entrepreneurs, deploying their capital to finance both the investment in distribution networks for cable/PayTV, and the content to pump through them.

And for that very simple reason, increased demand, the value of sports rights started to rocket in both the US and Europe, reaching new heights every time.

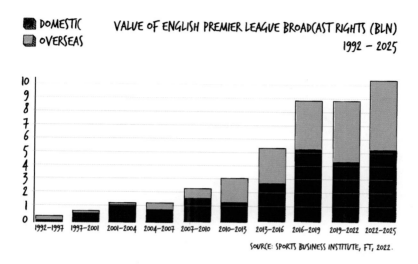

DOMESTIC
OVERSEAS

VALUE OF ENGLISH PREMIER LEAGUE BROADCAST RIGHTS (BLN)
1992 – 2025

SOURCE: SPORTS BUSINESS INSTITUTE, FT, 2022.

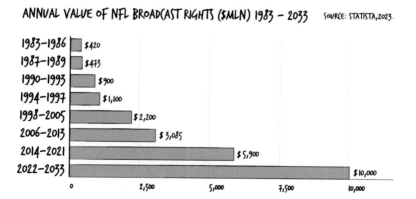

ANNUAL VALUE OF NFL BROADCAST RIGHTS ($MLN) 1983 – 2033   SOURCE: STATISTA, 2023.

1983–1986	$420
1987–1989	$473
1990–1993	$900
1994–1997	$1,100
1998–2005	$2,200
2006–2013	$3,085
2014–2021	$5,900
2022–2033	$10,000

As all big industries grow up, in pioneer new markets, there is usually a fierce fight for territory. And indeed, we saw our own media version of Gangs of New York.

In the late 80s, I found myself in the middle of a silly side hustle, working on Italian football content for new satellite broadcaster British Satellite Broadcasting, BSB. They had acquired the rights for Serie A, in a committed push for penetration of their platform. It was the height of the battle between the two PayTV rivals in the UK; BSB and Rupert Murdoch's SKY.

This remarkable full-page advertisement appeared in Variety eight months before the planned launch of the BSB service. It gives a taste of the bombastic frontier times, which does chime very much with this decade's Streaming Wars, and its land-grab for content and sports rights.

Both sides were, in reality, bleeding out, in hand-to-hand combat, and it just wasn't sustainable. On Monday 29 October 1990, Rupert Murdoch went to see Prime Minister Margaret Thatcher at 10 Downing Street and stated clearly that a merger of Sky and BSB would be needed, as both were losing serious money.

Three days afterwards, BSB merged with Sky Television to become British Sky Broadcasting (BSkyB), and two years later this new entity would be part of a story that would utterly change football and sport forever; namely the auction for the broadcast live media rights of the new breakaway super league of English football called the English Premier League (EPL). The idea of Murdoch was to generously fund the new league to allow the clubs to afford better players, and better stadia, which would in turn make the product much more attractive and valuable.

This virtuous circle worked, and over the following decades it would become the biggest, richest, and most followed football league in the world.

Back in 1992, the two bidders for the newly formed EPL were ITV, the terrestrial commercial broadcaster represented by Trevor East, and Murdoch's BSkyB, putting Vic Wakeling forward as Head of Sport.

One of the voting clubs in the EPL, Tottenham Hotspur PLC, was rather conflicted, because its owner also owned Amstrad PLC, which was the supplier of satellite dishes to Sky. Rumour has it that the owner of that club, Lord Alan Sugar, was a mole in the room back to Wakeling. The mythical phrase, delivered by telephone as he excused himself from the meeting was:

"They've bid X, so go now and blow them out of the (expletive) water".

If true, this phone call changed the future of English football and so much more.

Sky did indeed put in a knock-out bid, won, and then also stole Mr East for themselves.

For the next generation, *"Vic and Trevor"* would utterly dominate the UK sports industry, and the fortunes of almost every sport. ITV, as proxy for all European terrestrial broadcasters, instead never again played in these waters, as the table stakes had now become too high.

Murdoch's BSkyB would build a very significant business on the back of all this, ultimately selling itself to Comcast for $39bn in 2021. One wonders if that value could have been captured by sport itself, and this is a debate still very much alive today.

The business professionalisation, and the polarisation of football and sport in Europe, began. It was utterly driven by the rise of the media baron, the thrusting raider who immediately saw the true value of sport, and it would be totally changed on and off the pitch by the Rupert Murdochs, the Bernard Tapies, the Silvio Berlusconis, as they all wanted to get their tentacles around the industry, to boost their businesses and their egos. Indeed, the purchase of AC Milan by Berlusconi, and the way he used it for marketing, brand and synergies with his growing broadcast empire, and also his political ambitions, changed everything as to how sport was viewed. Murdoch tried to buy Manchester United, Tapie bought Marseille.

It was in fact a moment of heavy investment in disruption. Not only with the cable/PayTV build out, but also people realising what was going to happen to mobile communications. Governments started to auction spectrum for 3G mobile for serious amounts (in the UK alone, Gordon Brown managed to secure £22.5bn from telecom companies). And the

Internet was coming. New media platforms, mobile. All creating a sense of frenzy in the air, with the industry of sport right in the middle. Rights holders were inundated with bidders, for all kinds of deals, with a fragmentation in definition of what sport had to offer. It was no longer selling just live games and a highlights package.

People started offering to buy your mobile 3G and WAP rights. Your website started becoming an asset for which companies would bid serious money. Lawyers for big clubs and franchises were starting to get involved as to what rights were actually held at the centre, as opposed to what their clients could exploit directly. For example, it wasn't clear if the online streaming of an audio commentary of the live game was in direct conflict with the exclusive central radio deal done by the league.

These were street-fighting years, where every day brought a new challenge between the centre and the clubs, even over classic league deals like the match ball contract with Mitre, or the sticker contract with Panini.

THE RISE OF SPORT 2.0 AND A NEW KIND OF MEDIA COMPANY

At the end of the 90s, the sports industry saw the creation of fresh digital conglomerates that were combining all these new digital rights of clubs and leagues. They were helping rights holders open and build their websites and IP assets.

One of these groups, Sports Internet Group (SIG) grew quickly and exited even quicker, in a sale to BSkyB for £266m. The goal of BSkyB was to create a positive integration between television and online and be a leader of sports content and betting in the UK. One could argue they did exactly that, and SIG, whilst very expensive, was worth it.

SIG's competitor, Sportal, was valued even higher but sadly didn't quite get the same exit. The company, created in 1999 by Rob Hersov and Andrew Croker, was a global provider of online sports content. Sportal built and managed the websites of some of the major sports clubs and organisations, including Juventus, AC Milan and Bayern Munich. The pitch of Sportal to those clubs was to benefit from their knowhow and economies of scale in technology and software development.

The company grew dramatically on the back of the dot.com bubble, and eventually sponsored the Euro 2000. Unfortunately, 2000 was also the year when the bubble burst. Eventually, the company, which at one point was valued at around £250m, ended up being sold to online bookie UKBetting for just £1, almost overnight. In a similar vein, a joint venture, PTV, between the The English Football league (EFL) and cable company, NTL, crashed spectacularly, doubling the pain of the demise of ITV Digital, a spin off from the ITV parent, who had paid very expensively for the broadcast rights of the EFL. The ITV Digital case study is well worth separate study, as a didactic classic around lending and *"parent company guarantees".*

It is difficult today to comprehend the extent of the boom-and-bust magnitude at the end of the 90s, although the crypto frenzy during COVID was very similar. Extreme bull markets do that, and sport was mirroring exactly the irrational exuberance of the NASDAQ stock market bubble.

Those of us in charge of a rights holder in the 90s were very much holding a tiger by the tail.

It would get worse.

As the stakes were now obviously very high, market forces and Big Media money would soon demand sport be run very differently, with much more focus on the premium end of the product, on the stars, on big brand clubs, and super leagues. They wanted box-office attractions to efficiently drive penetration and eyeballs, and needed new business-focussed leaders in sport with whom they could do business.

They wanted modern leadership with easier structures of governance and decision making; it made, for example, little business sense to offer them a product of 92 clubs in the old EFL. It would need to be only the very top end of the game in England, and the EPL arrived as a natural consequence, if not without major angst and political battles within the game.

As the UK contemplates a new government regulator for football, many of the old battles fought, deals done, pay-offs made, to set up the EPL, will come back into focus, often with bitterness.

Those were difficult days.

By now, as market forces got going, some owners of sports clubs had realised exactly the direction of travel and what they felt they had to do to buy a ticket for this *"gravy train"*.

It wasn't just about being an owner of sport; it was about being an owner of *"winning sport"*.

That was how to create a brand. Kids like big, successful teams, and often end up becoming lifetime fans of the top team in their early formative years.

Many entrepreneurs and investors saw correctly the start of what would be a polarisation in the industry, between those clubs and brands seen as premium, and those not, all driven by what the media sector needed.

These people started to position themselves aggressively to invest in this future. People like Peter Risdale of Leeds United, David Murray of Glasgow Rangers, and Ken Bates of Chelsea.

THE RACE TO BE "PREMIUM"

Leeds United is a storied English team but was a rather run-down and unsuccessful brand in the 80s and 90s.

In 1997, Risdale saw the direction of travel and was desperate to get his club into the brand castle before the drawbridge was pulled up.

Leeds had ambition, and were going in the right direction, but Risdale was impatient. He did not have the squad to aim for the very top of the league and maybe a Champion's League spot, and went on the hunt for better players. The idea was to invest in the squad to guarantee future success which would in return generate brand and revenues long-term.

The elusive yet seductive virtuous circle.

Fortunately for Leeds they found Ray Ranson, an ex-football player who had transitioned to the insurance industry. His understanding of both worlds was crucial to finding a corporate finance solution for the capital Risdale needed. Ranson brought an insurer who would underwrite debt, where the credit default risk was transferred from the lender to an insurer, for a fee and premium of course. (This is a risk mitigation technique we discuss in later chapters, and there is no doubt that Ranson was an innovator.)

In 2001, Leeds reached the UEFA Champions League semi-final and finished fourth in the EPL. Risdale got very excited and doubled down on the same strategy, signing Dominic Matteo for £4.25m, Olivier Dacourt for £7.2m, Mark Viduka for £6m and Rio Ferdinand for £18m, that next summer. This was very big money in those days.

In a classic example about ambition, debt-financing, and risk in sport, Risdale went too far, as did Murray and Bates. He went to the corporate finance well again, taking out even more debt by selling forward income from the season tickets and corporate hospitality boxes. That way, they managed to raise £60m, the biggest loan raised by an English club at the time.

They bought even more players.

Results on the field more than disappointed, and the circle quickly turned vicious, as opposed to virtuous.

Ultimately, Leeds got relegated at the end of the 2002-2003 season and went insolvent soon after. They took a generation to recover and have never broken back into the elite circle of English clubs again. They are currently owned by the San Francisco 49s.

The lessons of Risdale, Murray, and Bates, who all bankrupted their clubs, are sadly often forgotten in the enthusiasm of bull markets.

This intense disruption in football wasn't an isolated phenomenon. Sport everywhere was being forced to evolve, by Big Media. Without mercy. 1995 saw the arrival of the professional game in rugby union, basically as collateral damage to another ongoing media war, this time between the Murdoch and Packer families.

Murdoch wanted to establish his PayTV network in Australia, and again needed premium sport rights to gain traction. So he went after rugby, and its top players, who at the time were not professional athletes and all had other day jobs. The monies offered to them were thus life-changing in every way.

Packer responded in kind.

This understandably destabilised the entire ecosystem of the sport, and the International Rugby Board (IRB) decided to embrace professionalism, as they realised that this was happening with or without them. Looking at what was happening in the southern rugby nations, northern hemisphere players also thought it was time for change, particularly in England where the RFU was becoming a commercial success, and not sharing any of this new money with players.

After all, they thought, these people were supposed to be amateurs only playing the game for fun, like back in the Rugby public school, with the old DNA as an upper-class game that should only be played by people who could afford it.

Players though weren't happy with the unfairness of a governing body getting rich, on their sweat.

"If the game is run properly as a professional game, you do not need 57 old farts running rugby. What I think gets me and a lot of players now is the hypocrisy of the situation. Why are we not just honest and say there is a lot of money in the game? It is becoming a professional game."
Will Carling, England Captain

The professionalisation of rugby was initiated by these external forces: the media industry designing and packaging content to allow them to attract subscribers, rebalancing the bargaining power between players and their governing bodies, forcing the latter to accept that rugby had to change.

Looking at how this sport of rugby union has evolved in 28 years; it provokes a pause for thought.

"It is clear that football is a gentleman's game played by hooligans; rugby instead is a hooligan's game played by gentlemen."
Chancellor of Cambridge University, date unknown (c.1890s)

Rugby Union, perhaps the most violent game in the world, has always had an implicit code of conduct. The brutality of the field could never change the decency and dignity of the players before or afterwards. No quarter was given or asked by players of this game, but friends they remained, and they looked on the comparative cheating, feigning injury, and lack of stoicism, prevalent in football, with disgust. There is an argument that as rugby union has become professional, these values are now dissipating. When it's all about money, that tends to happen. Media moguls didn't care, and saw a value in rugby, sport, that the industry itself didn't see, or want to see. And they used that value to rip up the old structures and governance.

To quote *Deep Throat*:

"Always just follow the money."

Cricket followed that money soon after.

Twenty20 cricket, also called T20, is a shortened faster-paced format of the game that has now truly revolutionised cricket. The idea was to boost the popularity of the sport with the younger generation. Cricket was dying and the game needed to be reimagined, to engage with a wider audience. The T20 World Cup in 2007 was a fantastic success, particularly in India where around 730m people watched it. New formats that attract media dollars always demand changes in structure and governance, and the Board of Control of Cricket in India (BCCI) decided in 2008 to create the leading T20 league in the world: the Indian Premier League (IPL). And who bought the rights? Murdoch again. More precisely, Lachlan Murdoch, son of Rupert, who acquired them for $67m. Since then, the IPL has been a notable commercial success: extremely popular and highly profitable. It has become a business, and model, very similar to the major leagues in the US.

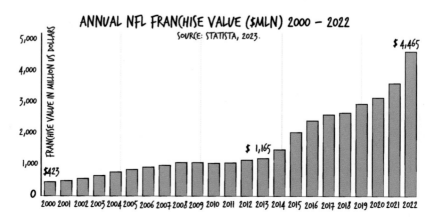

102

The media sector, its moguls and its money, were now driving a horse and cart through old traditions. This media boom had filled sports coffers everywhere, and sport became a true asset class. The valuation of clubs/franchises went up dramatically, especially in the US.

The conclusion, in hindsight, is simple and obvious. Once the industry of sport accepted the money of Big Media, its future would be, from that point, forever intertwined with it.

For good and bad.

Chapter Seven

THE DEATH OF THE SPORT SECRETARY

With so much money in the air, so many new bidders for sport, conflicts between leagues and their big clubs, the loss of control over player's remuneration, it was clear that the old way of doing things just couldn't hold. The game was starting to feel the need to professionalise its leadership.

Until the early 90s the role of the sports administrator in Europe was mainly about what is called *"rules and regs"*, namely the regulations, fixturing, registration of players and disciplinary issues. Today's CEO was back then called the *"secretary"*, just like the most prestigious golf clubs even today.

That rules-and-regs *"secretary"* just wasn't going to hack it going forward. The new world was demanding a new skill set; more strategic, more familiar with the media and entertainment sectors, more business-like. And almost always this needed to come from outside, from other industries.

Sadly, these outsiders were not always welcome. All those of my generation, coming of age in the 90s, will recognise the dynamic. The CEO title was distrusted, disdained, often quietly despised by the old people who inhabited the industry of sport.

This is my own story as that outsider.

FROM LAKE GENEVA TO LAKE COMO

In May 1998 I was 34 and sitting by Lake Geneva in Lausanne in tears. It was a beautiful Saturday and I had just heard by radio that my team Celtic had won the league, with a victory on the last day, depriving arch-rivals Glasgow Rangers of a record breaking 10 tiles in a row. I was living in Italy at the time, working at Virgin Records, and I had lost touch with Scottish football since I'd left home in 1986. But this was an historic season that needed to be followed, and the relief I felt was overwhelming.

Sport is like an old lover.

"Still crazy after all these years".
Paul Simon

The next day I bought the Sunday Times to drink in all the reaction and celebration. I wasn't in the habit of buying a newspaper, but that decision would change my life. The Appointments Section popped out and in bold on the front page was an ad, run by Deloittes, for the CEO of the recently established Scottish Premier League (SPL). The SPL was a cut-and-paste wannabe of what the English had done 6 years earlier with their EPL.

I hadn't followed any of all these developments. Indeed, since the late 80s, my passion as a football fan had been more than satisfied by Italy's Serie A, which in that period was the absolute pinnacle of the game. Every single top player in the world was, or wished to be, plying their trade in Italy. I had taken that fan passion into a casual hobby that kind of got out of control.

I had started doing research for BSkyB, who had the rights for Italian football. They quickly promoted me to an on-air magazine show, and, with that profile, I had started writing for the English broadsheets. Film crews were sent to Milan and Bari for me to "*produce*" pieces with the protagonists of the day, from Silvio Berlusconi to David Platt. When Channel 4 acquired the rights to Serie A the following year, they asked "*to see my tape*". I had no tape. I was a finance guy working in the music business. They chose James Richardson to front their show, Football Italia.

So, for me, football in Scotland had very much taken a back seat, but curiosity and ego got the better of me that Sunday. I applied half-heartedly, played difficult to get, but they still ultimately offered me the post.

I took it, for various personal reasons, with a view to going back to Scotland for a rights cycle of 4 or 5 years, although in truth I wasn't particularly sure what the job I had just accepted was going to be all about. I'd have loved to have read this book in May 1998.

In the interview process, one of the club owners had asked me what I thought would be the hardest part of the role. On reflection, I waffled horrendously, for the reason I know now, and can recognise in almost every new owner in sport.

Emotion blinds all at the start. And risk in sport is always not recognised.

One of my first tasks in the role was to attend the Super Cup final in Montecarlo between Real Madrid and Chelsea, followed by the UEFA summit the following day. What struck me was seeing what looked like a playground scene of the cool kids, huddled, all plotting some naughtiness. Owners of the big clubs in whispered conversations.

It turned out they were discussing the first version of the European Super League, at that time driven by Media Partners, a Milan-based advisory group.

The rhetoric was as it is today: UEFA was a restriction of trade, peopled by enthusiastic amateurs who didn't know how to capture the full value of the product. They left too many of the big box-office Hollywood clubs on the sidelines (only each country's league-winners got in), there were not enough guaranteed games.

A lot of these complaints had been generated way back by a first-round tie in the old European Cup in 1987, between Real Madrid and Diego Maradona's Napoli. When Real Madrid won, the product was stripped of its greatest star, the Argentinian. What kind of people organise the theatre of sport where it's possible that your biggest box office player dies in the first act?

I'd never thought of all these things until that day in Monte Carlo. It was like an epiphany that in many ways dominated my thoughts and career for the next 25 years.

• • •

Authentic sport adores risk and uncertainty; but it is detested by those trying to run it for a return on their capital.

These market forces would, as I immediately saw it, inevitably tend to polarisation, and rip apart old structures, telling box-office clubs and brands that they were undervalued, and could do much better in new formats or super leagues. The governing bodies would both resist all this and then eventually appease, in an attempt to hold onto power.

UEFA has done exactly this in the last 25 years. Appeasement never works, as we saw in 2021 with the Super League. They keep coming back for more.

All of which takes you to a natural conclusion. What happens to the rest of our game, the pyramid?

This would have been the correct answer to the question in my interview, and why I should have refused the SPL job:

"Celtic and Rangers will be seduced and tempted by riches south of the border. They will have no commitment to the Scottish league you want me to run. You have given them a veto on me doing anything. You have set this up to fail. "

Scottish football was, and is, too small a TV broadcast market to be able to compete. The future was going to be around the 5 big European leagues with major populations. Scotland would be marginalised, eventually also from the European stage, on which it had done so well until the mid 80s.

Seeing this future, I then spent my 4 years in that SPL job trying to deliver what was called *"environment change"* which meant in practice killing the existing structures of football in the Scottish game, and joining up with other small leagues, in what was known as the

Atlantic League. I also tried to merge the British leagues, to allow Scotland's teams to operate in the bigger UK market.

Many of the great and good of Scottish political and sporting life came to me rather surprised:

"but you are trying to do something that will make your own role redundant".

And this was the last insight I received into the industry I'd just joined: sport and its incumbent leaders won't change. The status quo is just too comfortable. They can't conceive of someone who isn't happy to just cruise along, but who instead wants to be a change agent.

I didn't last long in Scottish football or Scotland. Before I left, there was one final entry for my diary from my days as a sport commissioner, perhaps the most important of all. 21 years later, with a media sector again in turmoil, and smaller sports everywhere maybe not going to be offered the rights deals they expect, the topic of league-owned media channels is again in vogue.

In 2002, Scotland was the innovation lab for that whole concept.

THE STORY OF SPLTV: A VERY PERSONAL MEMORY

In 2002, the Scottish Premier League went down a road called SPLTV.

The media sector was on its back, after the dot-com bust and 9/11. BskyB was the only game left in town, and it rightly took advantage. Sky bid £12m, no increase on the previous rights cycle of 1998.

Independent work done by industry expert Mark Oliver had shown that the value of the underlying game assets of the SPL could aspire to £50-60m pa. To be fair to Oliver, he had done this work 12 months previous, at the height of the ITV Digital, NTL, 3G frenzy. Rights tendering was, and still is, mainly about timing and competitor pressures. Don't let anyone tell you that it's more sophisticated. If there is no competitor, you are in trouble, and in 2002, all rights holders were in trouble.

My clubs couldn't un-see Oliver's valuation numbers, and they told me to forcibly reject the Sky bid. They then asked for options, and that is when the SPLTV concept was born.

We put together the business plan and the operational structure. We did a beauty parade for all the outsourced services, from subscription management, to production, marketing, and programming creative. They all traipsed up to Glasgow to pitch in a who's who of the sports sector.

The thing about beauty parades is that you hear everyone's great ideas. Many of those pitches revealed that the problem with Scottish football was its narrative, far too restricted to the Old Firm culture war antagonism. As a result, so many great stories of passion and local community, of the glorious history of the Scotch Professors of the English Game, were being ignored.

I loved that thought. Don't just show Celtic and Rangers games. Sell an entire historical novel, brought bang up to date, based on the crazy soap opera of fandom.

A couple of Hollywood folks would do something similar in Wales a generation later, to prove the viability of that exact point.

Someone then tells me that you have an entire week of programming to fill, and you'll need more sports rights. Before you know it, the SPLTV plan involves buying the other rights to Cups and the national team. And it's becoming a mini DAZN or Eleven.The techies then tell you that once you've proven the concept of this delivery platform, you can sell it to other rights holders as a service provider. The MLB did exactly that years later with Bamtech.

It was a beautiful project, where my role was merely to open my mind, recognise the vision of others, see that the numbers were rooted in reality. And, finally, sell it to my clubs.

As a league CEO or Commissioner, you always need to get votes for your plans, as you yourself have no real power. You therefore start building your book. I needed 11 of my 12 clubs to agree to this. The EPL's 67% threshold was, in comparison, a wet dream for me. The SPL constitution was constructed with a built-in veto for Celtic and Rangers acting in unison.

How was I going to get clubs to vote for something where they would need to leave aside the safe B2B money, in exchange for a media startup that had never been done before?

I had two advantages:
- the clubs were angry at the lowball from Sky. "*Insulting*", I was told to refer back to Vic Wakeling;
- the second advantage was in pointing out very clearly to the clubs that Sky only wanted the Old Firm games and had no interest in marketing every other single club. "*Surely we can tell our own story better?*" That resonated.

To this day, Sky has only ever wanted the Celtic and Rangers games.

I started building my consensus. John Boyle, maverick owner of Motherwell and major shareholder in Wark Clements. He was a zealot. Chris Robinson, pugnacious owner of Hearts, always liked a knife fight. Stewart Milne of Aberdeen, started as an electrician, to then build the biggest home builder in the UK. Then the clubs that always trusted me, regardless. Bill Costley of Kilmarnock and his hotel empire. Geoff Brown of St Johnstone, another big house builder. The Marr brothers, in Dundee, with Ivano Bonetti. Lord Haughey, owner of Livingston. I had seven. Eight, with Dundee United, who – to be honest – just always went with the flow.

The advice I would give to any young person needing consensus: win over the hardest sceptic, because then they'll be a proponent in your favour. If you turn them, they become your main asset. Gavin Masterton, Managing Director of the Bank of Scotland PLC, and owner of Dunfermline, always believed in my SPL and gave his support immediately. I also knew he was the personal banker of Sir David Murray at Rangers and could maybe help when I needed to get his vote. I then went to Rod Petrie at Hibs, a hard-nosed investment banker. The plan needed to have the numbers and, therefore, I asked him to be my anti-Kool Aid guy. "*Tell me this isn't going to work, Rod*". He is a dry Edinburgh corporate finance guy, today president of the SFA. He was convinced. I had 10 votes. I needed 11.

Timing is everything in life. Celtic PLC, especially, had become very public in the media about how they saw it as "*inevitable*" that they and Rangers would be playing in the EPL soon. Brian Quinn, their chairman, was also vice-chairman of the Bank of England, and carried gravitas when he spoke in the FT, as he did with that quote. Sir David Murray at Rangers was an unpredictable maverick.

Celtic and Rangers gave their apparent support to the SPLTV project each month for the next 6 months. We had fortnightly update status reports. The beauty parades. The clubs and their staffs were a massive help to us at the centre. It was 6 months of green lights and shoulders to the wheels.

We chose our partners. Worth mentioning a particular incident that is such a learning point.

Sooner or later, if you get senior, you are going to run into a Logan Roy type. A hard man who doesn't have much time for your feelings or pronouns, or even your "*mental health*". They are proactively looking to bully you and test you. Alpha male stuff.

The last two bidders for the SPLTV production contract were IMG and Granada. Bill Sinrich with IMG had cleverly aligned with local partner Wark Clements. My clubs, nevertheless, decided for Granada, but wanted Wark Clements in our team. I was told to rip them away from IMG and get them to partner with Granada. Not the most ethical thing to do. It is here that a young exec learns how hardball business really is! I did this for my clubs (I had run them up to the top of the hill and wasn't going to go all boy scout at the 11th hour). I then had to explain to Sinrich that he had lost, inventing some lame reason. He knew exactly what had happened and let me have the most aggressive barrage of personal abuse I've ever experienced. I tried to deflect, but we both knew that he was right, and it was very fair. I just took it. Bill was a fierce and formidable man, and the sports industry lost a giant of a pro when he died.

May 2002 arrived, 12 weeks before the new season. The whole 6-month project was complete. At the meeting to sign all the contracts, Rangers and Celtic declared that they would not be approving. They cited doubts, and the vote didn't pass.

83% of my clubs had had the vision and courage. Tragically, however, the league threshold for approval was 92%. The 10 clubs in favour resigned from the SPL in fury, with a public statement on the steps of the stadium, slamming Celtic and Rangers.

The project died that morning at Hampden. So did the SPL. It has never recovered and is now irrelevant in the wider context of rights holders.

I was told to go back to Sky and get the best deal.

Vic Wakeling was magnanimous in his victory and in his office turned around his PC to show me our entire plan, and workings.

"You never stood a chance Rog."

I gasped. Business is indeed hardball.

Maybe that glorious old Yorkshireman was right. Getting, and holding, a consensus of clubs is an impossible task with so much at stake. Maybe the Old Firm never had any intention to commit to Scottish football for so long, and were surprised I got so far, in what they hoped was a negotiating tactic for Sky.

• • •

Sport is politics, and like that game, is full of personal relationships, favours and betrayals. It needs to be managed with that mentality. It is not a spreadsheet business.

It is 100% that Balanced Scorecard, with Machiavelli, and SunTzu (*Art of War*) thrown in.

The sports' CEO has a difficult and much misunderstood job. The sector is full of competing stakeholders; owners, coaches, players, TV, sponsors, betting companies, all playing their own tune. They're also all likely to be heavy on the ego.

It has fans and politicians, bursting with irrational populism and partiality. And, if that isn't enough, sport has a dreadful constitution, being under the same body legislative, executive, judiciary and marketeer.

Getting things done in sport is like getting a Supreme Court judge elected through Congress. It's set up to fail, at least in Europe.

In many ways, the old "*secretary*" had it easier and simpler.

They certainly didn't need to deal with Big Finance. Now they do.

Part Two:
What Really Is Serious Finance?

Chapter Eight

FINANCE IS NOT ACCOUNTANCY

People think finance is about numbers. It's not, it's about vision.

"Let me tell you something, Mr. Sullivan. Do you care to know why I'm in this chair with you all? I mean, why I earn the big bucks? I'm here for one reason and one reason alone. I'm here to guess what that music might do a week, a month, a year from now. That's it. Nothing more. And standing here tonight, I'm afraid that I don't hear a thing. Just -- silence."
Margin Call 2011

So much more will be asked now from the leaders of our industry, in having this vision, seeing trends, anticipating change, having different relationships with broadcasters, investors and banks.

The quickest shortcut is simply to follow the money. Understand the motivations, hopes and fears, of the person who pays you, and how they in turn make their money. Every serious financier and businessperson should do this exercise. Not necessarily to assess today and tomorrow, but to see trends in years to come, and skate to where the puck will be.

What funds the NFL?

One could say the traditional TV networks in the States. So how do Fox and CBS make their money ultimately? Via selling advertising around their programming. How will advertising hold up in a recession? And when youngsters just *"don't do TV"*? ESPN and Amazon also have deals with the NFL. ESPN makes its money as part of the old cable bundle, and how long will that last in the *"cut-the-cord"* trend? Will Disney sell them? If so, as a stand-alone business, what budget will they have for rights acquisition? Amazon is a play on the e-commerce purchasing power of individuals' disposable income. In a recession, how much will they be spending on Black Friday?

The idea should be clear; follow the money as deep and far as you can go, to try to hear the music. That's when *"you'll earn the big bucks"*.

Best placed to see and understand all of this is always the finance function in a company. They own the numbers, the forecasts, and the market info.

Who is this finance person?

Early in my career, as a young auditor, I would on occasion be lucky enough to attend meetings with senior executives of big firms, meetings often well above my station and experience. I remember one such meeting with a major listed UK buildings materials company where my superior had offered an opinion to the CEO.

"Thanks for that, but to be frank, you are just here to keep score!"

Harsh, brutal, and perhaps deserved. The profession of accountancy endures this branding to the present day. Why should people listen to mere scorekeepers?

The sector of sport has seen a growth in all kinds of commentator, on podcasts and Twitter, talking about the accounts of football club A, rugby receivership B, media company C's quarterly reporting. Many of these are decent, and very well researched. Others are truly depressing, with people totally bluffing a subject of which they know nothing, and making the most absurd statements. I suppose in general, in the world of ubiquitous social media opinions and hot takes, it's become normal for *"experts"* to opine on all things from virology to fusion energy, so why should financial commentary be immune? Journalists don't have accountancy qualifications. And accountants are not financiers.

Be careful to whom you listen. Look for a proper finance person.

Nakisa Badarian, a guest on our sports-biz podcast, AreYouNotEntertained?, was a crucial member of the team that negotiated the sale of the UFC mixed-martial-arts sports business, to the entertainment conglomerate Endeavor Group, at an excellent valuation. He is a modern, strategic financier, an entrepreneur, and anything but a bean-counter. Badarian has continued his career by managing the rise of one of the top YouTube influencers, Jake Paul, and turning him into a bankable sports star. Jake has parlayed his existing loyal audience, now becoming a boxer, creating prize-fights that have been very efficient in popularity and monetisation, mainly as PayPerView (PPV) events. With other YouTubers, he and his brother have dramatically disrupted the sport of boxing, much to the disgust of the noble sport's traditional community.

In one of these Badarian-managed events, Jake Paul fought and beat a UFC fighter, and then very publicly called out the UFC organisation for badly underpaying its fighters. Clearly, this put Jake, and his manager, firmly in the sights of the formidable and rather aggressive UFC founder, Dana White.

"That guy Badarian used to be an accountant for me, and let's just say this, he no longer works for me, and I think he is a scumbag."

The easiest put-down directed to a financier is this one. He's just the *"accountant"*.

It hurts, but it's probably a fair reflection of how little people understand about the true value that a financier, as opposed to an accountant, adds. We hope to improve this understanding over these pages.

In the main, accountancy is backward looking, after-the-event, scores on the boards. One could argue that no or little value is being added, especially when the published accounts being analysed could be for a trading period ending over 2 years ago, (many sports organisations are notoriously late in filing accounts). The sport and media sectors are changing too fast for that to be much worth at all.

Accountancy and financial reporting also have other limitations. Its KPI metrics of performance are rigid, favouring a standardised approach to keeping score, (generally accepted accounting principles called GAAP), as opposed to tailored relevant reporting on a case-by-case basis. In all this, the accounting profession is making a knowing trade-off between a well-understood, simple, commodity format, and a really valuable commentary and insight.

The *"output"* of the accountant-auditor is an opinion on whether the reporting offers a *"true and fair"* view of the company. It's binary as an opinion, with not a lot of colour. You are either true and fair, or you aren't. It's a pretty basic product if truth be told.

This cookie-cutter approach works well for its purpose and audience, as it allows banks, investors and credit agencies to benchmark apples for apples. But it doesn't offer any real added-value insight.

To really understand the accounting and auditing profession well, one must be clear on what it is not doing, what it is not set up to deliver. Financial statements have limitations, and just can't reach the places a sophisticated investor and corporate financier would want to go.

"Useful financial statements must enable a user to answer three basic questions about a business: approximately how much a company is worth, its likely ability to meet its future obligations, and how good a job its managers are doing in operating the business."
Warren Buffett

Inflexible GAAP conventions make these determinations difficult, and indeed almost any accounting system will be hard pressed to furnish these answers, given the complexities of business.

In trying to find out how much a company is worth; it is common to use earnings/profits as a guide, and the most common accounting metric is EBITDA (Earnings Before Interest, Tax, Depreciation, and Amortisation). For so many, it's become the holy grail of truth and insight.

Nonsense.

Buffet argues that it is incomplete and perhaps misleading, as it omits the future investment needs of the business to fully maintain its long-term competitive position and its unit volume.

An example in sports would be focussing on the EBITDA of Manchester United, without considering the deterioration in the stadium and squad, and the capital that would be needed to bring both up to speed.

More crucially, regarding the limitations of EBITDA, any accountant of skill and experience can "*massage*" reported profits so easily and quite significantly.

In the music industry that I used to inhabit, a world full of artist advances and the potential for supply chain return of product, one has so many ways to "*smooth*" earnings, as required, with the result that much of the accounting is really misleading.
- Will the artist sell enough for me to recover the advance?
- Will the retail stores send back all that product I stuffed into them before Christmas?
- Are these costs we incurred in November exceptional or extraordinary? Exceptional costs are included in EBITDA, extraordinary ones aren't and can be taken as "*restructuring*" costs (a term given to a whole range of manoeuvres that enable managers to engage in age-old earnings management techniques). Here is what passes as an accountant's joke: "*I see we had less returns than expected, how exceptional; oh my, that artist in rehab not able to record... how extraordinary*".
- How should accountants deal with employee stock options? This is a pet hate of Buffet. If options aren't a form of compensation, what are they? If compensation isn't an expense, what is? And, if expenses shouldn't go into the calculation of earnings, where in the world should they go?

To a proper financier, it really is child's play to make the trawling of financial accounts at best solely indicative, at worst utterly worthless. There is ample scope for good creative accountants, using aggressive revenue recognition, provisioning, and write-downs, to, say, reduce profits in boom years, all of which may return useful in barren years. This is how it really works:

"*What number do we want to report this quarter? OK, I can get to that relatively easily.*"

And yet, so many people get hung up and passionate about filed accounts. To quote, Warren Buffet's famously more direct, and recently deceased, partner-in-crime at Berkshire Hathaway, Charlie Munger:

"*I think that every time you see the word EBITDA, you should substitute the words "bullshit earnings"....I would argue that a majority of the horrors we face would not have happened if the accounting profession developed and enforced better accounting."*

I am a Chartered Accountant, and this is my profession. But I myself would never ever put too much faith in reported accounts. They are just too easy to manipulate. You need a far deeper analysis to be a serious corporate financier.

Accountants look at past accounts and take a photograph of a moment in time. The best ones look at those accounts over many years and look for trends in all those old photographs. The financier is seeing the whole movie frame by frame; and can even fast forward to see how the film will end.

Top-end finance is a fundamental differentiator in understanding and creating value, and knowing if it exists at all.

Reflect on that the next time you see someone reporting on Companies House filings or doing Twitter threads on the latest EBITDA of club A.

Corporate finance, for companies, is the art and science of managing money; its deployment into investment opportunities, that themselves are looking for funding. In short, someone has money (called capital) from which they want to earn a return; someone else needs money that they want to access, as cheaply as possible:
- protect and grow my capital (Buy-side finance);
- fund projects with the cheapest possible capital and without excess risk (Sell-side finance).

Unlike the accountant, the financier is not a scorekeeper, but the person with the ability to add most value to their company/client, and the numbers involved can be eye-watering. Corporate financiers and investment bankers are smart and know this. They will often demand as remuneration a piece of the value they create (*"clipping a coupon"*), which can be in a variety of ways. The fees, commissions and bonuses around finance are juicy, and most of the best and brightest of my own generation ended up on Wall Street.

For the entertainment and content industries, buy-side financiers and investors will look at sport for a return, with a thesis on what they are hoping for from their investment. Knowing their thinking should help the sport industry to attract, and build partnerships with these providers of capital, to negotiate better, to sell better and, ideally, to create a win/win.

When people come to me to ask my opinion about investing in sport, I always reply:
"What is your investment thesis? What are you hoping will happen to grow the value of your

investment?"

These are the type of answers we could hear from a serious corporate financier:

- invest opportunistically, where distressed assets and IP can be bought cheaply. This is known in the finance sector as a *"Special Situations"* market, or, most vividly, *"vulture investing".* Good finance people know that the best investments are made more by buying well, at the right time, than by selling well;

- run the asset better. Realise that the management of this industry has left significant room for operational and execution improvement. So, bring in better skills and people. Change the value chain of the industry, cut out middlemen, try B2C;

- structure the assets we buy for the best operational leverage, using as little capital as possible, and keeping most costs variable as opposed to fixed. Look for synergies and economies of scale with other investments made in the same business, all contributing to a conglomerate of more attractive unit economics. Many investors in sport are now using multi-club investment strategies, as this portfolio of assets in theory reduces the risk of individual clubs having a bad run of results on the field. It also allows for the sharing of central cost and knowhow. If you have a portfolio of events and races that you run efficiently with top central management, as in the case of the Y11 group, you can buy new races and immediately capture more margin by allowing them to use the central services of the group, and cut their superfluous costs;

- expect a general re-rating of an asset class (like European football clubs, which are traditionally valued less generously than their franchise counterparts in the USA). Many believe that European sports assets will inevitably be rated as valuably as similar assets in America, and in finance terms this is known as a convergence play. One of the ways this will happen is through the structural change of reducing risk in that sport. If you could remove the chances of relegation, with the introduction of closed leagues, the risk would go down overnight, and the asset class would be re-rated. The same result could be obtained if you could impose hard salary caps. And by creating real knowledge and rich data around your fan base;

- use debt and leverage to maximise returns on equity (ROE) for investors.

All of these reasons, and others, then allow for a grown-up conversation with the investor, even if you don't fully agree. It has given you an idea of the mindset of who you are dealing with.

Sometimes, or often, however, you may get other answers, that are equally as useful as a guide to who you have in front of you:

- when we get promoted, the asset is worth so much more;
- I think French league media rights will catch up with England;
- it's a glorious and storied club, and we can sell that to new generations, for growth;
- I'll bring in these top managers I know from the restaurant industry, and they will

shake this asset up;
- I have this fan engagement start-up, and my uncle works in the NBA, so we can sell it easily to this industry.

All of these answers would be scarlet-red flags.

So, ask the question about the investors' thesis for return, and you can make your assessment of how to deal with, and communicate to, this person.

This is corporate finance. It has little to do with accountancy.

It's about the capitalist, and his/her vision. And it is the oldest business skill in the world; seduction and persuasion, knowing well what the human in front of you wants.

Chapter Nine

CAPITAL AND CAPITALISM

Capital is money. The people that own it want to preserve it, and deploy it, for growth, and a return.

"It is not from the benevolence of the butcher, the brewer, or the baker that we expect our dinner, but from their regard to their own interest"
Adam Smith Wealth of Nations

This insight of Adam Smith articulates the power of free markets. Even though each individual is selfishly trying to maximise his/her own interests, such free trade will inevitably lead to a better outcome for the overall society.

Capitalism has been the cornerstone of Western economies since the Industrial Revolution. Individuals, corporations and governments allocate their money to what they regard as the most attractive and profitable investments, which in theory optimises an entire economy.

But, in reality, inefficient markets and malinvestment have been a constant theme since the days of Adam Smith and have accelerated significantly in the last 40 years. We shall see why in the next chapter.

Capitalism provides funding to:
- companies or organisations that need to grow, or to finance new products/projects;
- governments that need to finance the budget deficits they run every year;
- individuals who need to buy houses, cars, or fund credit card expenditure.

The purest capitalist would argue that all the world's great innovations and progress, at scale, have come to pass when someone started to believe in a vision that they thought would make them money.

And ultimately, it's simply about competing with the next guy. Since the caveman, we have tried to do better than our neighbour, in finding food, finding a mate, and protecting a family with better shelter. Now that *"competition"* is about getting a better education and set of skills, finding a good job and being promoted, having a superior product, and marketing it better.

Competition makes us improve and helps us survive against the challenges of new players and products. Unless you are thinking every moment about who and what can eat your lunch, lunch you will inevitably lose.

Arguably, if not for this philosophy, we would live in a world of monopolistic mediocre products of poor value. Soviet Russia would be a good example of exactly that.

Companies need capital to compete, and without it, our major corporates wouldn't be much different from the 1950s. Innovation instead has rewarded those companies who efficiently took capital from someone and created new products and new markets. It has also rewarded the providers of that capital, as it should do.

FAANG STOCK PERFORMANCE VS S&P500 (%) 2010 – 2023

SOURCE: BLOOMBERG, 2020.

- FACEBOOK (+702%)
- AMAZON (+1,825%)
- GOOGLE (+384%)
- NETFLIX (+4,732%)
- APPLE (+2,208%)
- S&P500 (+284%)

Compare the top ten companies in the S&P 500 index for 1980, the year I first read Brealey and Myers, with the equivalent data today. It really brings home how much Silicon Valley's venture capital funded disruption has changed the world. In 1980, seven out of the top ten were oil companies; today, eight out of ten are technology businesses. Of the class of 2022, only Berkshire Hathaway would have been immediately recognisable to the average 1980 investor.

Top 10 companies in S&P 500 – 1980 vs 2022

1980	%	2022	%
IBM	4.3	APPLE INC	7.07
AT&T CORP	3.9	MICROSOFT CORP	6.02
EXXON CORP	3.8	AMAZON.COM INC	3.62
STANDARD OIL OF INDIANA	2.5	ALPHABET INC (CLASS A)	2.19
SCHLUMBERGER	2.4	ALPHABET INC (CLASS C)	2.04
SHELL	1.90	TESLA INC	1.95
MOBIL	1.90	NVIDIA CORP	1.72
STANDARD OIL OF CALIFORNIA	1.80	BERKSHIRE HATHAWAY INC (CLASS B)	1.52
ATLANTIC RICHFIELD	1.60	META PLATFORMS INC (CLASS A)	1.41
GENERAL ELECTRIC	1.50	UNITEDHEALTH GROUP INC	1.21

This rate of disruption is only destined to increase going forward, and in maybe only 10 years' time now, this list will again be unrecognisable. AI, quantum computing, robotics, and so much creative destruction is now on our doorstep. It could be said that the magic formula that has driven our world for generations is:

Capital + Competition = Innovation and Progress

The above is the mantra of capitalism, of Adam Smith, and every single book on business.

One of the best, *"Competitive Advantage"*, by Michael Porter, lays out a number of, what Porter calls, generic strategies for obtaining an advantage.

These are: cost leadership, differentiation, niche.

Cost leadership is a race to the bottom, via size and economies of scale. It is why we have nondescript supermarket chains and DIY stores, replacing the old characteristic grocers and hardware stores, who now can no longer compete on cost. A niche market strategy is where a business wins its competitive advantage by meeting perfectly the unique needs of a specific, small market segment.

All this will become very common after-conference bar talk in the sports industry in the next 12 months.

"Are we going mass market to compete on cost, or are we going niche?"

Sadly, I think much of the industry suffers from the wishful thinking of sport being different and special as a product. Without realising, probably, they are in the *"differentiation"* camp, and that is going to lose them their jobs. Sport as a business, as content, isn't as special and differentiated as the legacy operators think.

Earlier in this book we discussed how sport, especially in Europe, accidentally and reluctantly evolved into businesses and companies, which were financed by benefactors and local entrepreneurs. We commented on how they were simple B2B businesses that got risk-free revenues upfront, passively selling its loyal fans to others. It didn't need massive marketing budgets.

This book argues that this is all about to change, and that sport now will need capital, lots of it.

And what does that capital look like?

At the simplest level, in any business, there are two types: Equity and Debt. Someone can invest in your company (equity) or can lend it money (debt).

EQUITY

Equity capital is where you own a company. You are a shareholder and are entitled to participate in the economics of the company, in its dividend payouts, and sale value on exit. You also get representation, perhaps formally on the Board of Directors, and voting rights in proportion to your stake. These equity shares may be publicly owned on a stock market or may be privately held.

If on a stock market, the price of the shares will change in real time, as buyers and sellers trade, and you will know what they are worth to you every day. You will also have pretty much full freedom to buy and sell your shareholding when you want. In private equity you have neither of these things.

Investors in equity capital get a financial return in 2 ways:
- dividends paid out of profits;
- increase in the value of the shares over time.

Crucial to understand is that, in the last 2 decades, dividends have been less and less prevalent, and seen as marginal to a world of investing and corporate finance. With the prominence of high growth tech companies like the FAANGs (Facebook, Apple, Amazon, Netflix, Google), the vast bulk of equity investor returns have been from share price growth. What need has there really been to get a cash return in dividends, when your shares have skyrocketed, and you had the ability to sell them for massive profits?

Big Tech companies have therefore accumulated mountains of cash over the last few years.

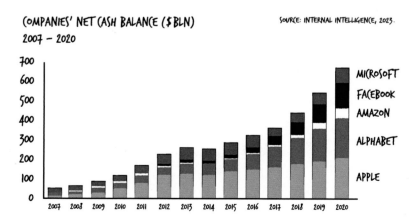

COMPANIES' NET CASH BALANCE ($ BLN) 2007 – 2020

SOURCE: INTERNAL INTELLIGENCE, 2023.

At the end of 2021, Apple had $190bn in cash on hand, Alphabet had $142bn, Amazon $79bn, and Facebook $58bn. These companies could all afford to pay significant dividends, but they didn't.

And that is simply because there are just fewer investors out there these days looking for dividend yield, and companies have therefore de-emphasised the need. Also, once you start paying dividends, it is rather hard to stop, as the markets always perceive cutting them as a sign of weakness, trouble and illiquidity.

So why bother? Especially when there is a better way to use that excess cash.

These companies have often preferred to buy back their own shares. Buying your own shares reduces the amount in circulation and is the opposite of dilution. It's arithmetically increasing the value of the remaining shares, and this phenomenon has undoubtedly been a major, if not fundamental, element in the rising stock markets in this millennium.

The FT reports that in 2022, the largest 1200 global public companies spent collectively $1.3tn in share buybacks. That is unprecedented, and three times more than 10 years ago. If (stock)markets are simply about the matching flows of supply and demand, share buybacks are what have fueled demand more than anything else.

Not all shareholders are equal.

There is a very simple yet profound distinction:
* majority equity (where you have the ability to control and influence the company;
* minority equity (where you don't, and are a passenger).

Unsurprisingly, a controlling stake in any company, making you a majority shareholder, is significantly more valuable. The *"premium on control"* can be seen every day in real life, or fictional TV dramas. The 2% holding in a company that takes the owner from 49 to 51% is significantly more valuable than the same 2% that takes the owner from 3 to 5%.

This notwithstanding, one of the most interesting themes in sport and capital in recent years has been the willingness of some investment funds like CVC, Silverlake and Arctos to be minority shareholders in sports leagues and clubs/franchises. The investment thesis of these investors often includes the idea to improve the management of underperforming assets proactively, yet, as a minority shareholder, you have no real power to do that. We have seen to date how little CVC has managed to influence and improve the prospects and performance of rugby union, seemingly powerless in dealing with horrendous governance. And yet there is an increasing appetite for minority equity investment in sport.

Several investment funds, including Arctos (already investors in Liverpool and several other US sports clubs/franchises), have expressed interest in investing in Paris Saint-Germain (PSG). It appears that the current owner of the club, Qatar Sports Investment (QSI), is ready to cede 5% to 15% of the club's equity.

One can legitimately question whether such a deal would make sense financially for an investment fund like Arctos, as the Parisian club has lost over €700m between 2019 and 2022 and expects a deficit ranging from €100m to €150m for the 2022-2023 season. What would be the investment rationale for Arctos to take minority equity in PSG? The club doesn't even own its stadium and, therefore, cannot expand it as desired.

For investors into US sport, minority equity might seem like a reasonable idea, where franchises are often profitable and cash positive, and make a tangible return on equity. But it is difficult to see how a minority stake in such a European club could be a good investment. What would be the point of owning 15% of an unprofitable business, especially when the majority owner is a nation state who isn't investing for financial return. To many classic value investors, this looks like truly asking for a bloody nose. So, what can the investment thesis of these investors be?

PSG will not be paying dividends, so investors are really in it solely for a future rise in asset valuation. What do they think will drive that growth in the value of their investment?

They must have a strong conviction on a simple metric: the value of sports broadcast rights in France. This is a binary bet, that perhaps will disappoint, and if it does, we shall see a massive destruction in investor capital.

I fear too many people, especially minority investors, are in sport for the showbiz and the status; the ability to hang out in the locker room and call themselves an *"owner"* (even if they only hold 1%). Someone once said that minority shareholding in a sports franchise is often just an expensive season ticket!

If sport media rights and resultant valuations come down, or even just plateau, there will be a lot of very embarrassed investors looking foolish with those season tickets.

For the existing shareholders in these sports assets, there is a very legitimate reason to allow external minority investors to come in. It is an opportunity to put a price tag on the club, and provides liquidity, meaning existing owners can get some cash out, *"take some money off the table"*, without giving up control over the franchise.

Control is everything in finance. The film Social Network highlighted very well how it can be used and abused. Protecting yourself legally as a minority shareholder is a major theme in investing.

A minority equity investor, especially if above 25%, will not easily accept being without a very significant say or influence on the company. They will, or should have, what is called a shareholders' agreement, giving them more than the usual minority voting influence. They will employ the best corporate lawyers to impose solid restrictive terms on the majority owners, and the Board, around:

- veto rights on *"reserved matters"* like major expenditures, hires, taking on debt, exit;
- the right of first and last refusal to buy all the company;
- liquidation preferences on insolvency. These are incendiary. In the case of a 1X Liquidation Preference, minority investors are guaranteed to get back at least the money they invested. They also get a share of the money in excess of that threshold in proportion to their share of the company (25% of the residual amount if they own 25% of the company). Likewise, for 2X liquidation preference, investors are guaranteed to get at least twice the money invested.

One wonders what terms, like these, CVC have secured with the rugby governing bodies?

Such legal protections can become devastating, especially for smaller companies, like sportech, and will become somewhat of a torture chamber in the coming years, when many early-stage companies run out of cash, and their minority investors suddenly point to all these clauses.

In good times, these weapons were unneeded, and left unused. Forgotten about. Now however, many founders will understand fully the meaning of the phrase,

"Your valuation, my terms".

DEBT

Debt capital is when, simply, one party borrows money from another, with a commitment to reimburse the loan over a given period of time, with interest.

A personal overdraft or credit card is one very common and simple example of debt, but in the case of corporate finance, the most obvious examples would be bank overdrafts/loans, or corporate bonds.

The interest rate on debt, called the coupon, is the *"yield"* an investor gets on lending that capital.

Debt, on the surface, involves no ownership rights for the lender, but anyone familiar with The Merchant of Venice knows the reality of being in debt, especially when unable to pay.

Debt almost always obliges the borrower to pay an annual interest payment, (whereas equity does not oblige a company to pay a dividend). Debt is in this way a harder taskmaster.

Interest expenses are tax deductible for a borrower, whereas dividends aren't.

Teaching the philosophies and practicalities of what capital one uses to finance oneself, debt or equity, is one of the main objectives of this book. But before diving deep into these matters, there is much to absorb about the world of interest. It is the kernel of all of finance.

"Compound interest is the eighth wonder of the world. He who understands it, earns it; he who doesn't, pays it".
Albert Einstein

It takes a genius to hit the nail on the head with such clarity and precision. Sadly, I fear the world of sport and sport investing will soon learn exactly what Mr Einstein means.

If you put £100 in the bank, offering 7% interest, and leave it for 10 years, it will be worth £197, almost double. Interest earned on interest.

Likewise, imagine you need to choose between two offers:
- offer A: $100m in 30 days;
- offer B: $1 today that will double every day for the next 30 days.

Offer B in reality returns over $1bn! Compound interest.

Compounding works like this also for a borrower.

You pay interest on interest due, and before you know it you are in a deadly debt spiral.

The finance industry likes to complicate the simplicity of what is debt versus equity, with what some call hybrid instruments.

HYBRID CAPITAL

These are a mix of both, tailored to the specific needs of investors. As in the world of fine cuisine, where the idea of strict separation of fish and meat, sweet and sour, has long since been superseded, high finance is the same. Creativity has no limits. If we have learned anything from the last few years in the markets, it's that smart operators can devise very complex and sophisticated capital instruments, with myriad conditions and characteristics. Here are some examples of hybrid capital:

PREFERENCE SHARES

In theory this is equity capital, but with many characteristics of debt. For example, holders of preference shares will have several additional benefits compared to regular ordinary shareholders. First, they will receive fixed reliable dividends, whereas ordinary shareholders don't. In case of bankruptcy, the liquidated assets will be used to pay back preferred shares in precedence to common shareholders, just like the infamous *"liquidation preferences".* Hence the name *"preferred"* shares.

In this category we can also find shares with different categories of voting rights (Golden shares etc). The rise of dual classes of shares, notably in examples like Facebook, is not a positive for corporate governance.

CONVERTIBLE BONDS

These are probably the most common hybrid instruments. They pay interest like a regular loan/bond, but also offer the holders the option to convert their bonds into equity shares at a future date. The conversion ratio is in the main predetermined. Investors like convertibles because it's giving them an option, optionality, on the future *"success"* of the company.

I myself have consistently used convertibles notes as a tool to invest in early stage, as I like the interest coupon yield. I am loaning the company debt capital, at say 8% interest rate, with an option to convert my loan in shares at a 25% discount to the next valuation round.

EXOTIC BONDS

These are debt instruments where the interest rate varies based on the performance of the borrowing company. Think of them as a loan where the interest expense is calculated like a revenue share, in relation to a fundamental driver of the business, like the oil price, or a specific operating variable. The more the borrower earns, the higher the interest payment. These types of bonds are as close to minority equity as you can get. But again, will have a precedence on liquidation.

ZERO COUPON BONDS

Zero Coupon bonds formally don't pay interest, hence the name. And, as such, cost less than the face value of the debt. But, at maturity, the full amount is redeemed. The difference is the equivalent of the interest payments. This is mainly a tax planning tool creating capital gains more than interest income. The finance industry is very good and constructing various types of instruments, also for tax reasons.

• • •

Ultimately, if one looks closely, minority equity capital isn't that different, in control and governance, from debt capital. It's all in the fine print. And this is where you see the difference between a superficial financier and a real quality operator: the crafting of the terms and protections.

Lending money on paper does not confer any ownership, and you have no right to vote in shareholders meetings. You just hope you get paid back. Well, not really.

Business is a hardball game, and no-one naive is going to last very long. The professional lender of debt will have those same corporate lawyers to protect their interests to make sure that they get repaid, even when things don't go as promised.

These are called *"lending covenants"*. Things like:
•   security and control over assets;
•   significant restrictions on the management operation of a company;
•   paid out first in the event of insolvency or liquidation.

This is very similar to what a good VC will be doing when investing in minority equity.

Unsurprisingly then, in recent years, the same lack of discipline we have seen around minority equity shareholder protection applies also to debt. Such that there is a specific term for bull market laxity from lenders.

It's called Covenant-lite.

Big banks financing debt capital generate a lot of commissions, arrangement and underwriting fees. There is thus a huge incentive to get these deals done, especially in times when capital is readily available and easy. Eyes get closed, corners get cut, and it's all about booking the transaction and earning a bonus. Problems are tomorrow's worry.

The 2007/2008 global financial crisis was a poster child of Covenant-Lite. Mortgages were getting approved with no controls; bad debts being re-packaged into what was sold as safe investments, rating agencies not paying attention and conflicted.

Now in 2023 we are arguably back at the same cliff-edge, with more and more loans Covenant-Lite.

In 2000, these loans represented only 1% of the leveraged loan market. In 2021, it was around 90%, and astonishing figure.

COVENANT–LITE SHARE OF TOTAL NEW BOND ISSUANCE (%) 2007 – 2021

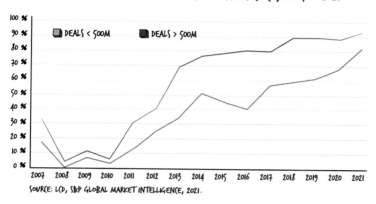

SOURCE: LCD, S&P GLOBAL MARKET INTELLIGENCE, 2021.

So, it is worth a second to reflect on so much similar debt now being offered to sport, eager to finance a binary idea that media rights always go up.

These bull markets end when something changes. Like the one Jenga block that collapses the tower. What will be the particular block (if any) that brings down the industry of sport? Piracy?

Understanding, as we now have, the basics of capital, whether equity or debt, is good. Understanding how money really works is something completely different.

Chapter Ten

THE MURKY WORLD OF MONEY AND CAPITAL

There is one obvious way to enjoy a standard of living beyond what you earn.

It's called debt.

Tyrion Lannister: *"For years I've heard that Littlefinger is a magician: whenever the Crown needs money, he rubs his hands together and - poof! - mountains of gold."*

Bronn: *"Let me guess: he's not a magician."*

Tyrion Lannister: *"No."*

Bronn: *"He's stealing it?"*

Tyrion Lannister: *"Worse: he's borrowing it."*

Game of Thrones

Money and capital has a cost, and that cost is not a constant; it changes. Over the years, I have found this concept - the cost of money, the cost of capital - to be one of the most difficult to grasp, even for people in business.

Now especially is the time to understand it very well. For 40 years we have lived almost entirely in an era of very cheap money, and very accessible capital. Maybe no longer.

Our story should really try and put this into context as to why. The truth is all around us, if we care to look.

For some *"The Wizard of Oz"* movie is a metaphor for the monetary system, with many economists and historians insisting that the book is actually a political allegory, where each character represents a person or group active in the late 1800s. The scarecrow represents the farmers in the West, most of whom had mortgages, and owed money to the bankers in the East. The yellow brick road is the gold standard. Industrial workers are represented by the tin man; his joints are rusted, and he can no longer work, much like the 18% of Americans who were unemployed in 1894. The lion is William Jennings Bryan, a populist leader and the face of the Free Silver Movement. He believed that adding silver to the gold standard would ease deflation and solve the nation's economic woes. And of course, there is a nod to gold in the title: the Wonderful Wizard of Oz or O-Z the abbreviation for an ounce of gold. The Emerald City is America's capital, Washington, D.C. where everything is seen through dollar-coloured glasses (which is why everything appears to be green). In the end, it is Dorothy's shoes that save her - her silver shoes. The shoes were silver in the book but were changed to ruby for the movie. It turns out, the solution was right under her nose the entire time: adding silver to the money supply.

This may seem all rather obscure, and a stretch, but understanding how money really works is perhaps deliberately hidden to most of us:

"It is well enough that people of the nation do not understand our banking and monetary system, for if they did, I believe there would be a revolution before tomorrow morning."
Henry Ford

Finance is an insider's game. What Ford refers to here is fractional reserve banking. In plain English, the man on the top of the Clapham Omnibus thinks banks merely lend out the money that they receive from depositors. But actually, they are much more ambitious than that, leveraging all deposits from you and I, and then creating more monies, practically out of thin air.

One can find oneself dragged into a rabbit hole of extraordinary conspiracy theories when speaking about bankers, debt, the creation of the Federal Reserve, the dollar's reserve currency status, the gold standard, and the dark power games of banking. Suffice to say, Henry Ford is onto something that I would translate into a simple reality: Banks do not hold in cash anything like the amount of money they owe their depositors.

I recommend the book *"Creatures from Jekyll Island"* for those brave enough to wander around this yellow brick road.

And as banking isn't about grandma's savings account and a simple loan, neither is corporate finance about accounting, balance sheets, and plain vanilla shares in companies. In this chapter we shall try and bring out the many elements that affect you and me, in business, and also sport.

It all comes back to the cost of money; the rate of interest.

So theoretically, what determines interest rates?

Economics basically works in cycles. In bad times, no one has any money to buy things, to consume. Inflation is low as there is no demand. Low inflation means low interest rates, and cheap money incentivises capitalists to invest in new ideas, new projects and new businesses. This puts money in people's pockets, they start to spend, the new businesses see demand rising, and make nice profits and returns. This encourages other capitalists to try and do the same, they invest also. This is known as boom times, called the bull market part of the cycle, where loads of optimistic capital, walls of money, push demand for goods and labour; wages go up, and so do prices. All this causes inflation (simple microeconomic supply and demand dynamics).

This forces the cycle to turn, into the bear market. There is over-investment, often malinvestment, causing overcapacity. Too many capitalists chasing the same return, profits go down at the same time as interest rates are going up to combat rising inflation. Companies start laying off workers, shutting down factories, people have less disposable income to spend if they are unemployed, inflation comes down. That is a recession.

Rinse and repeat. This is known as the *"business cycle"*.

Recessions in this way have always been seen as a necessary and inevitable cleansing reset. The business cycle is as natural as the moon and the tides, and used to work very well.

Recent decades however have seen dramatic changes to this old school reality. Politicians don't get re-elected in the down phase of the cycle, so folks looking to get elected will try to prevent and delay it, being much more *"interventionist"* in trying to game the system. The phrase used for this is *"kicking the can down the road"*.

So why would Hollywood make a film, full of hidden messages, about something so obscure as the gold standard? Is it that important?

"Gold is money, everything else is credit"
John Pierpont Morgan 1912

John Pierpont Morgan (1837-1913), more commonly known as J.P. Morgan, was the founder of the bank of the same name, that was, and is, one of the most powerful financial institutions of its time.

Almost all big finance deals in sport have JP Morgan in the background somewhere, like the proposed European Super League.

John Pierpont was also a key player in shaping the modern American financial system and stabilising the American economy during periods of financial crisis like the Panic of 1907.

In those old days, the economies of the world operated within the parameters of what was called *"The Gold Standard"*. Anything you did as a government was dependent on how much actual gold you had as reserves. Gold was indeed the only money that mattered, and, in theory, any paper currency was legally convertible into the physical metal, and this was in fact printed on the notes:

"I promise to pay the bearer on demand..."

Gold was the centre of the monetary system, and this limited all governments in what they could do. They couldn't print or spend money without having the equivalent holding of gold, of Fort Knox hard bullion. Debt was thus limited, and you had to live within your means. Your ability as a government to spend and invest depended on what you earned as a country.

Many of us will remember that this way of thinking was how our grandparents conceived money. Things were bought only when money had been saved.

But times changed. Richard Nixon abandoned the gold standard in 1971, as expenditure, like the Vietnam War, was making the US government tight on actual gold coverage. There are other very complex political reasons around international geopolitics at the time, worth further study for those that like rabbit holes.

Nothing after 1971 was ever the same and we entered the era of debt, (government, corporate, and personal). Credit cards, and paying on the *"never never"*, changed personal consumption.

The below graph tells a profound story.

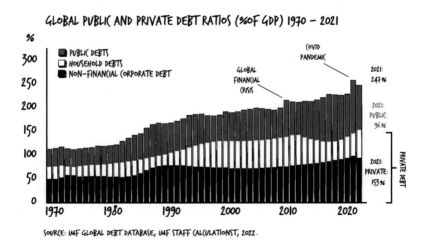

SOURCE: IMF GLOBAL DEBT DATABASE, IMF STAFF CALCULATIONST, 2022.

In 1970, the combined debt, of governments, companies and private individuals, represented about one year of the world GDP (Gross Domestic Product). That's a 100% debt/GDP ratio, as if a person had a total debt equal to his/her annual salary. Not low, but manageable.

As you can see, this ratio is now at 250%, and rising dramatically.

GDP comes from expenditure, and if debt allows you to spend more than you have yet produced, that's going to be a very significant driver of growth; meaning we are spending and investing with money that has not been earned, arguably stolen from future generations (who at some point will need to repay that debt).

Much of the world growth in GDP since the 70s has come from the massively increasing use of debt.

Debt is the truth whose name must not be spoken.

Legally, this end of the gold standard theoretically did not mean that the US government could carelessly borrow an endless amount of money. Constitutionally, debt is capped by the US Debt Ceiling. But of course, this hasn't worked at all in the profligate pork politics of Washington, and the US Congress has agreed to either suspend (ignore) or increase that ceiling over a hundred times since WWII.

US PUBLIC DEBT VS REPUBLICAN & DEMOCRAT CONTROL OF WHITE HOUSE, SENATE AND HOUSE ($TLN) 1980 – 2021

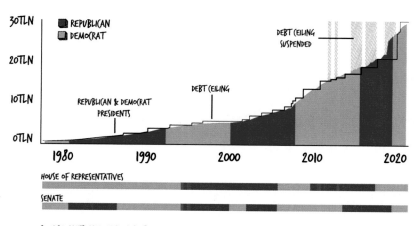

SOURCE: NATIONAL ARCHIVES, FEDERAL RESERVE ECONOMIC DATA, BBC RESEARCH

Debt has of course never been politically controlled, and has soared. We have funded our lifestyles and businesses with, in reality, a large mountain of I-Owe-You notes (IOUs).

These IOUs are obviously held by someone, by a provider of debt capital, a lender. This could be a combination of petrodollar states, China, our pension funds or insurance companies. And these investors lent their capital willingly, because they were getting an interest rate, a return, that is known as a yield. We will see in the next chapter the crucial importance of *"yield"*.

From the borrower's point of view, the interest rate is key, determining the cost of our mortgage payments, our credit card and our bank overdraft. A rising interest rate is painful, especially if you have a lot of debt.

2023 has seen a very significant rise in interest rates, and many governments, businesses, and family budgets are squealing in pain. The below graph shows that pain in the budget of the US government.

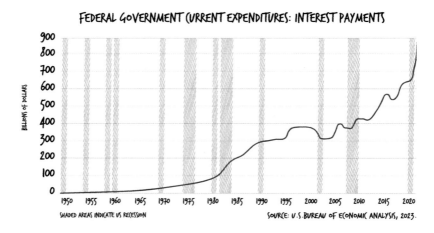

FEDERAL GOVERNMENT CURRENT EXPENDITURES: INTEREST PAYMENTS

SHADED AREAS INDICATE US RECESSION

SOURCE: U.S. BUREAU OF ECONOMIC ANALYSIS, 2023.

Debt always allows excess expenditure, and that in the business cycle creates inflation. In the 70s, for a variety of reasons, like the oil crisis, and being freed of the chains of Dorothy's gold standard, inflation took off. We reached 23% inflation when I started high school in 1975. That's simply unsustainable.

With the odd blip, we have for 40 years since then seen a downward trend. Our whole world today is explained by this simple narrative.

At the start of the 80s, it was felt that inflation was so damaging that it needed to be controlled with extreme zeal. Central banks increased interest rates dramatically, encouraging businesses and people to save money, instead of spending it. As a result, consumption (demand) slowed down and prices decreased. This was done, most painfully, by the US government, and the head of the Federal Reserve, Paul Volcker, reaching a peak in interest rates of 20% in 1981. Margaret Thatcher did something similar at the start of her premiership in the UK. In November 1979, the UK government raised interest rates to 17% in order to tackle inflation. This obviously harmed manufacturing industry and exports but did eventually have the desired effect on inflation. As always, a picture tells a thousand words:

HOW INFLATION HAS CHANGED SINCE 1970 — CONSUMER PRICES INDEX
SOURCE: OFFICE FOR NATIONAL STATISTICS, 2022.

To the sound of the screams of business and society, inflation was brought under control in both countries, allowing interest rates to eventually reduce. This was a time where Thatcher and her government were universally despised, and she would have lost an election had it occurred in 1981. The economy turned around in time, and she had the popularity of a win in the Falklands war to deliver her a landslide in 1983.

Timing is everything.

The 80s then, with decreasing inflation and interest rates, were the bull phase of the business cycle, the *"Greed is Good"* decade, the mantra of economic *"Laissez-Faire"*, and growth through the use of debt, untethered to the Gold Standard. Debt capital exploded, including the most aggressive and risky types like high-risk, high-return loans called junk bonds.

Michael Milken and his company Drexel Brunham took advantage of the huge appetite for high yield returns in the market. They simply gave investors and asset managers what they wanted, regardless of the risks. They needed to generate high returns to attract new customers, and junk bonds were the ideal product.The quest for yield and return in the capital markets drives everything, and debt introduced a new era for capitalism, the era of the corporate raider and hostile takeovers. With all its consequences and excesses. Leverage is a fancy term for this use of debt. But it isn't just cosmetic terminology or jargon. As Archimedes said, give me a lever and I will lift the world. In corporate finance, that lever is debt. It works like this:

I can buy Manchester United at a cost of 100, and then sell it in 2 years at 200, I have doubled my money, a 100% return. If, however, I use leverage and buy the club, using 20 of my own money, and 80 of external debt, and sell for the same 200, I pay back my debt of 80, and have 120. That is a 6 time, 500%, return on my 20 of equity invested.

It seems so simple, and indeed in many ways it is. It is the way most private equity (PE) companies have made their fabulous returns over the years. If you are buying, with debt, a company that is profitable and generating cash, you can finance the interest payments, and repay the debt, all from the cash flow of the company you buy. A genius business model, where the 80s was the moment when the leveraged buyout (LBO) became the entire zeitgeist in finance. It was a period typified by the phrase *"Barbarians at the Gate"*, taken from the book by two Wall Street Journal writers, Bryan Burrow and John Helyar. It describes the battle for one such cash rich company, RJR Nabisco, as rival tribes of barbarians came after a sleepy, debt-free company, throwing off wads of tobacco cash. They both saw the LBO play, using the lever of junk bonds.

Corporate raiders were more than happy to be able to finance transactions with very little of their own equity, and debt-to-equity ratios became ridiculously high. Milken and his friends made themselves a fortune by being the intermediary, and the volume of transactions rocketed.

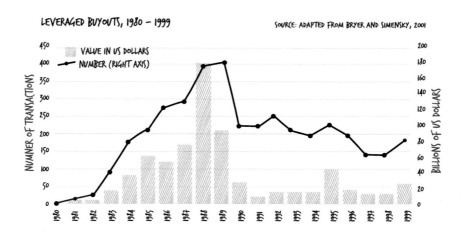

LEVERAGED BUYOUTS, 1980 – 1999   SOURCE: ADAPTED FROM BRYER AND SIMENSKY, 2001

But to be honest, everyone, not just corporate raiders, were all loading up on debt. With gusto.

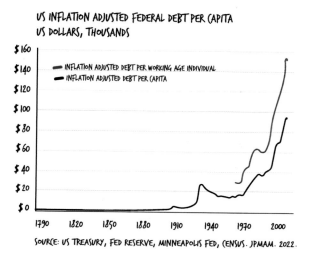

US INFLATION ADJUSTED FEDERAL DEBT PER CAPITA
US DOLLARS, THOUSANDS

SOURCE: US TREASURY, FED RESERVE, MINNEAPOLIS FED, CENSUS. JPMAM. 2022.

It all came to a crashing halt with the Black Monday stock market collapse of 1987. That was, in many ways, my generation's wake-up call. It wasn't pretty, and the fall-out looked dangerously contagious. Something needed to be done.

The Federal Reserve of the USA is the central bank of the American government and acts as the lender/saviour of last resort. Its chairman at the time, Alan Greenspan, in what would become known for the next 35 years as the Fed Put, came across the horizon like the cavalry, and interest rates were slashed drastically to boost confidence... and liquidity.
"Don't worry guys, the government has your back."

The Fed Put is known, by its critics, as capitalism when times are good, and profits go to private investors; but socialism when markets change, and the taxpayer has to pick up the bill of a bail-out.

This is a good point to remember Henry Ford. It's best that folks don't realise.

And to illustrate Ford's quote, Greenspan even likes to joke about his ability to make things look much more complex than they actually are:

"Since I've become a central banker, I've learnt to mumble with great incoherence. If I seem unduly clear to you, you must have misunderstood what I said".

153

These people are laughing at us.

This central-banker interventionist approach has stayed with us ever since, and indeed has become more prevalent, most obviously in 2008 during the Big Short fall-out. A classic case of provoking *"moral hazard"*, a fascinating phenomenon.

Moral hazard involves one party taking risks that others will have to pay for. Those who pay the costs often lack complete information about those who take the risks. Moral hazard may exist in a variety of spheres, including insurance, lending, investing, and more. For instance, in insurance there is always the risk that policy holders will adopt riskier behaviors once they have purchased insurance and are protected.

Greenspan and his successors at the Federal reserve brought in the era of the all-powerful central banker, who would vastly expand their role in *"managing"* the capital and financial markets. They would make a profession of denying all the cleansing benefits of the natural business cycle and would become Messi-level at kicking the can, the problem, down the road.

To those who believe in simple market price-discovery, the business cycle, the positive reset of any recession, and the Adam Smith invisible hand of the market, this *"managing"* of markets just isn't capitalism.

Adam Smith is the philosopher king of capitalism, with his masterpiece *"The Wealth of Nations"*. His statute stands in the university we both attended in Glasgow, and I am a disciple, if that wasn't clear yet.

There is a cadre of lateral macroeconomic thinkers who believe that markets, and interest rates, are now deliberately managed by the world's central banks to keep interest rates artificially low. These contrarian thinkers, including my colleague and friend Grant Williams, believe that rather than always letting the markets find the right price for everything, politicians and government central banks have deliberately distorted the normal business cycle, and done everything in their power to not let markets go down. They want to stay elected, and in power.

When markets appear to be collapsing, interest rates are immediately dropped, extra money is printed, extra debt taken on, all to prop asset values, and prevent bubbles from deflating. Today's superstar central banker in this way is so lauded for being the financial markets' elite fireman, when in reality they are better seen as the arsonist.

Regardless of intent and blame, the truth is that now if interest rates were to rise as they should, a load of people, companies and governments would just go pop under their gigantic debt burden. A debt burden created by central bankers. An Inconvenient Truth.

"You have to understand, most people are not ready to be unplugged. And many of them are so inured, so hopelessly dependent on the system, that they will fight to protect it".
Morpheus to Neo in The Matrix,

Low interest rates may be all that is preventing the system from collapsing, but it, by definition, leads to a bad allocation of capital, called malinvestment.

If you don't know what money and capital should really cost, because the interest rate is *"gamed"*, you will assess investment opportunities very badly. One could make a case that this is exactly what has happened in these recent decades, to the letter.

The purpose of capital markets should be to direct scarce resources to the places, the investments, of highest return. It's that simple. Capitalism is based on the idea of *"creative destruction".*

The concept, first used by economist Joseph Schumpeter, refers to innovations and new processes or methods of production that inevitably take over and destroy existing ones that are less efficient. This is an essential element of progress, but it can only happen if capital is allocated efficiently. Money needs to go to the smartest people to finance their best ventures. But if you don't allow the markets to find their level, capital is mispriced, and bad investments are made. You cut off Smith's *"invisible hand"* of the market.

This is the fundamental, foundational question of this book: if capital is not priced correctly, what remains of the Brealey and Myers Principles of Corporate Finance? And what does it mean for the valuations of assets in the sports industry.

"Capitalism without failure is like religion without hell."
Charlie Munger Berkshire Hathaway

Capitalism needs failure to filter good ideas, businesses and leaders from bad ones. Without such auto-regulation, markets do not fulfill their role.

Much economic theory talks about the efficiency of markets, but when the cost of capital is manipulated lower, and money is too cheap, efficiency and rationality go out of the window. Our markets and their valuations are, to quote *Marcellus Wallace* in *Pulp Fiction:*

*"pretty f***ing far from OK".*

This is not an opinion often heard in market commentary, even by the brand financial media. Or indeed by wealth management professionals. These people are all in the business of talking of valuations always going up; to attract even more assets under management for themselves and their remuneration.

All of this has been a long time in the making. At the start of the 1990s, something else happened which also dramatically changed the delicate mechanisms that link growth, debt, inflation and the interest rate (cost of money).

The world economy saw the start of globalisation, a process which culminated with the entry of China into the World Trade Association in 2001. Free trade everywhere was given a massive boost, and it was great news for the corporations of the world as this, overnight, put a huge and cheap labour force into the world economy, reducing prices for everything and keeping a natural but heavy foot on the throat of inflation. Jobs were moved to lower cost countries, workers in India and China started moving out of poverty, and with their new-found disposable income, they started buying goods and services from Western corporations.

Many would argue that the big losers in all this lovely story were workers, the labour force, in the West. Indeed, data shows that the share of profits going to labour, as opposed to providers of capital, shifted lower very significantly. The working man and woman, from Iowa to Ipswich, got quietly screwed.

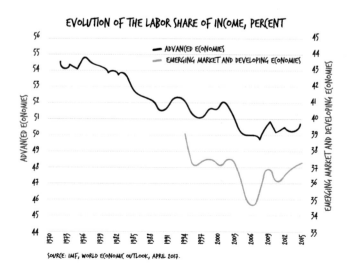

EVOLUTION OF THE LABOR SHARE OF INCOME, PERCENT

SOURCE: IMF, WORLD ECONOMIC OUTLOOK, APRIL 2017.

The 90s had all the characteristics of boom times, but crucially without the inflation and high interest rates. This new paradigm became known as the *"Goldilocks Economy"*.

Add in the moral hazard of the afore-mentioned Greenspan Fed Put, and it was clear that the business cycle, as we knew it, had altered very dramatically.

Many academics and central bankers around the world started to talk openly about how recessions could be more or less avoided.

Kansas no more indeed.

The world was entering a new world of more radical and experimental monetary policies as a consequence, led by central banks and their celebrity leaders.

Amid this New World Order, there was another very significant change adding to the punch bowl fueled celebrations. The 1993 release of Mosaic, and other browsers, gave computer users access to the World Wide Web, or the Internet, and this marked the shift to an economy based on information technology. At the same time, the decline in interest rates increased the availability of capital, so a lot of new tech companies were created. Alan Greenspan talked up the stock market, and people got more than *"over-exuberant"* in deploying their capital to make evermore speculative investments.

Between 1995 and its peak in March 2000, the Nasdaq rose 400%.

We started seeing a period where the *"return"* on capital employed was coming much more from asset appreciation, rather than yield. People became accustomed to asset prices being where they got rich. Whether in a house, or holding shares in Facebook.

No-one seemed to care about yield anymore.

Nearing the turn of the millennium, investment in technology was growing, as companies prepared for the Year 2000 problem, spending big on the Millennium Bug. Marketing also reached new heights for the sector: two dot-com companies purchased ad spots for Super Bowl XXXIII, and 17 dot-com companies bought ad spots the following year for Super Bowl XXXIV.

Sharp-eyed readers may draw comparisons with what happened with sport and Web3/crypto in 2022. Nothing in life and investing is new. The study of history is under-appreciated as a valuable skillset, in avoiding the mistakes of the past.

The bursting of these bubbles, bull markets and excessive optimism, is often flagged by the same combination of events time after time. We see iconic mergers that mark a top in valuations, (AOL and Time Warner back then), we discover mushrooming accounting frauds, and huge changes in anti-trust regulation in Big Tech (Microsoft back then). All of this is eerily similar today.

In early 2000, interest rates started to rise as things were just getting too white-hot crazy, and over in Asia, Japan had entered an old-fashioned recession. There are, again, parallels to today, as Japan now ends its *"Abenomics"* (hard yield control to deliver very low interest rates).

Tech and media values cratered: in 2000, the Nasdaq Composite Index, particularly tech-focused, dropped by 39%. Stock market start-ups were left orphaned overnight, as capital disappeared. Sportech founders in 2023 will empathize.

In less than a month after the beginning of the crash in March 2000, almost $1 trilllion worth of stock value was gone. 9/11 put the nails in the coffin of the party.

In normal times, this would have been a natural recession to cleanse and start again. But no, re-enter the hardcore Fed Put. The US government reduced interest rates dramatically, giving a clear message to the providers of capital at this point:

"you can risk all you want, because the Fed always has your back with bail-outs and reducing interest rates".

So, capital got the memo and started looking for the next asset that would benefit from low-cost debt. They found one: real estate. Greenspan himself encouraged individuals to take adjustable-rate (variable) mortgage loans rather than traditional fixed-rate mortgage rates. This is what Greenspan said in 2004:

"Many homeowners might have saved tens of thousands of dollars had they held adjustable-rate mortgages rather than fixed-rate mortgages".

Trusting Greenspan, Americans began to take out adjustable-rate mortgages, and in 2004, a report revealed that the number of adjustable-rate mortgages had soared from 5 percent to 40 percent in a single year.

At that time, the zeitgeist was:

"you should buy a house, because prices are constantly going up. You are certain to sell it for more in a short period of time".

That was the pitch to get the new party going again, and for a moment, that was true, because everybody wanted it to be true. But every bubble eventually bursts. You cannot buck the market forever. It will eventually get you.

The Great Financial Crisis in 2008. *The Big Short*. Banks, taking advantage of a hot housing market, decided to turn people's mortgages into securities/investments called collateralised debt obligations (CDOs), which they would then sell to the market. It was a very profitable product for bankers, so they became less restrictive on who could apply for a loan. Basically, they started lending money to people who should never have been allowed to borrow. We entered a period of *"Covenant-lite"*, or better *"Covenant non-existent"*.

"The work of Wall Street often is to introduce people who should not borrow to people who should not lend."
Thomas G. Donlan, former Barron's editor

As the whole scheme started to collapse, the financial sector was on the verge of bankruptcy. Once again, banks and insurance companies were blatantly bailed out by the taxpayer, and interest rates were dropped immediately. But it wasn't enough this time. Central banks had to *"manage"* the economy even more, to prevent a total crash. They had to go all in with quantitative easing (QE).

QE is a monetary policy action whereby a central bank purchases lots of government or corporate bonds to inject liquidity into the system and stimulate economic activity. When central banks buy bonds in large quantities, the price increases, and the yield goes down. In plain person's language, a government and its central bank print money to buy the debt of their own country. Because without them doing that, the interest rates in their country would be significantly higher, causing a stock market crash, corporate and personal bankruptcies and house-price collapses. Central banks have bought more than $10 trillion in bonds in the last 15 years.

Once again we should remember Mr Ford. All this has been executed in the shadows, as the taxpayer in reality has unwittingly paid for the excessive risk-taking of Wall Street. Many call this the greatest example of grand larceny in the history of the world.

"Few people are capitalists when threatened by losing money they regarded as safe, and nobody is better than a capitalist at explaining how essential their wealth is to the health of the economy."
Martin Wolf, The Financial Times

There were then a few years of calm, when people put the *"Big Short"* down to a one-off blip, and markets returned to going up and to the right.

COVID came along and transformed our lives, with a dramatic impact on the economy. Governments had to use gigantic QE and monetary stimulus to avoid a wave of bankruptcies as high street businesses and travel industries saw customers evaporate. This easy government money for corporations was supposed to fund operations and trickle down to employees. However, many big companies decided to use this money to buy back shares instead (2021 and 2022 were record years for share buybacks).

Again, companies were flipping from socialism to capitalism as it suited them.

You can see in the graph below how much *"new money"* has been created by the Fed in the last 40 years. The Federal Reserve printed approximately $3.3 trillion in 2020. That represents a fifth of all US dollars in circulation in that same year:

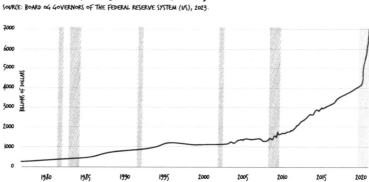

MI MONEY SUPPLY FROM 1960 TO SEPTEMBER 2023
SOURCE: BOARD OG GOVERNORS OF THE FEDERAL RESERVE SYSTEM (US), 2023.

This kind of unconventional (and very loose) monetary policy, which consists of printing large sums of money and distributing it to the public, to spur economic growth during a recession, is humourously called *"Helicopter Money"*.

The expression originates from a thought experiment proposed by the economist Milton Friedman in 1969. In his paper titled *"The Optimum Quantity of Money"*, Friedman used the metaphor of a helicopter dropping money from the sky to illustrate the concept of injecting money unconditionally and directly into the hands of the public as a means of stimulating the economy.

Unsurprisingly, the injection of huge amounts of liquidity into the system, combined with very low or even negative interest rates, led to the usual consequences:

- a new surge in LBOs. As you can see on the below graph, corporate raiders saw an opportunity to come back;

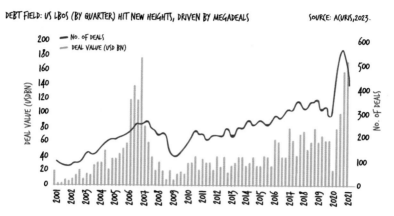

DEBT FIELD: US LBOS (BY QUARTER) HIT NEW HEIGHTS, DRIVEN BY MEGADEALS   SOURCE: ACURIS, 2023.

- companies that were already struggling had to take on more debt to survive through such difficult times. They would use what are called bridge loans. For some, these so-called *"zombie companies"*, debt is the only thing keeping them alive. They were, and are, on a drip;

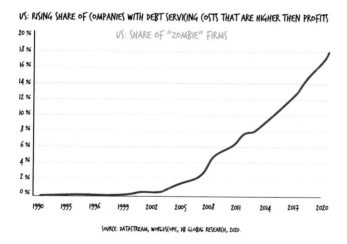

US: RISING SHARE OF COMPANIES WITH DEBT SERVICING COSTS THAT ARE HIGHER THEN PROFITS

US: SHARE OF "ZOMBIE" FIRMS

SOURCE: DATASTREAM, WORLDSCOPE, DB GLOBAL RESEARCH, 2020.

- another wave of malinvestment. But malinvestment on steroids this time, as the market welcomed a new type of unsophisticated investor. The arrival of Gen Z into exceptionally easy stock trading and investing, via user-friendly and cheap platforms like Robin Hood, created a *"meme-stock culture"* that has absolutely nothing to do with fundamental value, and all to do with momentum, social media pumping, and easy money. The *"trend is your friend"* they say;

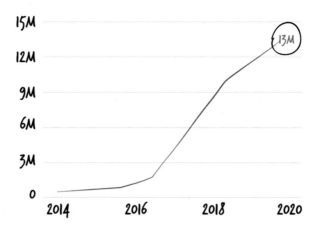

NUMBER OF ROBINHOOD USERS 2014 – 2020   SOURCE: NEW YORK TIMES, 2021.

- one could add that the "*Ok Boomer*" arrogance of these kids, thinking that their generation was somehow different, and that the older generations of the world just "*didn't get it*", has fuelled absolutely irrational malinvestment into things like Gamestop, Tesla, crypto and NFTs. In December 2022, Tesla's market capitalisation was bigger than the whole legacy car industry combined. When even the taxi drivers are giving you stock tips, hubris feeds on itself, but when sentiment changes, many inexperienced and innocent people get very badly hurt. One could argue that this could be the same for sports athletes piling into early stage sportech, or consortia buying sports franchises and assets;
- during COVID, thanks to QE stimulus, people had a significant excess cash to spend, and demand naturally increased. Simultaneously, the pandemic and most particularly the situation in China, generated huge supply chain shortages. Supply decreased.

For the first time, we had inflation coming from both a supply shock (disrupted supply chain) and a demand shock (consumption accelerating as a consequence of government stimulus). Automatically, the combination of both factors put tremendous pressure on prices and generated inflation. In 2022, central banks had to intervene and began to raise interest rates very significantly.

The risk-free rate in the USA has gone from basically zero to 5% in a very short period time.

This "*series recap*" of how we got here, can be summarised like this: debt levels have gone through the roof in the last 40 years. The only way this is sustainable and affordable is if the cost of that debt remains very low. So governments and central banks have been evermore interventionist and willing to deliberately manipulate interest rates lower.

But now they are stuck.

"Monetary stimulus is like the Hotel California, you can check out any time you like, but you can never leave."
Peter Costello Former Treasurer of Australia

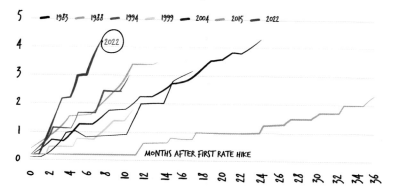

CHANGES IN THE FEDERAL FUNDS TARGET RATE IN PAST TIGHTENING CYCLES (IN PERCENTAGE POINTS)

All this has caused many bubbles, from real estate, to crypto, to venture capital valuations, to arguably what sport's assets and rights sell for.

2023: THE SEASON FINALE

"They pay me the big bucks... to hear the music of tomorrow."

The job description of the financier, and the corporate financier, is this. To have an idea of the future and deploy capital for best return, at lowest risk.

We have spent the bulk of this chapter explaining the massive risks in macroeconomics present in 2023. No-one can sensibly ask for capital, deploy capital, generate a return on capital, without knowing this story so far. What happens if the Fed Put disappears? If it is the end of cheap money, and interest rates now revert to mean? How can so much debt be sustainable?

2022 was the year we saw a very significant rise in interest rates and the cost of capital, and this will have very significant implications. Fewer investment projects will get approved; fewer startups will get funded; less product innovation and research will be green-lighted; most assets will be valued much much lower.

When capital is abundant and cheap, companies can take risks, and investors are happy to support them. Because, as there are no better alternatives to good yield, investing becomes a gamble on promising companies' asset valuations. However, when capital is scarce and therefore expensive, investors have to make choices about where to invest. They'll only invest in profitable companies or companies showing a clear path to profitability. Investors are more likely to invest only in de-risked projects.

THE YUCS: YOUNG UNPROFITABLE COMPANIES
% OF EQUITY MARKET CAPITALIZATION

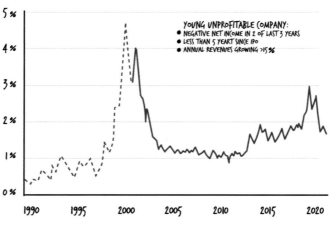

YOUNG UNPROFITABLE COMPANY:
● NEGATIVE NET INCOME IN 2 OF LAST 3 YEARS
● LESS THAN 5 YEART SINCE IPO
● ANNUAL REVENUES GROWING >15 %

SOURCE: FACTSET, JPMAM. DECEMBER 27,2022.

For so long, many startups have been focusing on growth, ignoring the need for a profitable business model. They were burning cash for the sake of acquiring customers. More than 90% of US unicorns were losing money in 2019 and 2020, and in fact, more than half of them were founded over ten years ago, which tells you how much the macro environment has distorted basic finance principles and common sense.

Running businesses this way means they always needed more capital to fuel their growth, and investors have been filling the holes. Investors were basically subsidising customers, who got a lot of products for free.

Now the subsidy is probably over, and those same companies will have to charge for what the service/product actually costs.

There is a scenario, at a significant percentage of probability, that we are now at the day of reckoning. For some, a Fourth Turning.

Even if the outcome is less dramatic, there is no doubt that the world has changed; capital will be rarer and more costly. That will automatically dampen valuations, and any investment strategy, based on ever-increasing asset values, is going to hit a brick wall.

For sport, which has seen tremendous growth in media rights, in franchise values, in sportech growth stories at *"fulsome"* valuations, it all means very stormy weathers.

Chapter Eleven

THE RETURN OF THE SEARCH FOR YIELD

For at least 20 years, with the emerging culture of Silicon Valley thinking, the hope and expectation of asset value increase has dominated finance and capitalism. The concept of seeking an annual return, a yield, has been, if not forgotten, then dismissed.

But yield is a crucial concept in finance. For an investor, an allocator of capital, it is a key factor in where you should invest. For a borrower, it is a metric, a KPI, to be evaluated carefully before accepting the money. Yield needs to be understood, as changes in it drive pretty much everything in the plumbing of finance, and hence capitalism.

Let's start with the simple definition and calculation.

Yield is the earnings generated and realised on an investment over a particular period of time, expressed as a percentage of either the invested amount or the current market value of the security. For equity investments the yield comes from dividends; for debt investments, it's the interest rate received.

Yield = annual return from dividends or interest / asset value

If you bought a share in BP PLC for £10, and its annual dividend per share is declared at £1, you have a (dividend) yield of 10%. That's a nice return, and very much how people used to look at investing in companies. Let's now look at the example of a debt yield.

"I will lend you $1000 for a year, and I'd like a 8% interest rate coupon. So, in 12 months you will repay me the $1000 (the principal), and $80 in interest. The yield on this debt is 8%"

So far, so easy. For the lender, the higher the yield the better, if risk is comparable.

Great investors will therefore compare yield opportunities from the markets and allocate capital accordingly. Should I invest in a yield of 9% in a Russian retailer, or take 4% from the debt of the German government? Or should I forget about yield and hope to get a 30% yearly asset appreciation from investing in a sportech start-up?

This is corporate finance.

"Over time, the skill with which a company's managers allocate capital has an enormous impact on the enterprise's value".
Warren Buffett

To use our sector's favourite phrase, it is really the whole ball game, and is actually much more sophisticated than the last decades have seduced us into believing. When all asset values were going up, you didn't need to think too much, frankly.

Understanding yield is instead difficult, as company shares and debt instruments are often traded on capital markets in real-time, and their movements have profound implications for both borrowers and lenders. Yield isn't fixed, it fluctuates, depending on the denominator in the formula, the value of the asset.

If investors start selling a company share, a government bond, a mortgage instrument, the price of that asset, the denominator, will naturally go down. Arithmetically then, by the formula, that makes the "*yield*" go up.

This is crucial to understand.

The share I bought before, in BP PLC, for £10, let's say hasn't changed its dividend of £1, but the share price has dropped (because it's had an oil spill) to £5. The real-time dividend yield is no longer 10%, but now 20% (1/5).

The rising yield, doubling in this example, is always seen by skilled observers as a sign of trouble, and a risk for your capital. A rising yield is like blood in the water; markets smell it out and often go in for the kill. No one borrowing capital can be ambivalent to rising yields.

Government and corporate debt is the biggest public financial market in the world, where you can buy and sell US treasuries, the bonds of a big bank etc. Most people don't realise that, thinking the capital markets are only about equity. In reality, the big beast is the debt markets.

THE RISE OF THE BOND MARKET SIZE ($ TN)

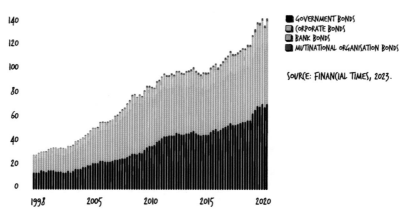

SOURCE: FINANCIAL TIMES, 2023.

Debt yields are an early warning system to all of the capital markets and corporate finance. They are pointing out the weakest of the pack. Like getting picked last at school for the playground football. It's a label of inadequacy. It's brutal and frightening.

"I used to think that if there was reincarnation, I wanted to come back as the president or the pope or as a .400 baseball hitter. But now I would like to come back as the bond market. You can intimidate everybody."
1990s Democratic political adviser James Carville

Glorious imagery. What does Carville mean? He means that the bond/debt markets are so big and so important, that they can make people, companies, and politicians dance, if they want to. They even have an intimidating name…*"bond vigilantes"*.

The term *"bond vigilante"* refers to investors who play an active role in financial markets to discipline borrowing governments and companies, especially regarding fiscal and financial policies. What these investors do is simple: they sell the bonds, reducing the price, to increase the yield. Letting the markets know that they smell blood, and that risk is increasing.

Borrowing costs go up, which penalises indebted governments and corporates, and is a way to punish policies considered irresponsible.

The phenomenon emerged in the early 1980s, at a time when inflation was high and government debt was growing (particularly in the US). To manifest their dissatisfaction, the vigilantes sold government bonds, which caused the prices to drop and yield to rise.

They can intimidate anyone. And do.

The debt that is issued by the UK governments, called gilts, is issued at its original value of, say, £100 a gilt, with the interest rate at 5% and repayable in 10 years. That is how it starts life as an investment. And if you were to hold it for 10 years you would get your £100 back plus 10 years of interest at 5%. Some people do just that; but most don't and will buy and sell, in and out.

Those gilts are traded in the market every day, like shares. The price goes up and down, basically based on people's confidence in the borrower; in this case the UK government, but it could be a big bank, or a pharmaceutical company on the same basis.

The public markets, especially the bond markets, react very quickly to news, and have an opinion. If they think someone needs to be *"whacked"*, be that a Prime Minister or a CEO, they always get *"whacked"*.

The demise of Liz Truss is instructive. At the end of September 2022, Chancellor of the Exchequer Kwasi Kwarteng announced a new fiscal plan of over £100 billion to address the energy crisis and cut taxes in the UK. Immediately, this had a negative impact on investor confidence, who were concerned that Kwarteng and Liz Truss's economic program would deepen the UK's public deficit, and boost inflation.

As a result, Sterling dropped dramatically against the Dollar and the Euro.

But the real concern was about the UK government bond market.

Investors anticipated an increase in the debt-to-GDP ratio and were concerned the growth generated by these fiscal expenditures would not offset the additional budget deficit. As a result, they sold their bonds and the yields on 30-year UK gilts rose to 5%, compared to 3.5% before the announcement.

In other words, investors were demanding much higher interest yields to keep holding long-term government bonds of the UK. Panic set in, leading to more gilt sales that further exacerbated their value drop.

The stability of the British financial system was threatened, as pension funds, which hold many gilts on their books as collateral, were facing significant liquidity issues, and they were forced to sell assets at a big loss due to margin calls. Some experts even wondered if they were on the verge of a major crisis like the one following the bankruptcy of investment bank Lehman Brothers.

Consequently, to stop the fire sale of gilts, the Bank of England (BoE) had to intervene and bought £1.45bn of UK debt securities themselves. The equivalent of the Fed Put.

Whilst the imminent catastrophe may have been averted, financial markets were still pretty nervous. Something had to happen, a positive signal to the markets.

Liz Truss got whacked, resigning only 44 days after she was asked to replace Boris Johnson.

The UK prime minister lasted very few weeks because the markets decided she wasn't up to it. Exactly the same thing did for Silvio Berlusconi in 2011, as the yield on Italian bonds approached 7%. He too was told to resign.

"Follow the money" as a principle refers to this.

The capital markets will always tell you what is going to happen.

The coolest and most sophisticated part of the capital markets, and corporate finance, is in smelling out these signals, looking at charts and trends. The various short sellers in the Big Short for example did exactly this. As always, they were ridiculed at the time, for basically having more vision and skill than the pack. Until they were seen to be right.

Yield curves tell you most things if you know what to look for.

This a metric monitored closely by investors and economists. It represents the relationship between the price of a government treasury bond and its maturity. In a normal situation, as the maturity of a bond gets longer, you tend to pay a higher interest rate. That is because long-term loans are riskier in theory. So, the normal yield curve is represented below.

In some instances, we have an inverted yield curve: the short-term rates are higher than long-term rates, which means it's riskier to lend money in the short term.

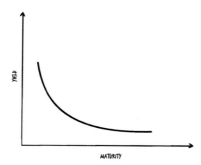

Inverted curves aren't normal, and it is often the first sign of an imminent bad economic outlook. This is why the yield curve is considered a great predictor of recessions. History has shown that, whenever we have had an inverted yield curve, there has been a recession soon after.

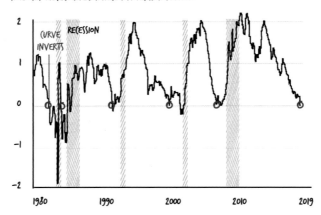

AN INVERTED YIELD CURVE USUALLY SIGNALS TROUBLE   3 PCT. POINTS

HISTORICALLY, WHEN THE YIELD ON 10-YEAR TREASURY BONDS DIPS BELOW THE YIELD FOR 2-YEAR BONDS, A RECESSION HAD FOLLOWED.

NOTE: ONLY THE FIRST INVERSION PRECEDING A RECESSION IS MARKED.

SOURCE: ST.LOUIS FEDERAL RESERVE, WELLS FARGO INVESTMENT INSTITUTE. THE WASHINGTON POST, 2019.

Investors of capital are assessing yield every day and will make changes to their favoured sectors constantly. Those changes can start a domino crash very quickly. If yield graphs are the equivalent of a crystal ball, let's have a look at the market value of the bonds of the people who finance sport; the media companies, and how they have performed in the last two years.

Remember valuation (asset value) is the inverse of yield. Valuation dropping is yield increasing. All of these bonds are decreasing in value.

News Corporation, Rupert Murdoch's media group (Maturity 2029, 3.875% coupon):

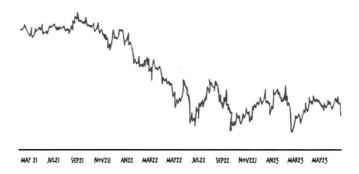

MAY 21   JUL21   SEP21   NOV21   JAN22   MAR22   MAY22   JUL22   SEP22   NOV22   JAN23   MAR23   MAY23

Disney (Maturity 2034, 6.2% coupon):

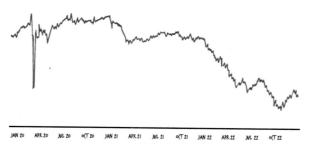

Sky (2027 maturity, 6% coupon)

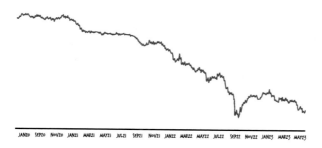

What is that telling us about the future of the media companies? (And hence, what does this tell us about sport?) The value of the corporate bonds of media companies has declined dramatically. The vigilantes have worked out what is happening. The business model is challenged, by cord-cutting, rampant piracy, and changing generational viewing habits. So capital providers are now asking for higher yield, to be compensated for the inherent risks of this industry. Hence, we have witnessed a downgrade in debt rating across the media sector.

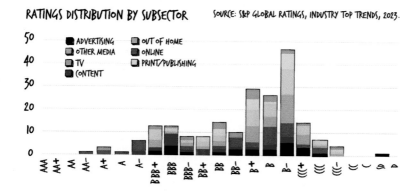

The Morningstar US High-Yield Bond Index (which measures the performance of high-yield corporate debt) shows that the media sector has issued more distressed debt in 2023 than any sector other than Healthcare.

All these datapoints, driven by bond vigilantes, don't point to a lot of confidence in Big Media.

Since early 2021, we have made exactly this analysis the core of our bear case for the industry of sport, in our *AreYouNotEntertained? podcast*. Interest rates were rising. The yield on the safest asset in the world, the debt of the US government, went from zero to 5% very quickly.

This made every single investor in the world stop for breath, and re-assess their investment strategy, their asset allocation, and their entire approach to yield. Unless they were confident that they could do better than 5% with an investment, they would just sell speculative assets, and say no to opportunities. Too risky, compared to what they could get just leaving their savings with Uncle Sam.

All investments, especially debt, now have to compete with the new benchmark yield of 5%, and how do they do that? This is the interesting part.

The *"art"* in finance. Markets, if left alone, do what markets do; they *"discover"* price.

This here is in my opinion the glory of the invisible hand of Adam Smith.

Asset values will drop until the yield is near the new market benchmark of 5%.

Let's say an existing bond worth £100 had an interest rate, and thus a yield, of 2%. Now the market benchmark has risen to 5%; the price of that bond needs to fall from £100 to £40 to arithmetically equate to 5% yield. That's more than halving, for what may seem as a trivial rise in interest rates from 2% to 5%.

This is critical to understand.

Assets prices always need to drop to bring yields back to the benchmark in the markets.

As 2022 has seen interest rates increasing, the value of existing debt/bonds everywhere has fallen in this way, causing utter chaos in the banking system in 2023, which is precisely what happened to the Silicon Valley Bank (SVB).

SVB

US venture capital-backed companies raised $330 billion in 2021. A record, and almost twice as much as 2020 (the previous record year). A lot of these early-stage companies were held their money with SVB, and that bank ended up with tens of billions of dollars of their deposits. SVB decided to invest its depositors' capital into US government debt. As interest rates started to rise, the value of the bonds they were holding arithmetically fell, causing SVB huge losses.

SVB had unrealised mark-to-market losses of $15 billion at the end of 2022. In other words, if SBV's assets had been marked down in the Balance Sheet to the current price in the market, they would have lost $15bn. This was almost equivalent to the entire company's equity of $16.2bn.

Unrealised losses means you only lose money if you have to sell the bonds. If you hold a debt to maturity, you will get your full money back. The value of bonds going down is not necessarily a problem...unless banks are forced to sell them to meet depositors' demands. In that case, bonds would need to be sold at a loss in order to cover withdrawals. And sadly for SVB, that is exactly what happened. Rising interest rates and a bear market for IPOs have made it difficult for startups to raise capital, forcing them to withdraw their cash from their SVB accounts to finance their operations. That started to put pressure on SVB's Balance Sheet.

Concerned for their investments in this scenario, VC funds were advising portfolio companies to withdraw their money from their SVB account. In fairness, there was a real risk for them to see most of their money disappear with the bank. Banks runs are immediate and absolute. In the US bank deposits are only insured up to $250,000, and SVB's clients had much more than that.

Consequently, the liquidity problem accelerated suddenly. The classic panic of bank runs: depositors run to get their money out, exactly because they see others doing the same.

Another important lesson for banks (and sports?) is not to overestimate the loyalty of customers.

SVB and other smaller banks and their depositors were obviously bailed out by the US taxpayer. Just like in 2007/08. Moral hazard never dies.

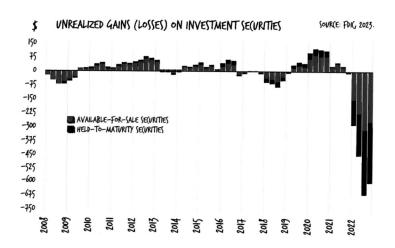

$ UNREALIZED GAINS (LOSSES) ON INVESTMENT SECURITIES — SOURCE: FDIC, 2023.

■ AVAILABLE-FOR-SALE SECURITIES
■ HELD-TO-MATURITY SECURITIES

For too many investors, commentators and asset managers, yield has been forgotten. Its power and its messaging is no longer front and centre. The skill has been lost.

In the sports sector, there is pretty much no understanding of any of this and of what is coming.

Look at the yield curve of the media companies. They are the financiers of the industry of sport.

They know.

Chapter Twelve

WHO ARE THE PROVIDERS OF CAPITAL?

Sport has become a very popular and growing asset class, considered by many as *"alternative"* and *"non-correlated".*

Alternative assets are considered a bit off the beaten track as a category but are an important part in any balanced portfolio of investment. They include real estate, cryptocurrencies, commodities, art, options, futures, currency forex, NFTs, peer-to-peer lending and venture capital. Alternative assets tend to be riskier than traditional assets, but not always, especially if they are non-correlated, meaning they act as a hedge against movements in the main markets. They should go up when other things go down.

This is classic asset allocation theory and one of the reasons why sport is interesting to Big Finance now.

Sport as an investment is also seen as having much upside in valuations, especially in Europe and Asia compared to the US. It is industry-adjacent to the media, entertainment, and tech industries, and in theory has significant room for operational improvements in efficiencies, value-chains and revenue-models. But it's also sexy, with the lure of celebrity, and intense passion from its fans.

People for all these reasons want to invest in sport, and the industry itself needs fresh capital. So it is high growth terrain for corporate finance, which matches the buy and sell sides. Private equity (PE) and venture capital (VC) firms are now very active in the sport industry. Major investment banks also see opportunities for debt and equity funding. Private wealth and family offices are diligent in looking to diversify and balance their portfolios with sport. And of course, sovereign governments are increasingly interested in sport as an asset class for a completely different set of geopolitical reasons.

All these various types of providers of capital have diverse aims and expectations, and sport needs to understand these, as they will offer a selection of forms of funding, with different conditions and structures, and changing costs.

Any good corporate financier will know the specific needs and preferences of the different providers of capital and be prepared for what they will expect:

"I know your fund likes to invest this amount of money, at this stage of maturity of a business, and you're looking for a return in this ballpark. Here is why we could be what you are looking for!"

That one sentence at the start of any meeting with Big Finance will save time, gain trust, and build credibility. If you are speaking their language, you are already well past first base.

Sadly, sports often can't articulate that sentence. And why should they? Up until yesterday, they were doing fixtures, allocating referees, and selling boards around the pitch.

Let's now look at all the providers in turn.

BANKS

The banking industry looks to lend against reliable asset collateral, steady revenues streams and IP. The famous old chestnut about banks is pretty accurate.

"A bank is a place where they lend you an umbrella when the sun is out and ask for it back when it starts raining."
Robert Frost

Banks have, and are, lending money to sport organisations, so it is important to understand that banks are not in the risk game, they are in the collateral game! Banks will only bear the risk of their customers defaulting on their debt if the risk is contained and there are valuable assets put up as collateral for the loan.

They do not lend money to anybody, but with the right collateral, debt will be a relatively cheap form of capital, at a low interest rate.

For this reason, banks often lend against future sports revenues like media rights, sponsorship deals or season tickets. In 2023, we saw JP Morgan interested in lending up to $1bn to Serie A (Italian football's first division), with the media rights used as the collateral. JP Morgan felt confident about Serie A's solvency and believed TV rights in Italy could only go up.

In 2022, banks like Goldman Sachs, Deutsche Bank and Credit Suisse offered €850m of high yield bonds (junk bonds) to finance CVC's investment in La Liga. CVC invested a total of €2bn billion in La Liga in exchange for 8% of the league's broadcast rights for the next 50 years. The debt resulting from this deal is expected to be BB-rated (pretty low).

In addition, banks can structure invoice factoring deals to provide clubs with liquidity. The player transfer market is a great example. Often, the transfer fees are too high to be fully paid upfront, and the buying club will pay for the transfer in installments. The problem for the selling club is that it will therefore have to wait several years before it receives the full amount. Of course, in most cases, clubs would rather get the cash as soon as possible, so that it can deploy it in its own operations (buy other players or invest in the stadium) and improve its working capital. This is where a 3rd party, usually a bank, comes in.

Let's say club A is buying a player from club B for £40m. Selling club B has an invoice receivable. The bank will pay Club B say £38m immediately to settle their debt. And then get the full £40m from club A, over time. The spread between the amount they pay and the amount they receive is how the bank itself makes money. This is invoice financing or factoring.

To mitigate any possible credit default risk to their loans, banks will ask for various covenants, and look at solvency KPIs, like interest cover (the space the operating cash flow has, to repay contracted interest payments). This ratio has been a bit overlooked in recent years, in a regime of low interest rates, but in 2023 onwards, banks will have higher hurdles as regards to whom they are willing to lend money.

Furthermore, as capital now becomes more expensive, many companies or clubs are under pressure on cashflow, and need to restructure and renegotiate their debt. Extending the maturity of a loan is an example of restructuring, as it enables lower monthly repayments. This activity has become frenetic in the last two years, not just in sport.

Sports organisations traditionally seldom go completely bust, but they do often go into different forms of insolvency restructuring. We started to see this unfold in 2022 with various football clubs (FC Girondins de Bordeaux for example) and rugby clubs in the UK.

Careless, superficial investors and lenders can get wiped out under such restructuring and always need to do good analysis of risk, and proper due diligence, up front.

Have they assessed well the asset value of their collateral (media rights), and given themselves enough power to change things via strong covenants? More fundamentally, as interest rates and yields are no longer zero, do these sports deals still work for them for return?

PRIVATE EQUITY

Private equity has become really important to society and the markets, so they cannot be ignored.

A Private Equity (PE) fund is made of investors, Limited Partners (LPs), and managers, General Partners (GPs). GPs are the ones setting up the fund, raising capital, identifying targets, and managing the fund during its lifetime. The LP investors, the ones investing capital, have no control or influence over investment decisions, and will be in the main institutional money from pension funds, mutual funds, sovereign wealth, high net-worth individuals, insurance companies etc.

PE has captured a bigger proportion of total institutional capital in recent years, attracted by the higher returns delivered. This, in itself, is of one of the great themes of Big Finance in the new millennium. It affects all of us, as this is where a lot of our pensions and investment savings are held, whether we realise it or not. In some indirect way, our own retirement nest eggs may have been invested by CVC into rugby.

The expected return on capital for PE firms will vary depending on several factors, like the stage of the investment, the industry, and of course the market conditions. However, private equity firms generally target a higher return on capital than traditional asset classes like public equities or fixed income securities: on average they will expect between 15%-20% per annum. PE investors are very numbers focused, with precise spreadsheet modelling. To make those numbers work, PE firms will very often boost these returns with the use of leverage, borrowing huge amounts of debt. This has been a central part of their playbook, absolutely facilitated by very low interest rates.

All this worked splendidly as interest rates fell to very low levels, but if rates now start to rise, and stay high, all of the above unwinds. Returns on private equity without leverage drop, making these PE funds far less attractive to institutional money, who will invest less, resulting in far less PE money chasing (sports) assets. With less demand for assets, valuations fall.

The GPs running these PE funds earn their money in two ways, known traditionally as the 2/20 model. Namely, they take a management fee of 2% of the value of the total fund, and a performance fee: 20% of the profits above an agreed minimal bar. As such, private equity is not cheap capital to accept. They need to extract a lot of juice to pay the GPs and the underlying investors. Assets will be sweated hard by them. Here is a visual to explain these structures.

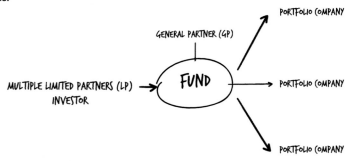

PE funds will usually be set up to operate for a fixed time period of about 5 to 10 years, and as such, they must obtain their returns in that timeframe. This is key, and part of the understanding of dealing with them. They need to get in and out within a couple of (sports)

rights cycles.

So, the lifecycle of any fund can be broken down:

- fundraising: raise capital from LPs;
- sourcing deals: identify potential target companies and investments;
- investing and managing: the period putting capital to work and operationally improving investee companies in the fund;
- exiting: the harvest period when the fund sells its positions and investors get their money back with a return (if the fund has been successful).

Again, easier to see visually:

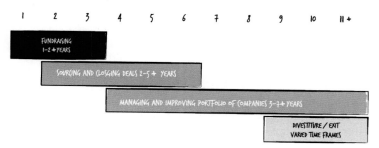

As PE money has become so central and fundamental, especially to sport assets and valuation, it is important to study each of these in turn.

FUNDRAISING

The PE industry has grown rapidly since 2000, particularly since the Great Financial Crisis. People will even talk about the *"privatisation of capital markets"*:

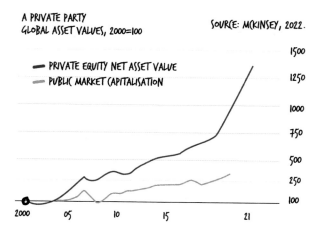

Its immense importance as a provider of capital cannot be overstated.

The distinction between public and private equity is absolutely crucial for 2 reasons. On the public markets you can see the market value of your shares, and you have the ability to sell them at any time.

In private equity you have neither of these, and I believe that understanding this sentence will be the source of much pain in coming years for investors in private equity. Valuations risk a significant drop, and investors will struggle to get their money out.

Regarding valuations, whilst, in public markets, you have price discovery every day, looking at the last share price, in private equity you just don't. Carried valued is decided by the PE fund itself, arguably marking their own homework. How do we know at what value they are valuing their private equity? Have they marked down valuations as much as they should have?

I believe that they haven't, and are holding assets, including sports assets, at above current market valuations. For example, the public valuation of sports and media assets has fallen significantly in 2021 and 2022.

That should be a good indicator for the valuation haircut that private equity assets should impose on their funds.

Do they? Has CVC marked-to-market its investments in rugby?

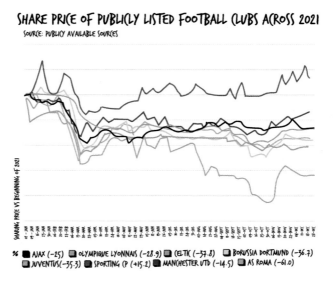

SHARE PRICE OF PUBLICLY LISTED FOOTBALL CLUBS ACROSS 2021

SOURCE: PUBLICY AVAILABLE SOURCES

% ■ AJAX (−25) ▢ OLYMPIQUE LYONNAIS (−28.9) ▢ (ELTK (−37.8) ▢ BORUSSIA DORTMUND (−36.7) ▢ JUVENTUS(−35.3) ▢ SPORTING (P (+15.2) ■ MANCHESTER UTD (−14.5) ▢ AS ROMA (−61.0)

We just don't know, but the truth will out.

Investors shift their money around, called asset allocation, depending on the various returns each asset class offers. In the past it was mainly public stock market equities, and government bonds, and this was called the 60/40 strategy, namely, 60% equities and 40% bonds. These so-called balanced portfolios did rather well throughout the 80s and 90s.

PE funds have replaced a lot of this old thinking, because they were giving you so much more return than the debt yield of the US, UK, or German government. And there has been this shift to private capital markets.

As a result, pension funds have started to pour billions into PE and similar *"alternative investments"*, and its weighting has increased significantly. This has huge implications well beyond sport. If you are looking to raise a PE fund, you will need to pitch to a lot of this institutional money, to get them to invest in you.

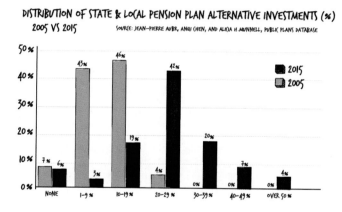

DISTRIBUTION OF STATE & LOCAL PENSION PLAN ALTERNATIVE INVESTMENTS (%)
2005 VS 2015   SOURCE: JEAN-PIERRE AUBR, ANRI CHEN, AND ALICIA H.MUNNELL, PUBLIC PLANS DATABASE

We can clearly see on this graph how the investment profile of Pension Funds has shifted to the right, towards more risk in PE. Valuations of everything that PE funds invests in, including sport, have consequently soared.

As a result, the public stock markets (shares to you and I) are losing even more ground. The number of share listings, called initial public offerings (IPOs) in the US, reached a three-decade low in 2022 as, with PE capital cheap and readily accessible, it just has been easier for companies to fund their growth without the need to go public, and all the scrutiny that involves.

In the dark rooms of PE, there is less scrutiny, whereas on public markets, everything is impacted by market sentiment, and you get a real time valuation of a company every second of every day. PE funds however are not exposed to this. They don't need to constantly mark-to-market the value of their assets (even though the value of comparable public companies has dropped). And when they do, they come up with the valuation themselves. The cold reality of fund performance and return doesn't come out until years later.

Private capital markets are not just about equity. The private debt market also grew significantly as an asset class after the global financial crisis in 2008. Banks and other traditional lenders reduced their risk appetite and lending activities, and this was an opportunity for alternative lenders to step in and address the needs for debt capital in the economy.

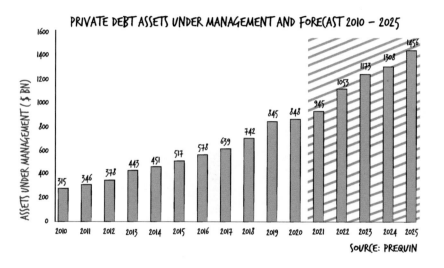

PRIVATE DEBT ASSETS UNDER MANAGEMENT AND FORECAST 2010 – 2025

SOURCE: PREQUIN

There is now a whole body of concern about what is called the "*shadow banking*" sector, and how healthy it is.

The shadow banking system consists of lenders, brokers, and other credit intermediaries who fall outside the realm of traditional regulated banking, not subject to the same kinds of risk, liquidity, and capital restrictions as traditional banks. It played a major role in the expansion of housing credit in the run-up to the 2008 financial crisis.

Examples of shadow banks or financial intermediaries not subject to regulation include hedge funds, private equity funds, mortgage lenders, and even large investment banks.

The shadow banking system can also refer to unregulated activities by regulated institutions, which include financial instruments like derivatives and credit default swaps.

The underlying size and fragility of the shadow banking sector, and the associated derivatives markets in options and futures, is beyond the scope of this book.

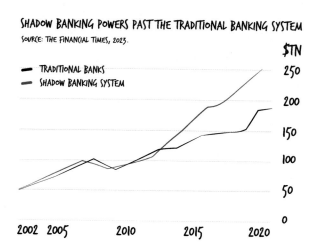

SHADOW BANKING POWERS PAST THE TRADITIONAL BANKING SYSTEM

SOURCE: THE FINANCIAL TIMES, 2023.

Suffice to say that there are trillions of dollars in assets and loans that operate pretty much without oversight.

Risk that doesn't bear contemplating.

SOURCING DEALS

What kind of assets/companies are PE funds looking for?

PE buys into existing established assets and businesses, usually with positive cashflows, where they can bring expertise to generate improvements both operationally, and financially (using debt and leverage to find a more efficient capital structure).

They like solid businesses, brands, and assets that are underperforming, because of inefficiencies and poor management.

PE funds, in sport, look to take advantage of the industry's need for upfront cash, especially since COVID. They can work out the time value of money better than most, and they will often capitalise on sports penchant for a bird in the hand, where they will hope to take three in the bush on the back end.

FROM BERLUSCONI TO REDBIRD

The Berlusconi family sold AC Milan to a Chinese investor, Li Yonghong, in 2017. AC Milan had a huge debt on its books, a big chunk of which (over €300m) was borrowed by Li, from Elliot Capital. Li never managed to turn around the club, and eventually missed the deadline to repay the loan. Elliot reacted immediately and took control of the club: Elliot (controlled by the Singer family) is a world class investor, the opposite of *"collateral-lite"*. When they found themselves in this position of being able to take ownership of the club, swapping their debt for equity, they asked me and many others, for a view.

"Can we take this asset, invest what is needed, and make a return on exit?"

I replied that if polished up well, and managed much better, it was worth at least $750m. Elliot did that and sold AC Milan to PE group Redbird in 2021 for €1.2bn.

MANAGING, ON THE OPERATIONAL SIDE

PE looks to improve underperforming businesses in various ways.

This applies generally, and to sport:
- upgrade sleepy management;
- improve operations by seeking synergies with other companies from their portfolio;
- better processes and data informed decision making;
- more professional governance.

If we look at specific sports examples, this is what PE funds are trying to achieve:
- improve topline revenue generation (Broadcast, Sponsorship, Licensing and IP monetisation). The investment of CVC into rugby is a fine example. They believe that they can improve what the sport gets for its broadcast rights, not least by taking out the middleman or rights broker. The CVC investment into various sports rights holders in rugby will tell a profound story as it plays out. Will the broadcast rights be as valuable as they hope they will be? And do they have enough covenants to exercise control, to improve things in terms of governance? I personally think this whole deal will turn out very badly and be seen with hindsight as the poster child of bull-market optimism into sport;
- player/squad planning and trading (often with more systematic and professional processes). This is now extended into multi-franchise strategies, for example Sapphire VC and City group. Shared central skills and processes, player pooling. 777 is another PE fund adopting a multi-club strategy in football;
- fan ARPU uplifts (fan loyalty can be leveraged to sell them more). Know your fan and monetise them much more strongly;
- cost cutting with cold impunity: the easiest way to improve the bottom line is to cut

expenses. Talking about CVC ownership of Formula 1 between 2006 and 2017, this is what Bob Fernley (Force India) had to say: *"All their actions have been taken to extract as much money from the sport as possible and put as little in as possible."* ;
- reorganise decision-making structures to streamline operations and eliminate conflicts of interests between stakeholders. This is where CVC has utterly failed in rugby;
- finance a stadium to generate new and diversified revenues;
- change sports formats to reduce volatility and risk, (closed leagues, salary caps, Super Leagues...). European sport is valued much less than American sports assets because of the different risk profiles of those assets. Investing in Europe is much riskier, PE funds know that, and they want to change it. CVC has invested in the commercial arm of various leagues like Volleyball World, 6 Nations, Premiership Rugby, Ligue1 and La Liga.

EXITING

PE funds have a finite lifetime (usually around 10 years). So, at some point, they will necessarily exit and sell even the most profitable companies of their portfolio. There are three ways to exit:
- an IPO (going public);
- a trade sale to another corporate;
- a secondary buyout, which means selling to another PE fund.

IPOs are now thin on the ground.

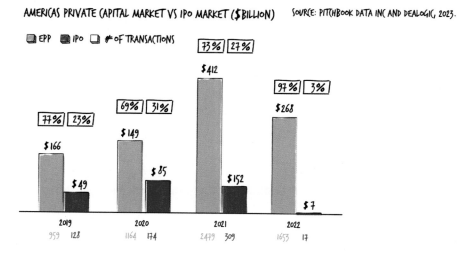

AMERICAS PRIVATE CAPITAL MARKET VS IPO MARKET ($BILLION)   SOURCE: PITCHBOOK DATA INC AND DEALOGIC, 2023.

Trade sales are always good but rare, and PE funds more and more now need to sell their investments to other PE funds. And sometimes, if needed, they will even sell to themselves.

That is called a GP-led continuation fund (or secondary fund). Basically, GPs create a second fund to acquire the company ceded by the initial fund.

We have witnessed a surge in continuation funds recently.

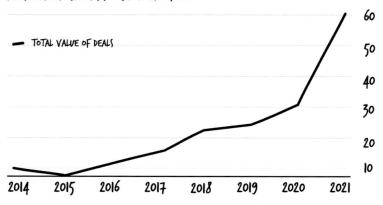

CONTINUATION FUND DEALS ARE ON THE RISE
SOURCE: RAYMOND JAMES (EBILE CAPITAL UNITE, 2022.

Officially, this gives more time to GPs to retain ownership, extract more value from their best investment and of course wait until the capital market improves.

Unofficially, it kicks the can down the road on having to mark-to-market, and admit the fund isn't working.

What if it all unwinds now?

SPECIAL PURPOSE ACQUISITION COMPANIES (SPAC)

Very much the child of booming equity markets and bullish outlooks, these organisations raise capital into a listed stock market vehicle, with the promise of subsequently buying an operating business. As such, they are what many call *"a blind faith investment"*, where investors are betting on the track record and reputation of the organisation's management team.

As the words *"blind faith"* suggest, risk and uncertainty are high. It is very much like giving your money to someone who tells you:

"I still don't know how; but don't worry I will invest it well".

A SPAC has 18 to 24 months to find a company to acquire and complete the deal. At the start of the 2020s, the popularity and use of such vehicles in sport exploded, bringing to the public markets such giants as Genius Sport.

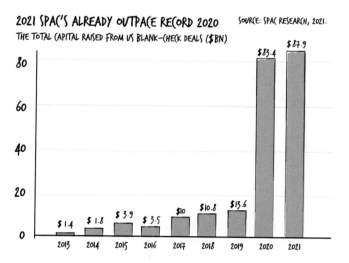

2021 SPAC'S ALREADY OUTPACE RECORD 2020   SOURCE: SPAC RESEARCH, 2021.
THE TOTAL CAPITAL RAISED FROM US BLANK-CHECK DEALS ($BN)

The *"promise"* of buying a company to insert into the listed SPAC has often not ended well. Many have just not found one. Even the biggest European SPAC, backed by Bernard Arnault of LVMH, got wound up after failing to find a company to acquire *"at a right price"*.

Some others may have found a target company to acquire but investors then pulled out. Indeed, once a SPAC's managers announce which company they wish to acquire, investors have the right to decline if they do not like it. This is called redemption rights. And many investors have been exercising their rights.

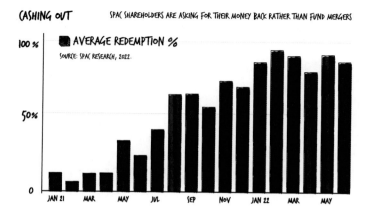

CASHING OUT   SPAC SHAREHOLDERS ARE ASKING FOR THEIR MONEY BACK RATHER THAN FUND MERGERS
AVERAGE REDEMPTION %
SOURCE: SPAC RESEARCH, 2022.

And for those that have found a company and managed to keep their investors on board, things did not always go very well. In fact, in 2021 around 70% of SPACs were trading below their initial share price.

One of the main characteristics of a SPAC is the use of debt to "lever" the return of the equity investors.

ICONIC SPORT

The recently launched Iconic Sport SPAC, launched by my friend Fausto Zanetton and the late Luca Vialli, which raised circa €350m in equity from investors, was planning to make an acquisition with a price tag of €1bn through the use of leverage debt. Iconic raised money via a SPAC in October 2021. Ultimately, they did find an opportunity by joining forces with John Textor in December 2022. Billionaire Textor, via his Eagle Football Holdings, successfully bought French football club Olympique Lyonnais, and this complemented its already existing portfolio of investments in other clubs like Botafogo (Brazilian Serie A), Crystal Palace (English Premier League) and Molenbeek (Belgian Pro League). Iconic Sports Management made a $75m investment in Eagle Football to fund the acquisition. Quickly after the acquisition of Lyon, Textor decided it was time for its Eagle Football Holdings to go public via a SPAC valued at around $1.2bn. Whilst Iconic Sports Management was initially supposed to merge with Eagle football as part of this listing, the deal eventually fell through in September 2023.

Olympique Lyonnais was one of the few publicly listed football clubs before Textor took over. It is interesting to understand why the American billionaire took it private before going public again. It is because not all public markets are equally attractive. The French club was initially listed on the Euronext, in Europe, and Textor wanted Eagle Football to be listed in the US. That is because increasingly the US has become the most attractive place for IPOs.

SPACs are very much fruit of a moment in time; a bull market, so it may be a while before we see them prevalent again.

HIGH NET WORTH INDIVIDUALS (HNWI) AND FAMILY OFFICES (FO)

There are many rich people and families around, as much new wealth has been created in the last generation. Yes, it has unfairly polarised, but suffice to say that there are now many more individuals with significant capital at their disposal. Not only what's called the ultra-rich, but also simply well-off people, managing their capital. Sport, as an alternative asset, is a favoured sector. Start-ups, early stage and alternative assets will all form a part of their diversification strategy and, indeed, their tax planning. Many early-stage investments attract a significant tax break.

These providers of capital can operate singularly, or in syndicates, or as part of groups of families in consortia. They often will have an advisor/gatekeeper who is evaluating and controlling all this.

In my experience, HNWIs and FOs will normally be quite entrepreneurial in outlook. They operate with equity, debt and hybrid instruments. They are sophisticated and know a deal. They form part of the category of *"smart"* capital, often being very astute and capable businesspeople in their own right and having an excellent network of contacts. Their process of due diligence and red tape can often be very easy and light, so finding a good HNWI is usually an excellent option as a provider of capital. But the best ones are picky.

INTERNATIONAL OLIGARCHS

Clearly, we have a different type of investor here, perhaps less financially focused. These too will be ultra-rich individuals, although oligarchs may have different reasons for investing capital in sport:

- the oldest reason of all: sport is a trophy asset. The prestige and profile, the fame and respect, that sport brings, is often the only thing missing in the life of the oligarch;
- with such popularity, it makes it more difficult for these people to be attacked by their home governments. Indeed, many say that with Chelsea, Abramovic avoided the fate reserved for other Russians who accumulated wealth in the 1990s, extracting their personal fortunes from their home country, often under a regime of capital controls. It is curious to note the Chinese involvement in sport, so prevalent in the late noughties, has disappeared.

CELEBRITIES, ATHLETES, AND MAJOR PLAYERS IN THE MEDIA/ENTERTAINMENT INDUSTRIES

These people, themselves by now likely HNWIs, and maybe ultra HNWIs, will have a vision for any sports asset or startup. In recent years, there has been a notable trend of celebrities investing their wealth and influence in the world of sports. Celebrities have emerged as influential figures within the sport industry, combining their passion, money, and expertise in the entertainment business. They are diversifying their wealth into alternative non-correlated assets, but also, they have a passion for the sector and maybe an idea on how to personally leverage that asset.

Celebrities investing in sports are more than simply fans or team owners. Many of them have taken a more active role by investing in sports franchises, sponsorship deals, and even launching their own sports ventures. These investments not only provide financial support but also bring a new level of media attention to the asset. Celebrities have been investing in basketball, with people like Jay-Z, Justin Timberlake, and Will Smith having purchased ownership stakes in NBA teams. It also happened more recently in football, with the success story of Ryan Reynolds and Rob McElhenney investing in Wrexham FC.

SOVEREIGN WEALTH

Again, these investors are not specifically focused on hard financial return, and it is more of a strategic macro approach. All of the Middle East petrodollar countries have a long-term vision around the diversification away from a reliance on carbon-based industries. Sport (and the general media/entertainment sectors) are a priority.

Some investments are made at the club level like the Saudi Public Investment Fund (PIF) investing $375m in Newcastle in October 2021, or Qatar Sport investment (QSI) which owns Paris Saint-Germain. But sovereign money is also being deployed at the league level with for example Mubadala Capital, Abu Dhabi's investment company, being very active in this space. In 2022, they acquired 20% of the Brazilian football league for just over $970m. A few months before, they also invested $50m in the Motorcycle Racing Series.

Similar to the oligarchs, certain sovereigns see sport as the most efficient tool of *"soft power"*, offering both influence and protection.

Many will argue that the glories and popularity of sport is the best way to clean the human-rights image problem these countries have. The phrase used is *"sports-washing"*. But as always, reality is nuanced.

It shouldn't be forgotten that many of the most active private equity and venture funds are largely financed by Middle East LPs. If one looks at the power plays around the ownership of Endeavor, under Ari Emmanuel, one realises that the influence of sovereign wealth is everywhere.

It is reductive to look at Middle Eastern providers of capital as merely sports-washing. That's missing the point.

THE FAN COMMUNITY

To date, in sport, direct ownership by fan groups or the local community has been rare. There are some very notable exceptions like the GreenBayPackers or FCBarcelona.

Fans subscribe for, and own, shares in the club/franchise, but it is not ownership in the normal sense, with a right to distributed profits or dividends, but more the ability to participate in corporate governance (to vote on a Board of Directors).

Sport, and particularly football, has a common refrain, when mentioning the relationship with the fans.

"No-one ever asks the fans" or *"another scheme to soak or exploit the fans."*

Only one country, Germany, has specific rules on fan ownership. The 50+1 legislation refers to the need for members of a club to hold 50 percent, plus one more vote, i.e., a majority. In short, it means that clubs, and by extension the fans, have the ultimate say in how they are run, not an outside influence or investor. This is now being challenged, as PE firms look to invest into the league itself, the Bundesliga.

In short, there has never been a culture in European sport of fan ownership, for a couple of simple reasons:
- sport loses money in the Old Continent;
- being irrational, fans are not the best qualified to take necessary but unpopular decisions. Indeed, the phrase used most often to criticise over-exuberant new owners is *"stop thinking like a fan."*;
- fans prefer someone else to pay.

"Leave your credit card behind the bar, and you're welcome to own our club, until you get maxed out. Once that happens, you will be told in no uncertain terms, how and when to leave."

European sport has always had this feudal type of relationship between ownership and the fanbase. A rich owner willing to invest/spend, maintaining popularity with the fanbase as long as he/she did just that.

That said, on occasions, (often under threat of insolvency), fans will get involved in investing directly in the club. These can be structured situations like Hearts or Motherwell, or more last-minute pass-the-hat-around initiatives to avoid an insolvency practitioner pulling down the shutters.

Wimbledon All England Tennis Club and some other clubs have used the debenture (debt) financing method, offering benefits/utility to investor/fans:
- the right to a certain seat;
- priority in ticket offerings.

In recent years, especially through alternative finance companies like Tifosy, there have been much more structured debt/bond offerings aimed at fan investment and participation.

We are now entering an era where such organisations may receive a major boost, through the adoption of blockchain technology and Decentralised Autonomous Organisations (DAOs), which are a way for fans to operate as a syndicate together to buy a club/franchise in a relatively frictionless way.

VENTURE CAPITAL

This provider of capital is so important that is deserves its own chapter.

Chapter Thirteen

VENTURE CAPITAL AND SILICON VALLEY

The story of recent decades, at least from the point of view of business and finance, is the story of Venture Capital (VC), and the cluster that has grown up around Silicon Valley. A nexus of skills, people and networks whose source has been, and is, Stanford University. This is more an eco-system than an industry, more culture than corporate.

If the mindset and sentiment around VC is now going to change, as it has started to in 2022, the falling dominoes need to be considered for what it all means.

In many ways, venture capitalism was not born in Silicon Valley, and this old idea has been funding the most ambitious adventures for many centuries. So many projects, with highly lucrative but low-probability payoffs, were funded by people willing to invest and take risks. If Christopher Columbus and Magellan were able to do what they did in the 15th and 16th centuries, it was only because they managed to convince the powerful and wealthy kings to finance their adventures. At that time, the promise was to come back with ships fully loaded with gold and spices. And, as for modern entrepreneurs, it was very hard for explorers to secure funding. By 1492, Columbus had tried to get funding from merchants in Italy, from the King of Portugal and even the King of England. Wherever he tried, no one was interested. Ultimately, persistence paid off and Columbus did get the support he needed from the King and Queen of Spain. Similarly, Magellan, born in Portugal, never got the recognition or the support he asked for from his own country. He too got the money he needed from Spain, Portugal's biggest rival at the time.

The VC funds of today are concentrated around the famous Sand Hill Road in Palo Alto. Whilst VC is still equity that is private, it is very different in outlook, culture and modus operandi from its private equity (PE) cousins. PE isn't driving disruption and innovation, but rather looking to back and improve companies already well on their way. VC is very different in how it thinks, operates and deploys capital. VCs are investing much earlier into companies, accepting much higher uncertainty and risk, and thus require much higher returns. The mindset is one of innovation and disruption, not merely of efficiencies and financial engineering. VCs look to make their return from a very significant increase in asset valuations as the company grows. They will not be looking at dividends, at yield. They fund young companies to grow so that they will be more valuable when sold or listed.

If we think of the biggest corporations in the world in 2023, most have been funded in exactly this way by the venture capital industry. From Facebook/Meta, to Google, from fintech to AI, most of the growth capital for these companies has come from the type of investment fund known as VC.

These funds take their investors' money, like all funds, mainly from what is called institutional capital. These are endowment, pension, insurance and sovereign wealth funds, family offices and HNWI (high net worth individuals). The investors have very clear ideas about the return they need on their money, and know it varies depending on risk. An investor into VC will expect an annual return of 30%. That seems a lot, but remember they are taking a very substantial risk that they will lose all their money. Private equity instead is looking to return 15-20% to its investors, as the risk is less and, normally, there is little chance of losing all your money.

When this is your bar, it obviously dictates the types of deals you need to do.

In my experience, start-ups, and my industry of sport, don't really appreciate the differences here. They just look for capital and fail to know with whom exactly they are speaking, and what they should be pitching. For too many, money is money; and they are often talking the wrong language.

VC is a mindset and a culture that has no doubt changed our world, and this must be understood well if you are pitching to them. They are looking for a new vision, an idea of something disruptive or transformative, that solves a big existing problem. They rely less on hard excel modelling, and much more on belief: in a founder, in an idea of a new product/ market fit, and in execution credibility.

This is what's now called a *"narrative pitch"*. Doing such a deck well is an elite corporate finance skill.

Investing like VC in early-stage sport technology start-ups (sportech) is the core business of our company, Albachiara. As an asset class, sportech has grown exponentially in the last decade. When we started, there were few funds out there, especially in Europe, and it was a cottage industry. Now it is an asset class of very high profile, with significantly more players on both the buy and sell side. It has arguably become an *"over-crowded trade"* with more and more capital scouting for deals. Sports athletes themselves have developed a penchant for investing their remuneration in sportech.

A good working example of VC money and thinking in sport is the Professional Triathletes Organisation (PTO), the new triathlon entity funded personally by Sequoia partner Sir Michael Moritz. The particularity of the PTO is that it is *"co-owned"* by the professional athletes eager to grow their sport. It is a unique model, where all profits (and risks) are equally shared between Crankstart Investments (Michael Moritz's investment vehicle) and the PTO's participant members. It is, in essence a governing body owned and operated by athletes themselves. It is our best case-study of new capital challenging the existing governance, and structures of a sport, and creating value through innovative models, side by side with the athletes.

So, whilst many people may consider this VC industry a bit light, a bit hipster, a bit woke, we all need to realise that it has been, and is, crucially important. Some geopolitical commentators would even say that this *"asset"* is one of the major geopolitical competitive advantages of the US, over China and Russia.

VC investment can have different flavours, as some funds prefer to invest earlier than others, specialising in what they call their *"sweet spot"*:

- seed - less than $3m, to prove a concept, MVP (minimum viable product), and product/market fit;
- series A - likely up to $20m, to expand commercial traction, and scale;
- series B - likely up to $100m, to consolidate revenues, build a global team, serious marketing.

One shouldn't get too hung up on these definitions and parameters as they are in constant evolution. In simple terms, all VCs will have their own idea of the kind of investment size with which they are comfortable. This won't be a secret. The best VCs, like Courtside, a specialist in sportech, will be very clear to you what they are looking for.

To explain this more clearly, let me quote Vasu Kulkarni, a founding partner of Courtside:

"We have a $35M fund. ~2% of that is spent on fund expenses each year, which means that over the course of a 10-year fund, $7M is gone in fees. That leaves you with $28M in investable capital. It's usually good practice to reserve between 40% and 60% for follow on investments in companies that are doing well, so that you can maintain your ownership percentage. So, let's go ahead and say $14M of that $28M is now reserved for us to put more money into our top performing companies. That leaves us with $14M to place early bets on companies. At roughly $500K a check, we're looking at about 28 shots on goal. Of those 28, unless we are the recipients of divine intervention, roughly a third will fail altogether, a third will maybe break even, and the remaining third, if the stars align, will make up for all our losses, and make us some money. So, basically $5M in initial investments (10 companies) are going to need to be responsible for returning $35M to our investors, plus their return.

A company can have a great 3x exit someday, and not work for us. That doesn't mean it's a bad business, it just means it's not a good business for a VC fund to be investing in. I say to that type of company: go take $2-3M in angel money, don't raise more than $5M or $10M, and if you have a $25-30M exit you're going to do really well, but we as investors just can't do that deal. I try to explain that as candidly as I can to as many people as possible."

This is so important a quote, and it is astonishing how poorly understood this simple explanation is, even amongst the best and most committed commentators on early-stage sportech.

They just don't get the concepts of required return on capital, and it is a classic communication gap that needs to be bridged. It is also misunderstood by young founders, who don't realise that they need to pitch a very big hockey stick growth graph.

VCs are looking to companies who can deliver outsized returns, even be a unicorn. VCs are not so interested in startups that could be very successful and maybe can aspire to doubling investors' money. That's not their profile. Because if it only doubles, it won't be enough to pay for the other failures in the portfolio. Such young companies should find their funding elsewhere, from angels, syndicates, FOs and HNWIs.

To get this size of return, VCs will therefore tend to look at and invest more in the sportech ecosystem, rather than sport properties themselves. It's very difficult to get a 700% return investing in sports clubs and franchises. In sports, VCs have mainly focused on the ancillary business to the industry; sport media, over-the-top (OTT) broadcast platform providers, anti-piracy, AI, data companies, smart stadia, wearables, betting, all in the main enabled by new tech. The daddy of them all, in recent years has been crypto and Web3. The graph illustrates the increasing investment into the crypto space over the last few years:

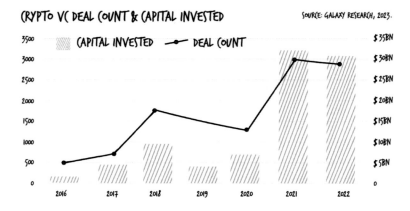

There have been many good sportech success stories.

Overtime is a digital media company that focuses on high school and amateur sports, aimed at GenZ, principally basketball fans. The company produces original content including highlights, interviews and behind-the-scenes footage, and distributes through its website, social media channels and its own mobile app. This became so successful that it then created its own sports leagues, especially Overtime Elite, which is a challenger competitor to the usual college route for the best high school players. At the last funding round in August 2022 (SeriesD), Overtime raised $100m which valued the company at $500m.

Barstool Sports is a digital media company that began as a sports gambling newspaper in Boston in 2003. It built its popularity on humorous and irreverent takes on sports news and commentary. Barstool's ability to connect with a younger audience, the Bro culture, as well as its fantastic use of social media platforms, is what drove its success. The company monetises its content through merchandise sales, a sports betting platform, and sponsorships. Barstool's founder, Dave Portnoy, has become himself a celebrity, contributing even further to the company's profile and following. Barstool was sold in its entirety to Penn Gaming in 2022 for a value of $450 million. It was sold back to Portnoy in Summer 2023 as Penn focused its sports strategy on ESPN.

Sorare is a startup founded in 2018 by two Frenchmen: Nicolas Julia and Adrien Montfort. When the two Parisian entrepreneurs discovered NFTs, they quickly recognised the potential of this technology and immediately decided to use it to create playing cards representing football players, and a fantasy game based on the Ethereum blockchain. Sorare allows users to collect player cards and be rewarded based on their real-life performance. It is an addictive game for football, baseball and soon basketball enthusiasts. The company has raised the largest amount of funding in the history of French Tech, €680 million in September 2021. This funding round values the company at $4.6 billion. Today, the startup boasts over one million users and has experienced rapid growth with a transaction volume in 2021 that is 40 times higher than in 2020.

There are other such amazing examples of value creation, and innovation in sportech, for 15 years at least, and this has shaped the evolution of content, distribution, fan engagement and monetisation. Sportech has for sure been a catalyst for much needed disruption. These start-ups sell into sport, and look to secure flagship deals with the big brands; the NFL, Manchester City, the All Blacks etc.

Seeing this trend, a lot of sport leagues are now themselves setting up their own investment arm to invest in sportech companies. For instance, 32 Equity, the Venture Capital fund of the NFL (and its 32 franchises) made an investment in Fanatics in 2017, which is now valued ten times higher in 2023.

All VCs will claim to be *"smart money"*, able to influence operationally the young company through their experience, synergies with portfolio companies, and extensive network of contacts. This is often very true, but like anything, you also get good and bad in VC funds. As tougher times have arrived, some very jolly VCs will now have a much sterner face in Board meetings.

When you take VC capital, they will absolutely be actively involved on your Board, and we now know that they will often have clauses in their shareholder agreements that give them powers, if projections aren't being met.

Remember *"your valuation, my terms"*?

VCs will give you money, but if you, the founders, don't perform, you may very well find some nasty surprises in the legal work you signed. These kinds of clauses will become more prevalent if market sentiment changes, as it has started to do. Another cliché in the VC ecosystem is *"sending the founder to the beach"*; sugar-coating language for firing the founder, with some get-lost money.

So, what do VC operators look for, and how should startups pitch to them?

As with anything, there is a *"playbook"* of what to invest in, when to invest, how to invest, and what are the signposts and milestones that a company can continue on the journey. Often, it's applied too rigidly, especially in Silicon Valley. But it exists.

Operators in sport should make themselves very familiar with this playbook. If we know what VCs are looking for, how do we pitch that? What mistakes should be avoided?

The biggest mistake made by most founders is that they go into these meetings hoping to sell their invention, their product. How amazing and unique it is and what it can do.

They have likely already condemned themselves to failure, as VCs just don't think like that. They don't invest in products, they invest in innovative business models that can scale, with product/market fit and, of course, people.

In the VC world, the best way to get money from investors is to convince them you're different. They are looking for a genius, so the logical thing to do is to offer them one. Whether that's true or not.

Some may feel this sounds like a snake-oil salesman, and often founders are, but there needs to be an element of selling a blue-sky vision, a high-growth set of projections, a future-looking visionary about to open up untapped markets. The clear reference is Elon Musk. If one looks at the fundamentals of his various businesses, there are no hard facts to back his promises, but he is very effective in selling an idea of mining asteroids or robo-taxis. To date, the capital markets have bought that optimism with conviction. To date!

Musk aside, the point remains that VCs are looking for a vision of a huge virgin market that a founder and his/her start-up can capture. Sell the dream in your pitch and make sure to use, in the rights moments, the language of the famous Silicon Valley Playbook. It's how they speak.

Start with the 10/20/30 rule. 10 slides, 20 minutes, no less than 30 point font:
- if you can't explain a business in 10 slides, you're not the quality they are looking for, as a business, as a founder;
- give yourself 20m. You may have a 45m meeting but after pleasantries, and tech setup issues, you may be tight; and they won't wait. VCs do 6 such pitch meetings a day;
- no smaller than 30 font. A big font restricts how much text you can put in your slides and forces you to think hard on what is key, and obliges you to know very well the other stuff you left out, in your head. It's a discipline.

So what's in the 10 slides?

1. what problem are you solving? This needs a succinct explanation. Punchy. Eg Piracy will kill sport like it did the music-biz;
2. what is your solution? Equally this should be tight and confident. Eg Doing not viewing. You can pirate a video stream, you can't pirate a multi-activity platform;
3. is this problem big enough for any of us to care? Eg Piracy costs sports $28bn a year. The Total Addressable Market (TAM) is worth the candle;
4. what is your product and how will you make money? Eg. Where are you with MVP and product/market fit?
5. tractions and milestones so far;
6. competitor analysis. Why can't someone else just do the same? Copy, steal and just outspend you?
7. team. Why you? Show me this amazing bunch of people;
8. GotoMarket strategy. How will you connect with the market?
9. financials. A summary, showing key levers and assumptions. Get ready to be asked scenarios: what if you don't get the assumed 2% market share in 18 months? When do you run out of cash?
10. investment request, valuation on your company, and a vision of where that capital will go. Here you will explain on what basis you value your company:
- per user;
- multiple of revenues;
- benchmarks;
- the more traditional valuation metrics based on profits or cash are rare. Companies in high growth are expected to be investing to build, not reap.

We re-visit The Truth About Valuation in detail in future chapters.

In my own experience, few do these slide decks well, and even fewer can handle the surgical questioning that you will find on Sand Hill Road. VCs are very smart, and often rather arrogant. They will like to point-score at your expense in front of their colleagues.

This is a real test of a founder, which is the way it should be as, in the end, a VC is investing in people, the founder(s). If you are still in the game at this point, there will be a process of follow-up meetings, more searching challenges to your pitch, due diligence into the "*data room*"; all hopefully leading to offers, called terms sheets.

In the boom times of start-ups in recent years, any founders perceived to be "*hot*" in the Valley were inundated by such term sheets. Indeed, the greatest sin if you were a venture capitalist wasn't not doing your full due diligence, but in missing the train with the latest hot founder.

This is hugely important, as it has negatively influenced the process and discipline that all good investors should have. The fear of missing out (FOMO) on the hottest start-ups has brought bad habits. Not being on the next big thing, not deploying capital quickly enough, has resulted in proper due diligence not being done, covenants and legals being "*lite*", all of which was justified because valuations "*always went up*".

Many VCs disregarded the yard-by-yard grind of strong due diligence and financial discipline, for the Hail Mary pass of maybe getting in early on the next unicorn ($1bn valuation).

That's how markets go. The bull and bear are two very different beasts and mindsets, and VC probably is the very best example of this.

For the last 15 years or more, VC-backed companies have had a scale-at-all-costs strategy, where companies would first raise money to fund growth and then try to figure out a profitable business model later. It worked. That's the scene in The Social Network where Zuckenberg chastises Eduardo Saverin for wanting to "*monetise*" too early.

In my work in this sector, I once asked a company why nowhere in their reporting was there a focus on profits and cashflow. It was a good company, very well considered in the market. This is the answer I got:

"Currently the main metric we most care about is: number of active users. This is because we believe that they correlate most with our Enterprise Value from the perspective of a Series A investor or a potential buyer (eg large games company). But that's of course not to say that revenue isn't important at all - eg ensuring we can show overall positive unit economics is important too. To take it to the extreme, if we cared most about generating early revenue at this

stage, you could make the case that we should optimise the business around signing up large enterprises only (eg Netflix, Disney, Ubisoft) but this would reduce our overall Enterprise Value and make us less attractive to Series A investors and a large pool of buyers. We've also gone through a process recently of validating the metrics that we need to show to a Series A investor."

It's an intelligent founder setting out his stall, his pitch, to be showing the most attractive metrics that justify a valuation. Which in his opinion at that moment were *"active users".* The main focus was growth in customers, even if non-paying customers.

And up until 2022 he was absolutely right. VC executives would look at some key business metrics for them to tick boxes on suitability for follow-on investment. Growth in users, annual recurring revenue (ARR). These are top line growth proxies, not profits, not cash flow. Frankly, this is the language that the VCs wanted to hear and rewarded. Unit economics and scaling.

The afore-mentioned startup had many active users, with a free product. When they started to charge for it, in the 2nd half of 2023, the conversion rate was 3%. They are now in trouble. Non-paying users is so "last year" in VC.

The culture of Silicon Valley was simple: you build a product, or a platform, that can scale.

"Scale" is the idea that, in the digital world, the entire globe is your potential customer if you have what is called product/market fit. In simple English, you have a product that is liked and works well. Once you have proven this, which is what the capital in your seed round is for, you are ready to get much bigger fundings.

Series A, B, C and even D to take on the world at *"scale"* and benefit from unit economics.

A core idea is that users will ultimately be monetised, and therefore if you can acquire them for a cost less than what they will eventually spend with you, you have a money machine.

Number of Users x (LTV - CoCA)
CoCA = the average cost of acquiring a new customer
LTV = the revenue from a customer over the course of his/her use of your product/service.

As a result, a business is profitable when: LTV > CoCA, and I like to call this the golden formula for third millennial businesses.

A simple example to illustrate this would be bookmakers. They have built a product (a platform) that efficiently offers customers betting products. They can now know very well what a customer will *"lose"* with them over his or her lifetime. The House always wins if you play long enough. It's just statistics, probabilities, translated into odds.

As Warren Buffet puts it:
"Gambling is a tax on ignorance".

Let's say that the LTV of a new betting customer is £500, and it costs you £135 to acquire them through marketing (CoCA). The unit economics are very positive at £365 margin per customer. So, the task is to *"scale"* that margin to as many people as possible with more marketing.

As a natural consequence, founders set themselves up to play this game. Focussed on the fastest growth possible, the quickest penetration of their product in the hands of customers, acquiring users. It didn't matter if this was generating profits and cash, because the VCs would always fund them in their next capital raise.

That is wonderful as long as it lasts, and all of this worked well in a world of cheap capital and excess liquidity. VCs were sitting on a huge amount of money that they had to spend. There were only so many great founders and start-ups opportunities in which to invest. As a result, there was a fierce competition between VC funds, basically competing to invest in the best companies. Consequently, founders had all the leverage, and valuations started rocketing, performance protection clauses started becoming less onerous.

Here is a striking fact: in 2013, there were 35 unicorns, whereas 10 years later, at the beginning of 2023, there were more than 700. In late 2021, with the rise of interest rates and the cost of capital, the party was over.

As explained beautifully by Michael Spirito of Sapphire Ventures, a big sport VC, on the AreYouNotEntertained podcast of April 2023:

"The VC industry sentiment when it changes always exaggerates its correction. It has gone from no valuation too high, no deal closed too quickly, no terms too light, to an overnight draconian mentality of immediate profits and cash flow. Neither of these extremes is correct."

Sentiment changed, approach changed and so valuations also changed. The tech sector started making massive layoffs, capital became difficult to find, and valuations were much lower. Businesses that looked attractive six months ago suddenly looked like too much of a risk with no profits.

VCs told their founders to immediately change back from scale at all cost, and monetise for profits and cash flow. That is obviously a dramatic shift. Uber illustrates all this perfectly as it became profitable for the first time in 2023. The company had to spend $32bn and it took them 11 years to get there.

This is what happens in capital markets. It moves quickly and it's utterly existential. The sportech landscape is now full of good young companies not making money, not able to pivot from growth to profits without more time and money, running out of cash.

"How did you go bankrupt?" "Two ways. Gradually, then suddenly."
Ernest Hemingway, The Sun Also Rises

Companies requiring a lot of capital to operate and scale will now struggle to attract investors. Peloton is probably the best example of this. VCs will be pickier, looking to find businesses that make more cash than they burn. If they want to be backed, companies will have to show at very least that they have a clear path to good margins and profitability.

Silicon Valley has been an amazing place for 20 years, since people saw the value creation at Facebook and Google. Some have always warned that this would not be forever, but they were ridiculed.

As always, it may seem obvious now, but for the last few years, anyone not drinking from the punch bowl did their wallet and reputation no good. The life of the contrarian thinker is a tough beat. No-one listens to you for ages, and then when you are proven right, the crowd shout:

"what a surprise, who could have seen this coming?"

VCs are now back to investing for capital efficiency and fundamentals. While this is very bad news for cash-burning businesses, it is probably positive news for good businesses. The latter will be more attractive than ever before, and in a way, that is for the best, since it means capital will be allocated more efficiently to fund the best businesses.

Basic capitalism principles are at play here.

VCs are now looking to invest in profitable companies. But what about their existing portfolio, the companies they've already invested in?

Remember, for years they deployed capital in cash burning businesses, and as we said, it is not easy for those companies to adjust and change their model quickly. So maybe investors should sell those companies?

Problem is, they are not very attractive assets and businesses, which means they will not offer good exits in the current context. That is a major concern for VCs. They might have to lower their expectations in this new environment. As capital is becoming more expensive and investors more risk-averse, there are less buyers out there willing to trade (at least, at the valuation of previous rounds).

According to Pitchbook, in Q1 2023, the total exit value of US VCs was $5.8bn. Although it seems like a huge number, it is less than 1% of the total exit value of 2021.

So here is the dilemma: VCs can sell companies at a discount, but that would of course hurt the performance of the fund, the return on capital invested. If instead they double-down and back them, they have to raise cash at valuations below the previous rounds. That's the case of Stripe, the Fintech company which raised capital in 2023, reducing its valuation by half and $50bn.

VCs can back those companies. However, if they do, they will have to keep injecting capital in order for them to operate and keep growing. And that is far from ideal. Remember, capital is more expensive now.

Either way, the outlook is not great for many VCs. They are going to take a haircut, and their funds' performance will look rather different from 2023 onwards.

The storm in early stage sportech companies has arrived. It will feed into the other black clouds on the horizon, perfectly.

Chapter Fourteen

WHAT IS THE COST OF CAPITAL?

To understand the cost of capital, we need to immerse ourselves in the basics and theory of corporate finance.

Capital should be thought of as the savings someone has accumulated. It could be a mother, a child, a company, a government, a pension fund for retired firemen. People's hard-earned piggy bank for a rainy day. Those savings can be spent/consumed for immediate need or pleasure, or they can be *"invested"*, to protect them or ideally make them grow.

Even in ancient times, as told in Matthew 25:14-30 (the *"Parable of the Talents"*), this simple concept is laid out. Many of the points in this chapter are contained in that gospel parable. It is the basic axiom of the wealth management industry.

People only invest their money because they expect to get a return. The return they require is the cost of that money for anyone asking to use it. One side's *"return on capital"* is the other person's *"cost of capital"*.

So what determines the cost of capital?

There are 2 components that comprise *"cost"*:
- the cost of money without any risk;
- the cost of risk. The riskier the investment, the greater the return expected by investors.

Let's start by excluding *"risk"* for a brief moment. Risk is where it gets complex, and where it is most often badly misunderstood. So, let's start from the no-risk part.

Historically, money owed by the United States government, US Treasuries Bills, has been seen as the safest and most certain form of investment, and the return on Uncle Sam's debt, the US 10 Year Treasury Bond, is used as the best proxy for the risk-free rate. (Given the absurdly high levels of debt owed by the US government, and their budget deficits each year, many commentators scoff at this idea of *"risk-free"* in Treasuries.)

This risk-free rate is the foundation for all discussions around the cost of capital.

Remember that in this simple way, the cost of capital is controlled in large part by American politicians and central bankers; and control it they have, in recent decades.

In the Summer of 2023, the rate on the 10 Year Treasury was 3.85%. For context, at the start of 2020 it was 0.6%.

This risk-free rate (rf) has increased rather dramatically in 40 months, and that's very important for corporate finance.

In theory the return of an asset is determined by the level of risk associated. So, you might be wondering why a risk-less investment generates any return at all. In a situation where there is zero risk that you won't be repaid; for what is the capital provider asking to be compensated for

Answer: The time value of money and inflation.

For example, if you have the choice between receiving $1,000 today or receiving $1,000 a year from now, it's not a hard decision. $1,000 received today is worth more to you, because you could spend it today (and enjoy immediately whatever you're buying), or you could invest it and get a return over the next 12 months.

The time value of money is an important concept in corporate finance, but it isn't a radical one. It's common sense. The true skill (in corporate finance) lies in knowing exactly how much more valuable it is to get the money today. Or put another way, how much would you want to get in a year, in exchange for not taking the money today. If you get that wrong, you will lose out; and be taken advantage of.

Alert readers will already see the exact importance of this concept to the sports industry, so beloved of safe and secure money upfront, versus the promise of future revenue streams. Sport loves the bird in the hand, called *"the minimum guarantee"* culture. Leave a cheque that we like on the table, get lost, and best wishes to you in making money from our assets.

One could successfully argue that the history of the sports industry, especially in Europe, has been in not wanting to evaluate professionally the *"two in the bush".*

There are reasons for that original sin, mainly in the necessity to know your available budget to contract and pay players (who want fixed certain money for their remuneration). We could argue that sport's desperate need for immediate cash like this has limited its room for manoeuvre, and the cost of that has been sizeable. The bird in the hand has probably cost the industry a lot.

Has sport been making the right decisions? To date, in almost all cases, no. Because it misunderstands the cost of money, mis-prices risks, and puts too much value, giving too much away, for the elimination of that risk. Others have built big businesses on assessing all that better. That said, however, if rights values do now fall back, some of the deals done, in selling rights on long term deals, will look very smart. It will have been the broadcasters and funds who ultimately got the risk assessment wrong.

The concept of inflation is closely linked to the time value of money, directly influencing the risk-free rate (rf).

Most people have a common sense understanding of inflation, because they experience it first-hand every day in housing, fuel, shopping and utility bills. Our money doesn't go as far as it used to. So accumulated money, savings or capital needs to generate a return to cover, at the very least, the rate of inflation.

For this reason, in finance, people talk about "*real*" as opposed to "*nominal*" returns. The nominal value of your salary is what you see on your payslip at the end of the month. For example, if your monthly salary is £1,000 and you get a 10% increase, you'll think your new salary is worth £1,100 a month. Nominally yes. But if inflation is 6%, your "real" salary increase is a 4% (10% - 6%), increase in purchasing power.

Real rate = nominal rate – inflation

So, whenever we see inflation rising (something we haven't seen seriously for maybe 40 years), strike actions and worker protests obviously aren't far behind. The world gets complex, and the work of the businessperson, politician, and corporate financier gets a lot more complicated. The providers of capital get very edgy, and they will ask for more protection and greater nominal return. Inflation eats your wealth.

The best, and most telling, phrase about inflation is that you can't easily put it back in the tube. Once it's out, it feeds on itself, as input prices rise, companies increase their prices to maintain their margin, workers ask for their wages to fully protect their purchasing power. All which creates more inflation. It is like a vicious self-defeating cycle, where people try to defend their own self-interest, their margin, or their wages, all leading to a worse outcome for everybody.

In the 1970's, the economist William Nordhaus compared inflation with what happens in a football stadium in moments of high excitement. Some people stand up to get a better view, obliging the entire crowd to rise to their feet to see the action, although they would all prefer to be sitting down.

Inflation is exceptionally destructive and cannot be kept in check when it gains hold of an economy. For many people, with a macro-finance upbringing and mentality, inflation is the deadly dragon.

"Inflation is how democracy dies"
Charlie Munger

Given that anyone under 45 probably has no direct experience of this, and hasn't seen its corroding impact, many of the best commentators feel that this is a totally underestimated danger, especially when so many of the world's governors and central bankers casually comment that they are targeting a rising rate of inflation, at say 2%, as if a good thing.

It's crucial now to understand the link between inflation and interest rates, and risk-free cost of capital.

The concept of interest rates is pure macroeconomics, and obviously then the best corporate financiers need to know about economics, to manage and mitigate the future cost of their capital.

The higher the inflation, the higher interest rates need to be to compensate savers, to slow down consumption, and potentially to try and keep prices under control. Higher interest rates have always been the tool used to try and get inflation back in the tube. The story of the early 1980s in Thatcher's UK, and Reagan's USA is exactly this: very high interest rates to kill inflation.

Why has the cost of the 10 Year treasury gone from 0.6% to 3.9%?

The answer is inflation. The concept is as old as civilisation. Its simplicity is only matched by its power. Many would argue that for centuries, all this worked fairly automatically, with the invisible hand of the market doing its magic. But for 25 years, we have seen a much more interventionist approach by governments and central bankers to keep interest rates deliberately low. As the graph below shows, the last 40 years have been an extraordinary period of reducing interest rates:

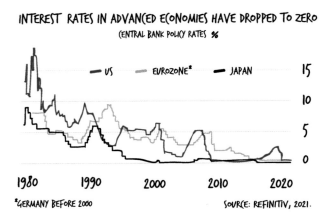

INTEREST RATES IN ADVANCED ECONOMIES HAVE DROPPED TO ZERO
(CENTRAL BANK POLICY RATES %)

*GERMANY BEFORE 2000

SOURCE: REFINITIV, 2021.

Now, Rf, one of the two building blocks of the cost of capital, has gone from basically zero to 4% very quickly. That leaves nothing unaffected.

We now need to bring in the second pillar: risk and its cost.

The full cost of any capital builds on the extra return, over rf, needed to compensate for risk. This is key because, the higher this cost of risk capital, the lower the asset financed by that capital is valued.

Risk in corporate finance is very costly and calculating that risk premium professionally and correctly is a real skill.

This is really what serious finance is about.

Chapter Fifteen

RISK AND VOLATILITY

"Reports that say that something hasn't happened are always interesting to me, because as we know, there are known knowns; there are things we know we know. We also know there are known unknowns; that is to say we know there are some things we do not know. But there are also unknown unknowns- the ones we don't know we don't know. They are the ones that get you."
Donald Rumsfeld

Business and finance, like life, is about decisions we make with incomplete information and finite resources, accepting the risk that emanates from all that, by concluding that the *"return"* will still be worth it.

There is a very simple definition of risk: it is a deviation from the desired/expected outcome, resulting in a permanent loss.

The unknown probability of adverse events potentially happening generates volatility, which is often used as a proxy to measure risk. It measures how far from the expected outcome all potential values fall.

To calculate volatility, you need two things: all the possible outcomes of an investment, and the estimated probability of each of those outcomes. With those two data points, it is possible for an investor to measure the volatility of an investment.

For any investment there will be a best case and worst case scenario, with plenty of possible outcomes in between. The bigger the gap between the worst case and the best case, the more volatility.

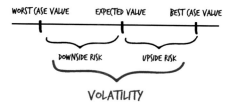

Imagine you have £900 you wish to invest, and you can choose between a shareholding in two rugby clubs, A and B. They are of similar size but operate in two different countries. To simplify the example, whether you invest in A or B, there are only two possible scenarios: the good one and the bad one. Both scenarios have a 50% probability.

If you invest in A:
- good scenario: your shares will be worth £1200 in one year;

- bad scenario: your shares will be worth £800 in one year.

Therefore, your expected return is: 1200*50% + 800*50%= £1000.

If you invest in B:
- good scenario: your shares will be worth £1600 in one year;
- bad scenario: you shares will be worth £400 in one year.

Therefore, your expected return is: 1600*50% + 400*50%= £1000.

The two investments offer the exact same expected returns, yet the level of risk and volatility is very different. That is because the standard deviation of their return is different. The standard deviation measures the dispersion of all the possible values relative to mean.

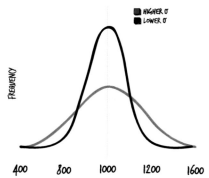

The graph plots the return distribution for investments A and B. The expected return (the mean) is the same (gray line) but club B (red curve) has the higher standard deviation/risk. The flatter the bell curve, the riskier the investment. It means extreme outcomes are more likely to happen which increases volatility. Club B has the possibility of a greater loss and is more volatile, and riskier. Club B, we would guess, is therefore valued less than A, despite the expected returns being the same. But perhaps in today's world of mis-assessing risk, maybe it isn't?

Note that on this graph, risk is symmetric. The gray line cuts the graph into two equal halves. The greater the risk, the greater the reward. But sometimes risk is asymmetric. It is not necessarily a bad thing if you can land in a situation where there is more upside than downside risk. That would be the case for instance if investing in club B could return either £1600 or £800. However, more often than not, in sport, it is quite the opposite, and shareholders are taking risks for which they are not being rewarded (e.g player injury or relegation). It's like investing £900 in club B and expecting a return between £400 and

£1200. You're taking the risk to lose £500 to maybe make £300.

As a rule, we can consider that 95% of all possible outcomes will fall 2 standard deviations from the expected mean. If the mean is 100 and the standard deviation value is 3, then 95% of all values will fall between 94 and 106. Everything outside this range is considered an outlier. To illustrate with a concrete example, we could say the chances of Bournemouth winning the premier league was much more than 2 standard deviations away from the most likely outcome. Equally so for Liverpool and relegation.

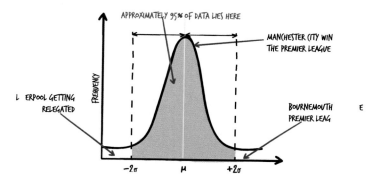

This understanding is particularly important for traders, and they will monitor the volatility on financial markets very closely. To do so, they use the VIX index, and some of the most advanced and complex corners of the corporate finance community will even trade volatility.

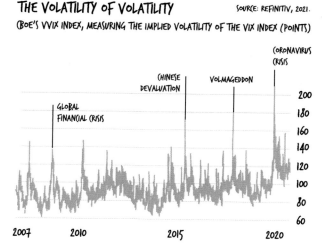

While the VIX index is used to measure volatility in the equity markets, there is also its equivalent for the bond market: the MOVE Index. In practice, the MOVE index is a much more reliable indicator of the overall economy.

Risk is necessary. For products to progress, for new markets to be opened, for money to be made, you cannot avoid risk. There is always a certain amount of risk that needs to be taken in the pursuit of value and profits. Indeed, risk and opportunities are two sides of the same coin.

"A ship in harbour is safe, but that is not what ships are built for."
William G.T. Shedd Theologian

What we really want to know is whether good things might not happen and how likely bad things might be. Knowing what can go wrong is more important than what can go right. That is because people are risk averse. They hate losing money much more than they want to make money. That has been demonstrated by Daniel Kahneman and his work on investors' loss aversion. Kahneman is a psychologist/economist who won the 2002 Nobel Memorial Prize in Economic Sciences. His work is particularly renowned for its application to behavioral economics. He showed that the perspective of losing money carries more weight with investors than the perspective of good returns. In fact, his experiments have shown that a loss affects an investor at least twice as much as the equivalent gain, to the extent that Kahneman argues that:

"the concept of loss aversion is certainly the most significant contribution of psychology to behavioural economics."

So ultimately it all comes down to a question: Is the risk worth it? Good investors, providers of capital, will obviously ask for a premium on their return as compensation for that risk. The risk premium is the major cost in corporate finance and hence business.

This book has a simple premise at its core: that sizeable risk in sport has not been seen, or has been poorly measured if seen at all, and has thus been mispriced, causing material malinvestment and out-of-whack valuations. Whilst this may not matter for investors who have wider objectives, like Saudi Arabia, it absolutely should matter to anybody looking for adequate financial returns.

One of the main reasons why Warren Buffett is a very rich man today is simply because he screens any investment to pick only the opportunities that pass his risk threshold.

"The difference between successful people and really successful people is that really successful people say no to almost everything."

Why would he phrase it like this? It seems bombastic. Perhaps because he knows that most people are always underestimating, and thus under-pricing, risk? Perhaps, by definition, they are too comfortable in assessing things around what are the Rumsfeld *"known unknowns"*, the consensus thinking. That's all understandable. We mentioned the phrase in finance is *"the trend is your friend"*, meaning that following the crowd in the main is a winning strategy. But perhaps these investors are ignoring the *"unknown unknown"* risks? In my opinion, this is what Buffett means. To be a truly great investor, you have had to see, measure, and price in, all risk, not just the bits everyone else can see.

The question then is: in sport, are providers of capital taking on risk that they do not really understand, and for which they are not being rewarded?

Almost certainly yes. Any debate would only be around the quantum.

Who would have planned and prepared for a global pandemic? A war in Ukraine? The dot-com bust? A dramatic geopolitical initiative from Saudi Arabia to buy sport, totally distorting the fair price of everything, and making competition with them almost impossible? Who in sport is correctly assessing the risk that most of the media value of sports rights could go down?

The new owners of AC Milan, Redbird Capital, have in the Summer of 2023 lost their legendary Sporting Director Paolo Maldini, and their captain Sandro Tonali. This has caused ill-feeling from the fans towards the investor, Redbird, and will have serious consequences. Was this risk recognised and factored in fully? These are all Black Swans, unpredictable events with dramatic consequences. But we now live in a world where black swans are more and more common.

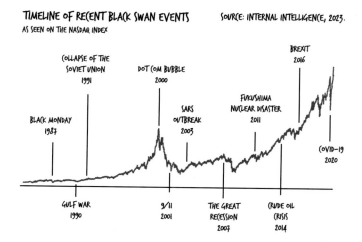

TIMELINE OF RECENT BLACK SWAN EVENTS
AS SEEN ON THE NASDAQ INDEX

SOURCE: INTERNAL INTELLIGENCE, 2023.

Since the dot-com bust 20 years ago, the capital markets have experienced myriad black swans of all types. None of these were, according to the financial media and the central bankers, *"foreseeable"*...but often they most certainly were.

They just weren't foreseeable by the consensus opinion.

The real added value of the corporate financier, calculating risk well, is in understanding black swans and the statistical bell curves of probability. The phrase *"more than 2 standard deviations away"* has entered common parlance and describes something extremely unlikely. Often followed by, *"so we can basically ignore that"*.

Something being unlikely doesn't mean you shouldn't price in that risk at all. If you don't price in black swans, you are using the wrong cost of capital, underestimating the required risk premium.

Finally, when identifying risks, we always must think about the contagion effect. It is sometimes tricky because although some events are not directly threatening your business, they might still impact it somehow. Good risk management is about looking at dominoes.

The FTX crypto exchange was the main sponsor of the Miami Heat Arena, paying $135m to acquire the naming rights to the stadium for 19 years. FTX went bust, basically overnight. Do we think that the famous athletes that endorsed the exchange thought through the full reputational risk properly? Or did they do what sport always does, and just looked at the size of the cheque?

This contagion effect makes it harder to anticipate what may happen and likely makes you underestimate the consequences, and true risk, of a particular event. We need to think about the impact on our customers and suppliers, and probably also on their customers and suppliers.

Ultimately it is not about getting the right answers, but more about asking the right questions. It's less about numbers and science, it's about the humanities.

How is the valuation of ACMilan dependent on the geopolitical and macroeconomic sentiment of Len Balvatnik?

Balvatnik owns DAZN, a sports broadcaster that buys sports rights globally. As a challenger brand, they have clearly overpaid for market entry, for example in Italy. They lose $2bn a year. At what point, and with what catalysts, does Len say enough is enough, and turn off the taps?

When the risk free rate (rf) increases to 4%?

When the Russians invade Ukraine? He is Ukrainian.

When the danger of piracy becomes accepted wisdom and common conversation?

If he does turn off the taps, the Italian football league Serie A has a major downside risk on the values of its rights. An aggressive bidder will have left the auction. Less money for clubs like ACMilan, who can't then afford the sporting ambitions of Paolo Maldini, or to match the salary of Tonali at Newcastle United. The point being that the state of mind and appetite for risk of Len Blavatnik, or indeed the new owners of BT Sport (also losing eye-watering amounts reported at £200m pa), is one of the most obvious sources of risk facing the sports industry? Are people pricing that correctly?

I don't think so.

Risk needs to be priced properly into all forms of capital.

We have seen that, in the main, we have two kinds of capital: equity and debt. So we now need to see what risks are inherent in those types of investments, to determine their cost.

Chapter Sixteen

PRICING RISK INTO THE COST OF CAPITAL

Understanding risk is mission-critical for a serious finance professional, on the buy-side or sell-side. Risk is expensive, and the challenge is to find some kind of tangible process to calculate the appropriate premium, to add onto the cost of capital, be that debt or equity.

Of those two types of capital, debt is by far the easiest to approach first.

DEBT

We have seen how the use of debt in the financing of governments, companies, and households has massively increased in the last 50 years.

It's been cheap and it's someone else's money.

The last generation has seen extraordinarily low interest rates that have become the norm for an entirely new cadre of financiers and businesspeople. The Millennials have no memory of 1970's interest rates of 15%, the union strikes for improved wages, power cuts and studying by candlelight. They struggle to conceive all of this.

I sense they are about to get a very painful refresher course now.

The cost of any debt capital, then translated as the interest rate charged, must integrate the risk of the borrower not being able to repay its debt. That is called the *"credit default risk"*.

Consequently, this is how we express the full cost of debt capital:

Cost of debt = risk free rate (rf) + credit default risk

There are many factors driving the credit default risk, like the nature of the industry or the maturity of the firm. It is less risky to lend to an investment banker than a metro busker, to lend to the All England Tennis Club as opposed to the Stevenage Community Sports Centre.

Lenders like and trust firms that have a proven track record (a credit history) of borrowing money and paying it back on time. If you are seen and known as someone who pays their debts fully, banks/lenders are likely to ask you for lower interest rates, as they assess your credit default risk as low.

Importantly, the existing level of indebtedness of a firm is a critical factor in assessing the credit default risk. The more a firm borrows debt, the more expensive that debt should be, as the more vulnerable the company is to a drop in performance, from a fall in revenues, or a general recession.

All of this is relatively intuitive.

The complexity comes in understanding that there are many different flavours of debt, suiting the different risk appetites of the providers of the debt capital.

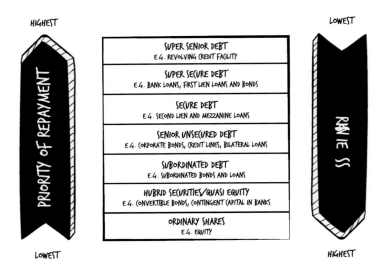

The risk of super senior debt, which gets paid back first, is much less than subordinated debt. So, providers of super senior debt capital will naturally receive a lower return, a lower interest rate.

Many of the lenders in sport today, and in general, feel confident that they are structuring deals where they are protected by the seniority of their debt. If you will, they feel they have positioned themselves sufficiently close to the fire exits.

A very good example of this is Inter Milan. They took debt from firstly LionRock, and now Oaktree. Both of those lenders felt/feel they were/are able to get out safe, even if things do go wrong. Elliot did something similar with AC Milan, with seriously strong covenants, and when they didn't get paid back, ended up owning the club.

In football, the priority and order of debt repayments is maybe less than clear, and could cause surprises. That is the case in the UK where, when a football club enters liquidation, the *"football creditors rule"* requires football-related debts such as wages owed to players and staff, and transfer fees owed to other clubs, be paid first. That was initially introduced to prevent a domino effect of other clubs not getting paid and going bankrupt themselves.

Assessing risk is always about the currency of knowledge and experience.

Determining the credit risk of companies is the role of dedicated organisations called rating agencies. The three biggest agencies are S&P Global Ratings, Moody's and Fitch. They are private companies whose role is to evaluate borrowers' ability to meet their financial commitments (to pay back the debt). They charge a fee for giving their assessment and evaluation.

By whom are they paid for this opinion? Well, like auditors, they are paid by the very people they are evaluating. A version again of Big Finance marking its own homework, and one could argue that these *"independent"* arbiters have a rather obvious conflict of interest. Students of the 2008 Global Financial crisis, and the film The Big Short, will be clear on this.

The ratings attributed to borrowers are in fact crucial since they basically represent the market's view on how risky, and therefore how costly, it should be for that company to borrow. They give us a clear idea of the credit default risk.

NUMBER	S&P	MOODY'S	FITCH	MEANING & COLOR
1	AAA	Aaa	AAA	PRIME
2	AA+	Aa1	AA+	
3	AA	Aa2	AA	HIGH GRADE
4	AA-	Aa3	AA	
5	A+	A1	A+	
6	A	A2	A	UPPER MEDIUM GRADE
7	A-	A3	A-	
8	BBB+	Baa1	BBB+	
9	BBB	Baa2	BBB	LOWER MEDIUM GRADE
10	BBB-	Baa3	BBB-	
11	BB+	Ba1	BB+	NON INVESTMENT GRADE
12	BB	Ba2	BB	SPECULATIVE
13	BB-	Ba3	BB-	
14	B+	B1	B+	
15	B	B2	B	HIGHLY SPECULATIVE
16	B-	B3	B-	
17	CCC+	Caa1	CCC+	SUBSTANTIAL RISKS
18	CCC	Caa2	CCC	EXTREMELY SPECULATIVE

SOURCE: GENC & BASAR, 2019.

241

The red line is the border between investment grade and non-investment grade. A very important distinction between those you can feel safe to lend to and those you should probably not lend to. This is the line Michael Milken decided to cross when he developed the junk bond market.

To illustrate credit risk rising in sport, we can take again the example of Inter Milan. In January 2022, the club decided to issue $468m of new debt to reimburse old loans. That's called debt restructuring. Like most clubs, Inter was hit by the pandemic, resulting in a fall in ticketing and sponsorship revenues. Capital control restrictions from the Chinese government, limiting the amount of Chinese capital flowing into European football, made matters worse. Unable to inject more equity, the Chinese owners had no choice but to look for debt-financing, and the club used their future media revenues as collateral to guarantee that loan.

The market mistrust was not tardy in arriving: Fitch downgraded Inter Milan's debt from 'BB-' to 'B+'. The table shows that this is a major change, as B+ is considered *"highly speculative"*, known in the parlance as *"junk"*. One pauses to reflect on all those sports brand valuation reports, with all their formulae. Do they factor in that the club has its debt rated as *"junk"*? How does that affect the brand?

We know that any interest rate charged, based on all this, is calculated as risk free rate plus the credit default risk. Fitch with its B+ is saying that the credit default risk is higher, and naturally, the interest rate goes up. The cost of capital for the club has gone up, and across the whole capital structure of the business, people start to lose faith like a virus.

Similarly, as a result of the China Grand Prix being cancelled in 2022, the debt of Formula 1 got degraded as *"Junk debt"* by Fitch (BB and BB+).

When companies are in financial difficulty and unable to repay their existing loans, the solution is often to restructure the debt, to extend the maturity and release part of the financial pressure on the company.

The Greek economic crisis in 2009, and the Troika *"rescue package"* was exactly that. That is also what the Glazers did with Manchester United after the initial takeover. They restructured the type of debt and its terms. Indeed, it is smart to restructure existing debt if the market conditions have improved and interest rates have gone down. Or if the credit rating of the company has improved.

A significant level of debt is not necessarily, of itself, a bad signal for investors. It's not just the level of debt that matters, it's how expensive it is and your ability to service it. For instance, a sports league with a 10-year contract (and guaranteed revenues) from ESPN can handle a lot of debt. Much more than a 4th division football club with a nominally smaller bank loan.

All good financiers would use a very simple KPI to monitor the ability of any lender to meet their repayment obligations:

The interest coverage ratio = EBITDA / interest expense

This ratio shows how much of the earnings will need to be dedicated to pay back interest, and gives a whole new level of insight. Companies who lose control of their interest coverage ratio are in a debt cycle, a debt trap. They are called zombie companies.

And, as we showed in chapter 10, they are (unsurprisingly) becoming more common. And that's before the recent rise in rf.

All the signals we need are within our sight; we just need the will to look at them.

There is no bad risk, there is only bad risk assessment and bad pricing.

It's the same in insurance. Nothing is too risky with the right insurance premium. Otherwise, how could life insurance companies make money, when every single insured person is going to die eventually?
- It is risk they are well aware of, and they have a lot of data to build their models and forecasts.
- It is risk that can be diversified. Companies will insure people from different background and different geographies. You obviously don't want to be only insuring smokers and drinkers.
- It is risk they are well paid to take. If their model forecasts you will die at 92, they will charge you on the basis you will die at 80 (that is a great margin of safety).

EQUITY

Equity investors (providers of equity capital) need to be compensated for more than just the risk-free rate (rf) and the credit default risk.

Equity capital gets paid out last and the investor isn't just interested in whether his/her capital will be repaid. They are looking for the equity asset to grow and pay a return in dividends or asset valuation.

The lenders of debt to Inter Milan are assessing the risk of not getting paid back; of the club not being able to afford its interest and repayments. The equity investor in the club instead needs to think about so much more, including sporting performance, directly correlated to revenues.

Risk, uncertainty, and volatility always have a cost. We have laboured this point to death.

Thus, equity investors will only accept to take the risk to invest if they are appropriately compensated.

The extra return they ask for is called the "*Equity Risk Premium*"

Cost of Equity = Risk free rate (rf) + Equity Risk Premium

How does one calculate the appropriate risk premium for equity capital?

Is the cost of that risk, and hence the cost of equity capital, the same for investing in football at Southampton, Salernitana, or a club in a closed league? Clearly not. MLS franchises are worth more than Southampton because there is no relegation risk. The traditions so loved, of promotion and relegation, have a financial cost for the industry of sport that few truly grasp.

Many factors influence your equity risk, including regulatory and political circumstances. The creation of a UK football regulator immediately increases the risk for that industry, and makes EPL clubs less valuable overnight. Why else would the English Premier League be lobbying so hard against it?

The graph below illustrates how the risk (and therefore the equity risk premium) also varies depending on the asset class of equity. The return expected by investors increases with their exposure to risks when buying certain assets, or classes of assets. This is a very powerful graphic.

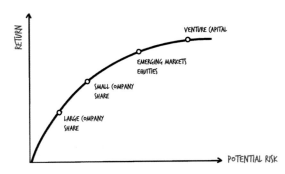

Note where Venture Capital sits in this graph. And when we realise that it is they who have dominated the corporate world for a generation, we can start to understand what we are dealing with.

For any business, there are two main areas of risk; market and specific risks, also called systematic and systemic risks. The latter is confusing, so we shall use the former.

MARKET RISK

Market risk is the macro uncertainty and volatility that the whole economy faces, such as a rise in interest rates, inflation, war, currency crises, elections, unemployment, a pandemic etc. It's the holistic risk of our world, our economy. Market risks will impact everyone, and we will be exposed to those risks no matter which sector of the economy we invest in.

There are investors who solely involve themselves in trying to predict these elements and place their capital accordingly. Those in macro investment funds, often hedge funds, are some of the smartest people around because all the elements above are correlated to each other to a greater or lesser degree. The best of these people see linkage that makes them fortunes.

As the risk-free rate is represented by rf; the market risk is called rm.

The proxy to identify and quantify market risk (rm) is to use the actual return of the stock market of the country involved.

Return and risk are, let's not forget, the mirror image of each other. So the actual return of assets is used as the proxy for their risk. So, to assess market risk (rm) in the USA, you'd look at current returns to investors in the S&P. The FTSE UK for the market risk (rm) in the UK. Same idea for South Africa, Peru, Russia.

This tells us the risk premium an equity investor is currently needing to be rewarded for, by country.

But market risk (rm) does not affect all companies in that marketplace with the same severity.

The impact of macro factors on a company is determined by the specific characteristics of that particular company and its sector. Those characteristics can either amplify or mitigate the exposure to macro risks (rm). In a market downturn, an economic recession, not all sectors and companies will be impacted in the same way.

SPECIFIC RISK

We need to understand this specific risk and find a way to measure it.

Specific risk results from the intrinsic characteristics of an individual business and its industry.

In financial terms, this specific risk is called Beta.

The finance industry loves Greek letters to create some kind of mystery and jargon. Besides Beta, you will come across Alpha, its alter ego in finance, to describe excellent skills in beating the market index. One of the best publications in the sector is called Seeking Alpha.

Gamma has also become popular in recent years as more and more people invest via options and derivatives. The term *"Gamma Squeeze"* has entered the lexicon of finance, albeit in a very niche corner full of more conspiracy theories. The complexities of Gamma go beyond the confines of this book.

°Industry level specific risk

Some industries will by nature be less risky than others. For example, *"defensive"* industries selling *"essentials"*: like food, pharmaceuticals, and utilities (telephone, water and electricity), have low Beta, and are pretty oblivious to market risk (rm).

Conversely, any industry closely linked with discretional purchasing behaviour, like advertising, has high Beta, and gets hit quicker and harder than the market.

As an industry, sport is renowned to be quite a safe investment because it is seen as *"stickier"*, and less correlated with the rest of the economy. Fans are hugely committed, potentially the most loyal customers a brand can have. That leads to a less volatile demand, which enables sport properties to predict revenues more accurately. Loyalty is synonymous with low price-elasticity, which means customers are unlikely to go elsewhere if the price increases. That enables sport to protect margins when inflation hits. In addition, the recurring multi-year cash flows from TV rights also make sport a safer asset class for investors. Stability is the opposite of volatility.

The important and germane counter argument is that sport is hugely influenced by the media sector, itself driven by the advertising industry. The advertising industry has high Beta and is the first to be affected by downturns. So, sports' fan-driven revenues like season tickets and replica shirts may have low Beta, but its media revenues have high Beta.

All the debt financing of leagues from banks and PE in recent years is focussing on the media rights. Do they know that's high Beta? Have they priced that Beta correctly?

°°Individual Company specific risk

Within the same industry, some firms will be more or less risky, depending on several factors like how well they are capitalised, their competitive landscape, the level of debt, or the maturity of the firm.

In sport, these could be: Does it have tangible assets? Does the club own its stadium? How significant is the relegation risk?

To put all this into a formulae, the cost of equity is equal to:

risk free rate (rf) + equity risk premium

The risk free rate, rf, is, we know, determined by the safest possible investment: Treasury bonds.

The risk premium is made up simply of the combination of 2 elements:
- rm: The market risk;
- beta: The specific risk of that industry and that firm.

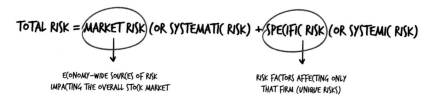

TOTAL RISK = MARKET RISK (OR SYSTEMATIC RISK) + SPECIFIC RISK (OR SYSTEMIC RISK)

ECONOMY-WIDE SOURCES OF RISK IMPACTING THE OVERALL STOCK MARKET

RISK FACTORS AFFECTING ONLY THAT FIRM (UNIQUE RISKS)

Let's use a visual to summarise clearly the components of cost of equity:

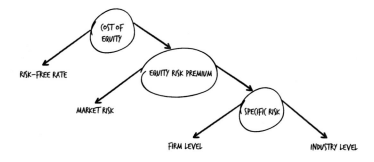

COST OF EQUITY

RISK-FREE RATE

EQUITY RISK PREMIUM

MARKET RISK

SPECIFIC RISK

FIRM LEVEL

INDUSTRY LEVEL

Now we have identified the various components of the cost of equity, we still need to measure it somehow. We need a number.

Luckily there is classical finance theory that computes everything described above to find out the cost of equity. The Capital Asset Pricing Model (CAPM) puts all the above into a formula to estimate the cost of equity:

Cost of equity = Rf + (Beta x (Rm-Rf))

Note that (Rm-Rf) is also called the market risk premium. In other words, how much riskier it is to invest in equities instead of risk-free assets.

See below the average market risk premium (i.e the excess risk to invest in equity instead of investing in risk-free assets) in Europe as of 2022.

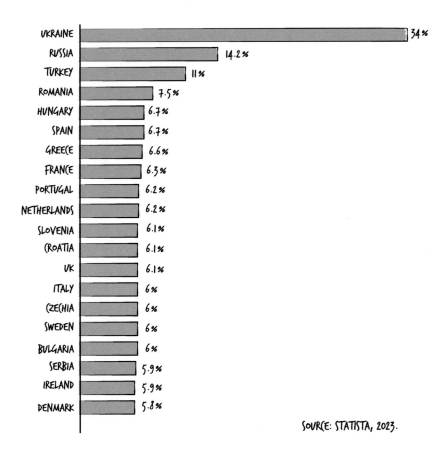

SOURCE: STATISTA, 2023.

This is telling us exactly the equity risk premium for investments in these countries. These datapoints and charts exist throughout the world of finance. They offer amazing insight.

I personally wouldn't have Serbia that low, given its recent tensions with Kosovo, as highlighted beautifully by sport's own Novak Djokovic, who called Kosovo the *"heart of Serbia"*. That is a lot of risk not currently priced in.

One of my own personal axioms after 40 years of career in finance and sport is this: the best way to interview a candidate for a finance job in sport, or indeed any industry, is to ask them to explain in one page the BETA of their industry, and of the individual organisation they are aspiring to join, and how they think it will change over the next 5 years.

This question will take out 95% of people who frankly won't make any material difference to your organisation.

To help answer the prickly interviewer question, and understand low versus high Beta, let's start with what is the average for Beta, as a number.

The answer is 1. A Beta of 1 means an asset is perfectly correlated with the market and has no material specific risk. The asset should react in the exact same way and in the same proportion as the general market. Eg, when the return of the market increases (or decreases) by 10%, the individual asset return increases (or decreases) by 10% as well.

If Beta is less than 1, like for the food and pharmaceutical industries, the asset varies in the same direction as the market, but in smaller proportions. When the overall stock market increases by 10%, these assets increase by less than 10% (anything between 0% and 10%). Same with decreases.

If Beta is zero, the asset is totally uncorrelated with the market. In this instance, the asset is not vulnerable to market risks at all.

If the Beta is more than 1, like say in early-stage sportech, the asset varies in the same direction as the market but in greater proportions. When the market increases by 5%, the asset increases by more than 5%. Same with decreases. The valuations of all sportech companies are all now realising this in spades, in 2023.

Finally, if Beta is negative, the asset is negatively correlated with the market. It moves in the opposite direction. Gold is an example of a negative Beta asset, and why the shiny metal is so prevalent in the wealth portfolios of bear investors. These are for sure the very hard yards of our book, and for that I apologise, so maybe the best way to explain all this is with examples in sport.

Many will argue that sport is quite a low-risk, uncorrelated industry with a Beta of say 0.5. But sport is joined at the hip with the media and advertising sector which one could put at a Beta of 1.5. There are also many more substantial risks at the individual company level of sport (particularly in Europe). Clubs are often badly run and struggle financially, driven by suboptimal decision-making caused by fan pressure and hubris. Overall, I personally believe that for the sports industry as a whole the beta is 1.25 or so; but mindful that some assets may be very significantly higher. For example, Glasgow Rangers football Club I'd put at 3! The below graph may help to understand the CAPM better.

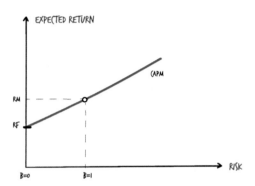

How to read the Graph:
- it shows the relationship between risk (horizontal axis) with cost of equity (vertical axis) Remember cost of equity is the mirror image of "expected return";
- every asset should stand somewhere on the CAPM line (blue line);
- we can see where the risk free (rf) asset sits. Today at 4%;
- as Beta (B) increases, you can see where the asset stands on the line, and the cost of equity (expected return) on the vertical-axis.

Now let's compare different sports assets to apply what we have just explained:

An American NFL franchise : New England Patriots
- Rf: US 10- year Treasury bonds
- Rm: S&P 500
- Beta: very low as they have longterm media deals.
  - The popularity of NFL franchises
  - Strong brand globally
  - Absence of relegation risk (closed league)

An English football club: Let's take Liverpool
*   Rf: UK treasury bonds
*   Rm: LSE
*   Beta: fairly low
    *   Relatively low relegation risk
    *   Owns its stadium
    *   Huge fan base across the world
    *   Plays UCL every year. Or does it?

A French football club like Bordeaux
*   Rf: French treasury bonds
*   Rm: CAC40
*   Beta: quite high
    *   Unstable TV rights revenues in French Ligue 1
    *   Low popularity domestically and very low globally
    *   High relegation risk

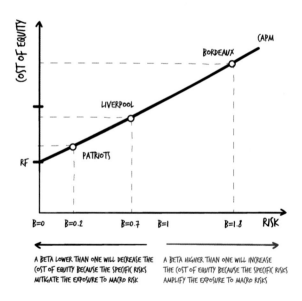

But as we said, we do need a number. So we shall calculate the cost of equity of two English football clubs playing in the EPL, Bournemouth and Chelsea, who both changed hands in 2022. We can try to estimate what could have been the cost of equity applied to those deals.

In both cases the risk-free rate (Rf) and the market risk (Rm) are the same because both clubs are in the UK. These were the numbers for 2022:

- Rf: 3%
- Market risk premium (Rm-Rf) = 6.1% (see table above)

However, their Beta will be very different. Bournemouth has a very high relegation risk, and a relatively small fanbase so their Beta is estimated to be 1.8. Chelsea is one of the most successful clubs in England over the last 15 years and is a true global brand. Chelsea's Beta would gravitate around 0.8.

Therefore, if we were to calculate the cost of equity of both Bournemouth and Chelsea in 2022, this is what we could have ended up with:

- Cost of Equity Bournemouth: 3% + (1.8 x 6.1%) = 13.98%
- Cost of Equity Chelsea: 3% + (0.8 x 6.1%) = 7.88%

This is the logic that is (or should be) applied when investors are looking at the cost of equity before acquiring any company. Naturally, the risk assessment of both clubs needs to be much more rigorous. Todd Boehly's management style wasn't factored in to the 7.88%!

Ultimately, you have no control on the risk-free rate or the market risk. Those two elements are given and tend to be broadly the same in most advanced economies. The real variable you need to assess in the cost of equity is the specific risk (Beta): the business decisions, capital structure, and industry characteristics.

It is critical to understand and assess Beta very well. Getting the risk premia wrong means getting the cost of capital wrong, which means getting the discount rate wrong. All that implies getting investment decisions very wrong.

For many years, none of this seemed to matter.

A rising tide of bullish sentiment was lifting all boats, covering a multitude of sins of very poor decision-making.

Now, in a changed world, we should revisit the good practices of elite corporate finance.

Part Three:
The Techniques Of Elite Corporate Finance

Chapter Seventeen

FINDING THE RIGHT CAPITAL STRUCTURE

Every company or business has its owners, its shareholders, its equity capital. Often, especially in VC, you will hear the phrase:

"Who is on your cap(ital) table and in what weighting?"

Having the right shareholders is key in business at any time, but in a storm, it's essential. Anyone with good experience in business will have seen all kinds of drama in Boards; proxy battles, extraordinary general meetings, power-plays, betrayals and double-dealings. Sport is no stranger to all of this.

The weighting of the cap table is also key. How much equity is still held by founders? How much of a voice does that PE firm have, in reality? Where will the minority shareholders vote when push comes to shove? Is there a punchy shareholder agreement?

Taking fresh capital, and from whom, is much more important than it seems. If cash reserves are getting low, many CEOs may understandably just want the oxygen of any money, from any direction, regardless. In good times that's probably OK. But in tough times, you will see that you need the right people on your cap table. Those of us who have seen the horrors unleashed when this goes wrong know exactly how crucial those questions are.

All that is before asking yourself whether you want to take on debt capital.

A main job of a strategic CFO is to find the correct capital structure to look after current shareholders' interests and maximise their value. Don't buy this stakeholder nonsense, that there is a whole community of interests to serve. The CFO is personally motivated and legally obliged to work for one set of people: the existing shareholders, the holders of equity. To maximise the return on their capital.

In raw terms, outside of VC, the creation of value in the corporate world in the last 40 years has been more driven by finance, and choices around capital, than product/market fit, operational excellence and scaling. So, it is important to understand how funding decisions affect the creation of value.

A company's overall cost of capital is called the Weighted Average Cost of Capital. (WACC). As the name suggests, this is the arithmetical average of all the different types of capital being used.

In a company with no debt, no leverage, WACC is obviously equal to the cost of equity. However, as soon as the company borrows money, we need to use the Weighted Average Cost of Capital (WACC) formula:

$WACC = Cost\ of\ debt\ x\ (Debt\ /\ Debt + Equity) + Cost\ of\ equity\ x\ (Equity\ /\ Debt + Equity)$

Don't let the heavy-looking formula confuse you. It's easy.

For instance, we explained that the Glazers used a lot of debt to finance the acquisition of Manchester United in 2005. They bought the club for £790m, but brought in only £250m of equity, and borrowed £540m. Let's assume the cost of equity, calculated via CAPM, was something like 10% and the cost of debt was 8%. These are not real figures of course, and the original debt was very onerous, but if they were these, this is how we could calculate the WACC, the average cost of capital:

$WACC = 8\% \times (540/790) + 10\% \times (250/790)$
$\qquad = 5.47\% + 3.16\%$
$\qquad = 8.63\%$

This WACC will then be used as the discount rate, which is the key parameter when valuing a company through discounted cashflow (DCF) modelling.

Finding the right capital structure enables companies to create value. In particular, the use of debt capital, which has often been cheaper than equity capital, and leverage, has regularly and systematically improved the return of shareholder capital. Let's take another sports example to labour the point of the attractiveness of debt capital.

A club is wanting to finance a new stadium. The cost of building the new venue is £100m. It can be funded by equity alone, or a mix of both debt and equity. Let's add as well that the stadium generates an annual net income of £10 million.

If the project were to be fully financed by equity, it returns:

$10/100 = 10\%\ pa.$

Now let's assume instead that the project is half-financed from debt, and the other half equity. Debt is never free and we can assume the net income is now down to £9 million due to say £1m in interest charges. What is the impact on equity returns?

$ROE = 9/50 = 18\%$

We can clearly see here that choosing to finance half of the project with debt improves dramatically the return (ROE) for equity-holders. We could go even further and imagine a situation where 20% of the project is financed from equity, with the remaining 80% coming from debt. Not uncommon. Again, the net income would be reduced, due to increased interest charges. So, let's say it goes down to £6 million per year.

ROE = 6/20= 30%

Same project, same underlying profitability, three times the juice. That is the Archimedes lever. It can indeed lift the world.

This most simple of concepts has dominated the world of business and finance for 40 years.

It's therefore logical to repeatedly pose the question: why wouldn't you use as much debt as possible? The benefits seem clear by now: lower cost of capital, levered returns on equity capital, no dilution of existing shareholders, tax efficient.

In the earlier stages of my career, I took some serious strategic finance courses at Stanford and Wharton business schools. Smart people were asking themselves, and us, why we shouldn't just use debt as much as possible. Why not take the arithmetic to the extreme and use excessive amounts of debt in your capital structure to reduce WACC?

Many business people and empire builders have in fact done exactly this, and gone all-in on debt. From Milken onwards. In today's world, PE funds are not shy about using massive leverage. Major companies like IBM and Apple have also taken on material debt to aggressively buy back their own shares and pump their share price. So make no mistake, there have been, and still are, many who will push the envelope on debt as far as possible.

But is there an optimal amount of debt? What are the downsides of excessive debt?

This has been the question that has dominated dry PhD research in academia since the 1980s. One could spend an entire career studying all this theory.

The most notable analysis is the Modigliani–Miller theorem by Franco Modigliani and Merton Miller. Modigliani won a Nobel prize for his work, which is referred to as *"the capital structure irrelevance principle"*. It basically says that the value of a company as a whole is not affected by its capital structure. Whether it uses debt or equity is irrelevant.

As with all research, it has found both proponents and acute critics. As a student, I had issues with it.

It was, for one, developed in a theoretical world without taxes, bankruptcy and agency costs. It also assumes efficient markets, which for me absolutely don't exist. But most importantly, it is talking about the value of an overall company, not the value of the equity capital.

For the returns of equity shareholders, which is all that really matters at the end of the day, low-priced debt does absolutely have an influence, and the reality is that Big Finance in the last four decades has made outstanding returns on equity capital by the ever-growing use of debt. It has been the weapon of choice of the all-dominant private equity industry.

The disadvantages have been less clear, especially in the good times of low interest rates.

We all know what it's like to be in debt. There are legal obligations to repay, and consequences if you don't. These commitments to pay every month can get on top of you if you exaggerate with your mortgages and credit cards. Interest builds on interest, and this reduces your flexibility, and room for manoeuvre (called "optionality"). If the deal of the century comes along, but you are already fully levered, you may not be able to take advantage.

Essentially, then, academia aside, what we really want to know is: how much should a firm borrow? It is very common to assess a sensible level of leverage by comparing the debt-to-equity ratio of the company with the average ratio of similar companies within the same industry. There is always safety in going with the crowd!

This approach is incomplete because it treats the quantum of debt all in the same way, when it is not.

$10m due in 3 years is not the same as $10m in 15 years. Equally, $10m at 3% interest is not the same at $10m at 8%.

The real risk of taking on debt is not being able to stay on top of the repayments of interest and capital.

That's why the *"interest coverage ratio"* is a much better representation of financial health. It measures the ability of a business to actually afford its interest cost. In other words, is the cash flow of the business sufficient to cover the interest to be paid over the same period? Is there a margin of safety?

A common-sense conclusion in the theory of the optimum capital structure, and best WACC, suggests that debt is a good strategy, but just don't exaggerate. If you use too much debt, the lenders will eventually get nervous, and charge you more interest.

The graph in the next page explains this idea. It even suggests that there exists some kind of theoretical sweet spot.

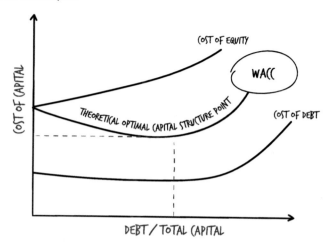

When there is no debt, the WACC is naturally equal to the cost of equity. Debt has been cheap capital, so borrowing helps bring the WACC down. However, the trend holds true only up to a certain point. Beyond the optimal capital structure, two things happen:
- the cost of debt starts rising as the risk of default increases. The more you borrow, the more the bank will be worried about lending to you, and interest rates will increase. We showed this in the example above, of 80% leverage for the stadium. We assumed that interest costs increased more than pro-rata;
- the cost of equity rises much more rapidly. Shareholders will ask to be compensated for the higher financial risk inherent in a highly leveraged firm.

As a result of this, the overall WACC automatically starts going up.

The reality of capital structuring, as opposed to this theory, is, as always, more pragmatic.

When the sentiment in markets is positive (bullish), and the direction of travel looks to be encouraging (interest rates on a 40-year downward trend), then CFOs and companies will likely load up on debt. When there always seems to be another big bank or investor willing to lend you more, if needed, you don't need to worry too much about leverage restricting your flexibility and optionality as a business.

When all that turns, debt capital is extremely dangerous. You risk losing everything.

We have seen since 2021 a rise in the cost of debt and interest payments, and this has changed the game entirely. Interest coverage and the ability to service debt will now deteriorate, and lenders will demand more risk premium for credit default risk.

To most commentators and operators, rising interest rates in this decade was a black swan, totally unforeseeable, and was blamed conveniently on the war in Ukraine raising oil prices.

To the elite financiers in the world, those who know about *"the murky world of finance"*, the Yellow Brick Road, the Fed Put, QE, and money printing, this was all utterly inevitable, and indeed long overdue.

So, the skill and technique of elite corporate finance boils down to this: can you perceive, in time, when those bull trends may reverse? Or, conversely, when the bad times have bottomed?

The role of the enlightened and strategic corporate financier, as opposed to the accountant, is in seeing, well in time, the changes in sentiment and mood, to position their company accordingly.

That is when they *"pay you the big bucks"*. Hearing the music in time allows you to take action; building up more robust reserves of cash, paying down debt on variable interest rates, and starting to look harder at cost efficiencies.

Not only will that protect your shareholders, but it will also allow you to be ready to take advantage of those who didn't prepare; those thinking good times would never end. They will be vulnerable prey.

So finding the right capital structure isn't about academic theory, isn't about weighted average arithmetic. It's about reading the weather patterns and seeing from where the storms are coming. Understanding the business cycle.

That is an art. The art of seeing risk and change on the horizon.

Chapter Eighteen

THE MANAGEMENT OF RISK

In the 1950s, when UK Prime Minister Harold MacMillan was asked what the greatest challenge for a leader was, he replied:

"Events, dear boy, events."

This is the British erudite version of Donald Rumsfeld's *"known unknowns"*, and *"unknown unknowns"*!

Harold MacMillan knew that risk is always inevitable and to be accepted.

"The key is not to predict the future but to prepare for it"
Pericles, Ancient Greek Politician and General.

Young professionals sometimes ask me advice about job offers they receive, and employment paths they are considering. My splendid colleague in researching this book, Etienne Dussartre, was one of them.

I replied to him, as to all others:

"don't choose a job, choose a boss".

My own career has been most influenced by some of the people I have had the privilege to work alongside. It wasn't the business cards and logos of my employers that created my experience, and resume; it was individual human leaders. One of them always had a simple question to his team.

"What are we doing today to reduce risk in this business? Risk is expensive in one way or another, so let's see if we can earn our crust by reducing it."

The stunning power of this simple wisdom opens this chapter. I have never forgotten it, and many of my own opinions about our industry of sport is really a scream against operators and investors seemingly under-estimating and under-pricing risk. The recognition and management of uncertainty, volatility, and risk is a cornerstone of corporate finance, as well as business and politics. The skill is in knowing the techniques of risk management and setting out your business to fit an agreed risk appetite.

In Summer 2023, Max Verstappen, the best current driver in F1, was asked why he had taken the risk of a pit spot to change tyres and claim the fastest lap. He had the race in his pocket and was risking the whole Grand Prix in Austria for a marginal extra point. His team told him not to do it (correctly, as the risk reward profile was clearly not beneficial).

Max did it anyway with the glib risposte:

"all of life is a risk".

Your risk appetite, like an F1 driver, may vary over time depending on the circumstances. For example, when you have nothing to lose, it's best to take on maximum risk. Businesses on the verge of bankruptcy are often *"gambling for resurrection".* The *"Hail Mary pass"* in American football is a useful sport analogy.

So the objective of the financier is not to completely avoid risk but rather to see it, manage it and take advantage when it is mis-priced.

This is now a competitive world on a global scale, reacting at break-neck speed. Products will get copied, and hold their first-mover advantage for only a small period. Tesla's EV advantage has gone now; cars from the traditional manufacturers are now objectively superior.

Being better at managing risk, instead, will always be a major source of competitive advantage, regardless of products. But you cannot mitigate/avoid what you cannot measure, and you cannot measure what you don't see.

To be elite level at all this, we need to:
- Identify risk
- Measure risk
- Manage risk

IDENTIFYING RISK

Most people do this very badly, and by far the biggest explanation for this is misaligned incentives.

The reward structure of leaders is often not in sync with the real interests of the company and its investors. *Charlie Munger,* of Berkshire Hathaway, articulates this best:

"Show me the incentives and I will show you the outcome."

Humans are incredibly motivated by their own self-interest (and remuneration) and will take action to maximise both. Many of the world's bankers saw the excesses of the great financial crisis brewing in 2006/7, and yet ploughed straight ahead anyway. The monies being made, the bonuses being earned, were too significant, and the associated risk wasn't theirs personally. Citigroup CEO Chuck Prince explained in 2007 his attitude to what he recognised as a potential major crisis coming, and why he would basically ignore it.

"When the music stops, in terms of liquidity, things will be complicated. But as long as the music is playing, you've got to get up and dance."

Many CEOs running businesses in this way will often accept higher risk than their shareholders actually realise or would want. Almost always, top management is being rewarded with stock options that strike gold on hitting short-term targets of share performance and growth. So that naturally is what is targeted by them, (and why precisely they so often do share buybacks).

In the Great Financial Crisis in 2007, investors in Northern Rock bank in the UK would have not realised the risky funding strategy being adopted by their CEO. That plan, of long-term illiquid assets funded by short-term debt, created outstanding growth and pushed up the share price. For a while, and with a fair wind at its back. In the long term, investing long when funding short, is always a horrendously risky corporate strategy.

If CEOs are personally incentivised to take risk, they will. If this is also juiced up by naked moral hazard, you are lighting a match in a gunpowder factory. It is human nature and will never change.

Bad incentives and misaligned interests are why organisations regularly fail. And why risks are often totally ignored. Good corporate finance, ergo, is in the true identification of risk, and the proactive alignment of interests, setting incentive plans that are balanced and all facing in the same direction.

The construction of remuneration packages, especially around hiring, is key. Even the negotiation itself gives so much insight. Someone willing to take a lower base salary and hefty bonuses is confident in their ability. Conversely, someone resistant to aligning interests like this is a signal in itself.

Having the right leader, correctly incentivised, is by far the biggest opportunity to create value in business.

Getting it wrong, in the corner office, or the head coach's boot room, is so costly.

"I try to invest in businesses that are so wonderful that an idiot can run them. Because sooner or later, one will."
Warren Buffett

Sport is full of these risky misalignments, across so many diverse stakeholders. Here are only some examples:

- a PE fund looking for a return in a 7-year timeframe, compared to a sport's CEO looking to foster the game for the long term. One will have a completely different vision, over cost and investment, than the other;
- the old chestnut of club versus country in football, cricket, rugby etc, and what that does for a congested and saturated calendar;
- a player with a relegation clause in his contract secretly hoping to go down, opening up more personal options around next year's employment;
- a coach needing short term results for his/her own future, thus prioritising older players, and ignoring the interests of the club to blood new stars;
- in American sport, you get *"tanking"*, deliberately losing games, so as to secure a better and earlier draft pick;
- the most obvious is what is/was called the *"bung"*. This is a personal backhander bribe to a coach to buy and sell a player, which may be the opposite of what his employer, his club, would need. In football, it is truly astonishing how many major decisions around the huge expenditure of player trading is left in the hands of friends and relatives of coaches.

Once the incentives of the top management are aligned with that of the organisation, there is, only then, no impediment, or conflict of interest, for good CEO/CFOs to try and identify other risks.

But they still often don't, as they are too busy in the grind of the here-and-now, to look up and ponder. Most people deal with today's inbox rather than imagining what it may look like in a month's time. Sport is a week-by-week results driven sector. It doesn't often do *"pondering over the horizon"*. This, in my experience, is true in all the creative industries. They are looking out of the window of the train, rather than sitting on a hill and being able to see where the train is headed.

It is unfair to criticise this too much, as we are in an industry where a run of bad results can end careers in a month. It is an industry of weekly pressure and assessment, and that is its weakness.

Less understandable is watching CEOs put no weight on possible scenarios that are not in the mainstream thinking of the moment. It's disappointing to see so many people always prefer the comfort of the consensus opinion, but it was ever thus. A common axiom of my generation in business, referring to relying on the industry bellwether in IT, was:

"No one got sacked buying IBM."

This safety-first thinking, in a moment of amazing disruption and opportunity in tech, seems absurd now. Back then it was how you kept your job.

Few leaders are motivated to be contrarian thinkers on potential risks because, when in a bull market of growth, with endless cheap available capital and universal optimism, no one likes the sceptic in the corner counselling about the need for change.

In sport today, the example of this would be the groupthink view that the value of sports rights can only go up. They may or may not continue to rise, but there is a good chance that they do not. There is also a chance that they fall, perhaps significantly. These risks are not being identified, and if they are, being ignored, even by some of the biggest brand name institutions in Big Finance.

"Long comforted by the ample and predictable injection of liquidity in markets by central banks, investors have been willing to take more and more risks. Some have ventured further and further into highly speculative strategies, causing outsized price moves that then attract others."
Mohamed El-Erian, CEO Pimco Capital

Risk is never well identified by the pack, and instead is perhaps imagined best by the outside contrarian with no skin in the game.

THE 10TH MAN RULE

If 9 people in a group of 10 agree on an issue, the 10th member must take a contrarian viewpoint and assume the other 9 are wrong, no matter how improbable it may seem. He/she is performing the role of seeking the *"unknown unknowns"*, of trying to envisage Harold McMillan's *"events"*.

Especially in turbulent times, find your 10th man or woman, sit them on a hill to watch the train, and tell them never to be afraid to be contrarian. Because the era of cheap and plentiful capital is over, and that won't bail you out anymore.

MEASURING RISK

Once you've identified the various risks, the next question is: what is the impact on my business if those events occur? What is my risk exposure?

Essentially, we are interested in two things:
- the severity of impact if the risk does materialise;
- the probability of that risk occurring.

Risk exposure = Severity of impact if event happens x Likelihood

Always consider the two components separately. Having a 90% chance of losing $10M is not the same as having a 10% chance of losing $90M. The risk exposure is the same ($9M), but the implications are different, meaning the necessary mitigation and hedging strategies will certainly not be the same.

To measure the severity of impact, we use sensitivity analysis. This simply means playing around with the inputs of your models. How sensitive is the investment to a change in a particular variable?

This is why it is also called a what-if analysis:
- What if the interest rate goes up 1%?
- What if attendance decreases by 5%?
- What if the club gets relegated?

That way you can observe how a slight change in one of the variables affects the outcome. It tells you the weight of the various parameters to consider and how critical they are.

In VC meetings, these are the questions you will get. To test you to see if you have done proper risk assessment.

Sensitivity analysis of impact of course doesn't estimate the likelihood that change actually happens. In other words, it tells you what the impact will be if interest rates go up 1% but does not tell you how likely they are to go up 1%.

This is where techniques like Monte-Carlo simulation becomes useful.

With Atomic Bombs You Need a Good Idea of Probable Outcomes!

Monte-Carlo simulation was invented by Stanislaw Ulam and John Vin Neumann (who were both working on Project Manhattan) to reduce uncertainty around complex, multi-dimensional problems with several unknown parameters. The name Monte-Carlo comes from the fact it is based on modelling the outcome of card games or roulette. The foundation of Monte-Carlo simulations is the law of large numbers.

"As the number of identically distributed, randomly generated variables increases, their sample mean (average) approaches their theoretical mean."

The more simulations, the more accurate will be the estimation of the various outcomes' probability. For instance, if we wanted to find the probability of throwing two dice and getting a 5, you simply need to divide the number of outcomes where the sum of both dices is 5 (which is 4), by the total number of possible outcomes (36). That is obviously straightforward and returns a probability of 4/36, or 1/9.

But sometimes, problems with greater uncertainty can be much harder to compute. Imagine, doing the same exercise two 24-sided dices. Or imagine we don't even know how many sides there are.

With Monte-Carlo simulation, it is still possible to find the probability of getting 5. You could throw the dice a hundred games and record the outcomes. You might get a 5 maybe 6 times, implying a 6% probability (6 times out of 100), but it is not accurate enough. However, if you keep doing it again for another million times, the law of large numbers starts applying.

Monte-Carlo simulations can be applied across various fields like finance, physics and project management. Basically, any field where there is uncertainty about multiple variables.

MANAGING (MITIGATING) RISK

Once you know what the potential risks are, and how significant your exposure could be, the question is as posed by my old boss:

"What are we doing today to minimise and reduce risk in our business."

The exercise starts by asking if the balance of risk and reward is acceptable.

As the influential muse of Buffet and Munger, Ben Graham, says, it's not that risk should be by definition avoided. It's whether the equation of risk and reward, loss and gain, is in your favour.

Risk is bad if it hasn't been identified and if it has been underestimated and underpriced. But if it has been seen, and perhaps over-estimated, that in itself is an opportunity for capturing value.

THE VALUE BET

A useful way to look at this is in sports betting. It's surprising how many people don't have a firm grasp on the concept of a *"value bet"*. Say that you're considering a punt on Tottenham Hotspur FC winning the EPL. We are not asking if it is likely, but whether the odds given for it to happen are generous or not. If the reality is maybe 20-1, and the bookmaker is too pessimistic, offering you 30-1, that is a value bet. And a good risk operator would take it on. And vice versa (better to avoid).

In inefficient markets, value bets appear, just as badly priced assets/companies appear. The very best operators and corporate financiers will accept the opportunity, but also have processes and techniques to get out with as little damage as possible if it starts going against them. These techniques are called *"stop-losses"*.

All the great traders know exactly how and where to pitch these, and have the discipline to use them, if their thesis isn't playing out. If it's not working, avoid further exposure, take your medicine, and get out of *"Dodge"*.

Risk assessment is a real-time activity. It can change rapidly with events, and we need to adapt.

Much academic research over the years has been written on whether markets are efficient. I wouldn't bother reading them. Markets are not efficient, and there is mis-pricing of risk and return all around us. That, for a competent corporate financier, is opportunity. Maybe the very definition of opportunity.

Finding this edge is all about information and data. Information is currency.

"... he'd know if the quarterback was on coke. If his girlfriend was knocked up. He'd get the wind velocity so he could judge the field goals. He even figured out the different bounce you got off the different kinds of wood they used on college basketball courts, you know?..."
Nicky Santoro, describing Sam "Ace" Rothstein, in Casino

The field of statistics, probabilities, big data, algorithms, AI and elite techniques like MonteCarlo, have empowered us enormously, and they now offer us amazing tools to give a little currency, more edge, in calculating risk. Quantum computing will astound us with what it will be able to do with this stuff.

All this is called quantitive analysis. The people who do it are called quants, and they are obviously much sought after in today's job market. One of Albachiara's first VC investments was in a quant shop called IoSport. Two physics graduates were using applied maths and hedging stop-loss strategies to trade sporting events, based on their better insight on real risk. This company didn't stay independent for long, and the founders decided to sell out, snapped up by major bookmaker, Superbet. Against my advice as a shareholder that it was too early.

The serious betting professionals like Tony Bloom, the owner of Brighton and Hove Albion Football Club, have made fortunes by finding an edge like this, measuring, avoiding and mitigating risk. It is no surprise that his stewardship of the sport club is equally as successful, via this type of outlook.

Risk always exists. Sometimes its just better to keep it at arm's length if possible. Avoid.

"Keep away from ventures in which you have little to gain and much to lose."
Ben Graham

But if we conclude that it is something in our interests to accept, for whatever reason, we should then try and mitigate and/or shift it onto someone else.

TRANSFER

°Insurance

When we talk about risk transfer, the first thing that naturally comes to mind is insurance. In exchange for a premium, you acquire protection against a particular risk.

Understanding insurance, using it well, is a superb tool in the corporate financier's toolbox. We remember Ray Ranson and his insurance wrapper with Leeds United.

Insurance is actually a really interesting concept and product, because it defines well the finance technique of diversification. Insurance companies can be more relaxed in accepting potential loss as they are spreading the probabilities across multiple clients, and not all of them will suffer the event being insured. The profession of actuary, in a simpler world, is who used to calculate all this. Now it's quants.

In sport, practically, insurance is extremely useful to lay-off and hedge against event cancellation. Some sports organisations came out smelling of roses for having had the foresight and the legal drafting techniques to have perfectly covered themselves against pandemics like COVID.

Another important area of sport insurance is around athletes' injuries. As the cost of employing athletes increases exponentially, finding a way to transfer this risk is essential.

Today it is a poorly served market, and so much more could be done, as injuries aren't just bad luck. They have patterns and are more predictable than some old sports doctors and physios would let you believe. Another classic example of Upton Sinclair's axiom:

"A man won't understand something if his position and livelihood depends on him not understanding it."

Owners in sport should reflect well from whom they are taking advice, and trusting, in addressing what is a very major cost for the industry. Insurance will eventually help them reduce the cost of injuries, when machine-learning is widely accepted.

Insurance in sport, with more sophisticated products across the board, will become much more prevalent and mission critical.

°°Invoice factoring

Previously we highlighted the benefits of invoice factoring to provide liquidity, but there is another aspect to it. It often enables a company to get rid of credit default risk. By selling the invoice to a third party, you can maybe transfer the bad debt risk, all for a cost. If the debt isn't paid back, it isn't your problem anymore.

For example, when a player is being transferred, the buying club will ask to pay in multiple instalments. In that situation, the selling club might not be willing to bear the multi-year counterparty risk before getting paid the full amount. FC Bayern, for instance, refused to accept instalments from FC Barcelona for the transfer of Lewandowski. The German club said there was a risk FC Barcelona would not exist anymore in two years!

Similarly, when a sports league decides to sell a share of its future TV rights to a fund or private equity firm, it is arguably transferring two types of risk:
- the counterparty risk of their broadcaster going bust. Or at least that risk is now shared;
- the risk that sports rights values start going down. When La Liga sold 8.2% of the value of its TV rights for the next 50 years, they were clearly offloading part of the risk in a drop in values onto CVC's books.

Invoice factoring in all forms has a cost. Crucially, when times are becoming more uncertain and volatile, it is likely that this cost will become more than acceptable.

°°°Outsourcing

Companies always have the option to outsource part of their activities to someone else, to reduce risk. This isn't always apparent, and may seem nothing to do with risk mitigation, but it is.

Not having a youth academy is an exercise in risk management.

Brentford FC suspending their youth academy is an interesting example of outsourcing. They decided that it didn't make sense to bear the risk of investing significant capital to develop young players, many of whom ultimately wouldn't make it. They assessed the risk/reward profile, and believed, for right or wrong, that it was better for other clubs to bear that risk for them, and to enter the player market later, by signing more proven players from other clubs, (who had instead accepted the risk/reward profile of working with teenage athletes). Even if Brentford didn't frame their decision around risk, and I'm sure they didn't, that is what they were doing.

Sports organisations in general often also outsource their risk on the commercial side of the business. They sell their rights, they license their brand, they even maybe think to let someone else monetise their database and loyalty program.

"We are a sporting organisation whose core business is in excellence on the field. That is hard enough. Why should we take on the execution risk of being flawless in developing our own TV channel or being perfect in strategic marketing. It's clear all of that is potentially more profitable, but it is a risk profile that we are not ready to accept yet."

I often criticise sport's B2B approach of *"a bird in the hand"*, but if it is a well-thought-out analysis of risk and reward, with complete scenario planning, it is valid corporate finance thinking.

The WWE, always a B2C business, recently decided to sell its broadcast rights to NBC Peacock, old school B2B, as the risk/reward profile for them had been shifted by such a high bid. This is intellectually sound as an approach.

Outsourcing also creates dependencies with suppliers. That can be problematic if the supplier goes bankrupt overnight, or if it decides to increase its prices. Apple, in outsourcing so much of its manufacturing to China, was badly affected by the counterparty risk of the zero-COVID policy of that country. Risk/reward profiles aren't a constant. They evolve, and the assessment and management of risk is always a trade-off. If done well, and there is full transparency, it is real added value.

All too often, it isn't done well. The dominoes of contagion aren't fully assessed. For example, outsourced risks don't stop being risks. They are just transferred, and that brings into play other potential contingent liabilities.

The industry of sport has often outsourced rights and activities to others and then had major issues. The collapse of the broadcasters ITV Digital, Setanta, Mediapro, Diamond Sport and the MP Silva agency, were all underpriced, counterparty risk.

In the *"Big Short"* financial crisis of 2007/08, companies had laid-off, transferred, their risk to the insurer AIG, but they did not envisage that AIG itself would not survive. Indeed, if it weren't for a full bailout of AIG by the US government (days after Lehman Bros was allowed to die with no bail-out) many major corporates would have had their insurance coverage rendered worthless, blowing in the wind, and they would have gone bankrupt. Why Lehman was allowed to die, and AIG wasn't, is a didactic lesson in itself in understanding *"the Murky World of Finance."*

A corporate financier needs to assess well the option of outsourcing, as opposed to the opposite; maximum vertical integration, which reduces the dependency on suppliers or distributors, and gives greater margins. It is always a trade-off to be assessed coldly.

°°°°**Derivatives**

To mitigate and transfer exposure to risk, companies and investors have recourse to more complex financial instruments called derivatives. Derivatives are contracts between two parties where one is actively paying to transfer a risk to another.

One of the biggest risks for any investor is movements in exchange rates. If you owe, or are owed, money in a currency different to yours, there is exposure. Imagine you are a Turkish club like Galatasaray, and you need to pay 5m in Euros to a Spanish Club for the next 5 years, following a player transfer (€1m per year). In 2021 alone, the Turkish Lira lost half of its value against the Euro.

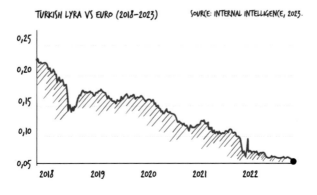

TURKISH LYRA VS EURO (2018–2023)   SOURCE: INTERNAL INTELLIGENCE, 2023.

Therefore, while at the end of 2020, Galatasaray had to pay just over Lira 9m to cover its €1m debt repayment, the same amount represented almost Lira 20m at the end of 2021. The debt, and the player, essentially became twice as expensive.

Derivatives exist to transfer that risk, at least in part. Their use in corporate finance has exploded in recent years.

If in the past, derivatives were very much focussed solely on operational and business risk management, eg, in the protection against the rise/fall in the prices of commodities like oil or pork bellies, today, sadly, they are now used more for aggressive naked speculation in the capital markets.

It is one of the most opaque and worrying corners of modern finance, and many people think that derivatives, linked to shadow banking, is a totally unregulated Wild West of risk, largely unknown to almost everyone, including central bankers and politicians.

The three types of derivatives commonly used are: options, future, swaps.

*Options

An option is a contract that gives its buyer the right (but not the obligation) to trade an underlying asset at a given price up until a specified maturity date. Although the buyer has flexibility, the counterpart (the seller) must deliver if the buyer exercises the option.
There are two types of options:
- a call option (calls) gives its holder the right to buy an underlying asset at a given exercise price for a period of time. Eg the right to buy sugar at today's price for the next 3 months. You are simply transferring the risk of a price spike. Calls can help you cap your input costs, which is extremely useful when budgeting. The principle applies to almost everything by now. Apple shares, currencies. It gets very complex and quants are extremely well paid to do the maths. The valuation of options is explained in the formulae developed by Black Scholes and Merton. Beyond the scope of this book;
- a put option (puts) works in exactly the same way, except it gives the right to sell the underlying asset. A put option is used by companies and short-sellers who wish to protect themselves (or profit from) the fall in an asset value. If you are selling oil, you can buy puts to lock in a price, to make sure you will not sell the barrel below a certain price. If the price rises, you do not exercise the option.

**Futures

Similar to options, forwards and futures are contracts allowing two parties to agree on the price of a future transaction for a specific underlying asset. However, different to options, here both parties must fulfil the contract: the buyer must pay the agreed price and the seller must deliver the asset on the date specified in the contract. There is no flexibility, no "*optionality*".

***Swaps

As the name suggests, a swap is an exchange around the future pricing of assets. The best way to explain a swap is to use a concrete example.

Firms and individuals often borrow money at a variable interest rate, where if rates increase, the impact is severe. Those personally now on variable rate mortgages will need no further explaining of this risk in 2023. Finance has devised swap products to transfer that risk to someone else. The whole of the Big Short film plot is around betting on a CDS (credit default swap), and working out complex graphs like this, all beyond the scope of this book. It's just too complicated.

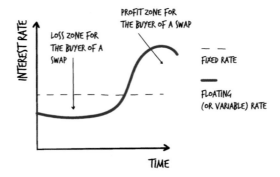

"You're completely sure of the math?"
"Look at him, that's my quant."
"Your what?"
"My quantitative. My math specialist. His name is Yang. He won a national math competition in China he doesn't even speak English! Yeah I'm sure of the math."
The Big Short

Transferring or laying-off risk can make or break your business, and reduce its cost of capital materially if done well. As can actually eliminating risk.

ELIMINATE

As we saw in the insurance examples, diversification is important, and is also the foundation of portfolio theory, which is a body of research I would recommend studying.

"Diversification is the only free lunch in investing".
Harry Markowitz, Nobel Prize Winner for his work on portfolio theory.

"Don't put all your eggs in the same basket", in finance, is shorthand for having good diversification and natural hedges across all your assets and investments, and indeed your liabilities.

Portfolio theory suggests that a well balanced basket of investments, will actually diversify away a lot of the inherent risks contained in individual companies and projects.

We should remember that investors like the asset class of sport because of this; it is seen to be non-correlated in a very useful way.

One remembers again the question on Beta to interview candidates. Just dropping the Markowitz name, and mentioning diversification, portfolio theory, is going to score you so highly. Learn it, I'd suggest.

But is diversification of investments really Markowitz's free lunch? Does it really work in 2023? Passive, index investing, which is sold as *"diversification off the shelf"*, now dominates wealth management and asset allocation today.

This idea of diversifying away individual company risk, by buying entire stock indices and (Exchange Traded Funds) ETFs, has become almost an unchallenged truism in capital markets in recent years.

But this is faux diversification and risk elimination.

Stock indices in reality distort their own maths. The bigger the market cap of a company, the bigger its impact is on the overall index.

The ETF index of the US stock market, even though it is generally considered a well-diversified barometer of the whole economy, is now mainly driven by 5 mega-cap companies: Apple, Microsoft, Alphabet, Amazon and Nvidia. These are all tech companies, all heavily correlated on the same themes, like AI. That isn't in any way Markowitz diversification and is a powder-keg of risk. This, many fear, is going to be the exact source of a major crash in all stock market and asset valuations, as too much risk has been accepted around too few companies, and when it reverses, the passive index algorithms will be ruthless in selling automatically, like 1987.

THE BIGGEST COMPANIES IN THE S&P 500 BY MARKET VALUE BECOME A LOT   SOURCE: BLOOMBERG, 2023.
BIGGER RELATIVE TO THE FIELD

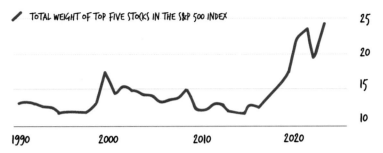

Another *"foreseeable"* black swan? Do investors realise how much their portfolios and wealth management is dependent on Nvidia, even if they don't directly own it?

In our industry, investors seem keen to diversify their equity across multiple geographies, leagues and even different sports. The most obvious example of diversification in sport in probably the multi-club ownership model. The examples in football are Man City Football Group (8 clubs), Red Bull (4 clubs), RedBird Capital which has now added AC Milan to Toulouse in France.

Multi-club ownership can help to reduce risk in a number of ways:
- diversity of revenue streams: Owning multiple clubs can help reduce the impact of any one club experiencing financial difficulties. More importantly, it decreases the exposure to relegation risk. It is unlikely all clubs of the portfolio will get relegated at the same time;
- shared resources: It creates synergies (cost efficiencies), allowing the implementation of a common coaching philosophy which can facilitate players' integration when they get moved around clubs within the portfolio. It also reduces information asymmetry when you recruit a player from your own portfolio;
- having a larger pool of players gives more chance of finding the next superstar. This is very similar to what VCs do with startups. Clubs just need to find one major success to pay for 19 failures. Venture capital by definition is all about diversification theory;
- geographic diversification also offers significant benefits in terms of brand development, especially in growing markets like the US and Asia;
- finally, this strategy also gives increased bargaining power to a group of clubs when negotiating with sponsors, broadcasters, agents and other partners.

Speaking to many financial investors in sport, they may even say that this is the only way to manage risk and get a return on their capital.

But is it real diversification when one only invests in sport assets? Does owning several football clubs offer real risk diversification? Smart diversification is not just about investing in various different things, it is about investing in things that respond differently to the same factors. We could argue all clubs are roughly exposed to the same risks and react the same way to macro changes. You do spread the risk, but you don't, properly speaking, diversify.

To a certain extent Red Bull is maybe the closest thing you can get to pure diversification. First of all, they are an energy drink company which is a completely different business. But even focusing solely on what they do in sport, it is unique. Not only do they have several football clubs, but they also diversify in other sports like *Formula 1* or Extreme sports. A football club and a Formula 1 team are naturally less correlated than two football clubs.

In summary, the *"spray and pray"* approach of diversification undoubtedly has its benefits (eg with a proper balanced portfolio of bonds and shares), but my own belief is that the trend for totally passive index investing has gone way beyond its natural equilibrium, and people have got complacent and inured by the great returns.

Value investors like Buffet, and stock-pickers like Ben Graham, don't believe in diversification as a risk management tool. They think it is better to invest more narrowly in something you know about deeply; an industry you know, a company you're familiar with, a technology you understand. Some call this approach *"rifle shot"*. One bullet, aim very well, know all your facts, and fire.

This ancient skill and technique of stock-picking and short-selling has sadly been forgotten, because it is there that the excellent corporate financier lives. Assessing companies isn't just about looking at them as investments, but also as clients and suppliers, to identify and manage risk holistically.

One way to truly eliminate risk is through innovation, and rethinking the way things are done and have been done for years. A business model might be fundamentally inefficient, risky or unsustainable.

Professional Rugby in England realised it had to change in the most brutal manner. In recent years, two clubs (out of 14) have gone bankrupt in the middle of the season (Wasps and Worcester) forcing Premiership rugby to rethink the way the league is actually structured.

Similarly, Super League was also an attempt to change the business model and risk profile of European football competitions. As more and more US investors invest in European football, they and their corporate financiers will likely try to reduce risk in these ways, focussing on closed leagues.

Fans will resist this till the end.

Yet, maybe fans do not know what is best for their sport. After all, As Henry Ford famously said:

"If I had asked people what they wanted, they would have said faster horses."

Sport has barely scratched the surface of proactive risk management. And that's because at the bottom of its heart, it loves it, on the field. It's the essence.

Off the field, it needs to be dealt with by elite corporate finance, because as it stands, its cost is far too high to be sustainable.

Chapter Nineteen

CAPITAL IS EXPENSIVE SO USE IT LESS. CASH IS KING

The best solutions to challenges are often the simplest.

In an era of cheap capital, husbanding cash just hasn't been such a priority, as there was always more available just around the corner. People have forgotten the importance of cash management.

Early 2023 has seen that sentiment change very significantly.

"Where's my cash, and how do I access it?"

If capital is now costly, and rare, the best businesses will just use less of it. The top organisations will ask treasurers and CFOs to minimise the amount of capital required to run their company.

The best businesses won't need to hold much stock, will get paid quickly and be able to pay suppliers with lengthy credit terms.

Let's use two different businesses to illustrate this concept: a kebab business near a football stadium, and the business manufacturing the scarves of the football club.

Let's assume the kebab business is open every day. It buys ingredients every morning and then makes and sells 100 sandwiches per day. The cost to make a kebab is £3 while the selling price is £6. This way, we can actually calculate the annual income of the kebab business:

- total annual revenues = 100 x £6 x 365 = £219k
- total annual costs = 100 x £3 x 365 = £109.5k
- profits = 219 – 109.5 = £109.5k
- margin= 50%

Now let's look at the numbers for the scarf business. It buys raw materials, produces 730 scarves a month and sells those directly to the club which pays for them at the end of the month. The cost of raw materials and production is £12.5 per unit, while the sell price is £25 per unit:

- total annual Revenues: £25 X 730 X 12 = £219k
- total annual Costs: £12.5 x 730 x 12 = £109.5k
- profits = 219 – 109.5 = £109.5k
- margin= 50%

These businesses show exactly the same financial results both in terms of revenues, costs, profits and margin. So surely investors should be indifferent to investing in one or the other?

Yet the answer is no, because, in corporate finance, not all earnings are equal. You need to go beyond profit. In this particular case, the two businesses generate the same annual income but require different amounts of capital to achieve this.

The kebab shop is clearly a better business since it requires less capital: an initial investment of £3x100= £300 of capital whereas the scarf business requires a £12.5x730= £9125.

Successful investors always look for businesses that, by their structure, require little capital. Here is what Buffet was saying in 2017 about the FAANGs:

"I believe that probably the five largest American companies by market cap…they have a market value of over two-and-a-half trillion dollars…and if you take those five companies, essentially you could run them with no equity capital at all. None."

In Europe, in sport, capital investment is required in a very costly stadium. Ask Tottenham Hotspur FC. In the US, instead, franchises often require their host city to build the stadium, with the threat that if they don't, they will up sticks and leave that city, for one that will. This is why Las Vegas has been without many sports franchises. It is convenient to have them as the *"threat of leaving"* city.

US sports franchises are therefore capital-lite, compared to their European cousins, and that matters.

By nature, some industries are more capital-intensive than others as they require massive investment in fixed assets.

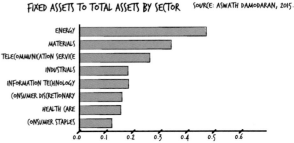

FIXED ASSETS TO TOTAL ASSETS BY SECTOR   SOURCE: ASWATH DAMODARAN, 2015.

Currents assets, as opposed to fixed assets, are called working capital, and represents the capital required to fund the day-to-day operations. It is simply the difference between a company's short-term assets and its short-term liabilities:
- short term assets are cash, account receivables (payments yet to be received from

clients) and inventories (raw materials and finished products yet to be sold);
- short term liabilities are the account payables (the payments yet to be made to suppliers), taxes, and short-term debt.

Essentially it is the cash trapped in the operating cycle.

So naturally it is critical to optimise working capital as it is a signal (for investors) of operational efficiency and financial health. Warren Buffet has always invested in the insurance business for this precise reason.

The beauty of insurance is that companies collect premiums up front, before having to pay any claim. Therefore, they have excess cash at hand, which they can deploy/invest elsewhere.

Working capital must be monitored closely. And as much as possible, companies should aim to optimise the three components of net working capital simultaneously:

Inventory: It is critical to try to transform raw materials into the final product, and then sell it as quickly as possible. That is the whole Just-in-Time philosophy. Holding a lot of slow-moving inventory/stock is a classic red flag that something is going wrong in a company.

Accounts receivable: Make sure you collect the cash from your customers rapidly. One of the most crucial departments in any company is Credit Control. A top operator chasing down unpaid invoices is invaluable. At the start of the 90s, I was asked by Amstrad PLC to help them understand and recover what looked to be a very bloated number for overdue invoices in their Italian subsidiary. It took about a day to realise that there was a fraud. Sales targets were being met and bonuses were being earned by selling to clients, with an implicit understanding that the invoices would not be chased aggressively. When Charlie Munger tells us that incentives always dictate outcomes, he is speaking from experience.

Accounts payable: this is the opposite mechanism: you need to try and get as much time as possible to pay your suppliers. Find ways to delay payments. Get good at *"cheques in the post"* excuses.

These are the components of working capital, but how do you assess if you are managing it well?

Calculate the number of days it takes for a business to convert the money invested in operations & inventory into cash through sales. This is called the cash conversation cycle (CCC).

CCC = Days sales outstanding (number of days to receive client money)
    + Days inventory outstanding (number of days you hold inventory)
    - Days payable outstanding (number of days before you pay suppliers)

Amazon is the ultimate illustration of good working capital and cash management. The company even manages to have a negative CCC. After it enters Amazon's warehouse, a book stays there for 28 days on average before it is sold to a customer. The customer pays upfront online, and it usually takes 2 to 3 days before Amazon receives the money. That means days sales outstanding + days inventory outstanding = 31. Amazon however pays the book supplier back after 50 days.

Amazon's cash conversion cycle is -19 days.

A negative CCC is a free loan from suppliers to finance operations. And that is the true competitive advantage of Amazon. It is the cheapest way to finance your business operations: make someone else pay for it!

Supermarkets are similar. We pay for groceries immediately and they pay suppliers with all the tranquillity in the world. Every supplier wants to be distributed in the supermarkets and has to just accept the terms.

Some industries will have good CCC naturally, like the insurance business.

And not every company can negotiate such favourable terms with suppliers. It all comes down to bargaining power and how much leverage you may have over people you do business with.

What about sport?

Think about the upfront revenues from: season tickets, sponsorship deals and TV rights. These revenues are received on a regular basis and should provide financial stability. Yet, sport in Europe is rarely a healthy business, and is often cash-strapped, as it can't control its cost line.

If European sport, football and rugby above all, cannot get a serious handle on its player costs, it has little future as an asset class. The EPL, the most commercially successful league in the world, has 2/3 of its member clubs losing money.

Working capital management is an underrated technique of good corporate finance, and one of the most difficult and least understood situations in business is how a very successful sales growth can actually bankrupt the company? This is counterintuitive and hard to grasp.

The answer again is in the CCC. If you need to pay your suppliers in 15 days, but your own clients pay you in 90 days, you need to finance 75 days of working capital. The more you sell, the more those 75 days cost. If your sales are £100k a month, then 75 days equates to £250k of working capital you need to fund. If your sales go to £1m a month, you need to find £2.5m of working capital. If you don't have it, it's over.

Making more sales is not necessarily a good thing if working capital isn't managed well.

• • •

This book is perhaps unkind to the humble accountant, as opposed to the all-powerful corporate financier, and this merits a better explanation.

There are different types of accountant, and the ones adding least value are the scorekeepers and the auditors. The first one is looking backwards and telling us what happened. The second one sadly often isn't even looking at all (they miss all the really big frauds).

There is one accountant that has all my respect: the management accountant, the person in a company working out the realities of business models, helping make better decisions, planning and budgeting, managing working capital and cash, and giving excellent MIS (management information systems).

One of the errors I've seen in my career is the trend for people who do not have the training, skills and technique of the management accountant, (but do have say an MBA), to be given the CFO role.

You can't be a great CFO without being a great management accountant. You can't separate out the sexy fund-raising, IPO, strategy and M&A (mergers and acquisitions) stuff from just knowing your onions as an accountant.

For too many decades now, in this era of cheap and easy capital, even poorly prepared CFOs were managing to raise capital. As things change, and the due diligence questions get harder, they will all be exposed.

Here are some examples of the corporate finance techniques used by a very good management accountant around performance and business models: focus, liquidity, operating leverage, strategic budgeting.

THE FOCUS OF THE PARETO PRINCIPLE

The easiest way to assess a company and its management is to ask questions like:

"What percentage of your revenues come from your top 5 clients, your top 5 geographies, your top 5 product lines?"

You would be surprised by how many C-Suite management really struggle with that question.

In 1941, Italian polymath Vilfredo Pareto came up with the 80/20 rule, which states that 80% of your output/profits come from 20% of your population, called the *"vital few"*. It doesn't just apply to business, but life in general, and I have found it to be very accurate. The good management accountant will know this backwards, and be able to reply to the question of the top 5s with ease.

But the real elite technique of corporate finance is to ask the next question:

"Why do you bother investing capital in the 80% of your activity that only gives 20% return? Why bother serving the 80% of your customers that generate so little? Why bother making the 80% of your products that don't really move the needle? Why bother being in 80% of the markets that don't really matter to your bottom line? What type of revenues available to you would you actually say no to?"

Every single time that I have found myself asking this type of question in a company, the reaction has always been animated.

Surprise, epiphany, then anger. Not always in that order.

"If we just stopped investing capital in that 80%, we would be so much more efficient and profitable, using much less capital, and giving a better return to our shareholders."

Again, through direct experience, the answers you get back tell us everything. The following push-back to Pareto I myself have heard many times, and is always a worry:

"If we did that, we'd reduce our revenues in half. And we need to be seen to be growing the top line."

"Our management is bonused on revenues and market penetration. That would kill them".

"That division, that market, is historic for us, and politically sensitive. You may be right, but we'd never let that go."

The corporate and Big Finance world has for 40 years rewarded growth, not profits or efficient use of capital, but perhaps now we are entering the era of Pareto, as the way to minimise the capital needed in a business. Focus on the 20% that really moves the needle.

In sport, in broadcasting, some may already be making the leap as to what that will mean. Polarisation of content towards premium, the 20% that matters.

LIQUIDITY AND THE MONARCHY OF CASH

Good management accountants and corporate financiers will also never forget the difference between liquidity and solvency. Ultimately the control over working capital and the operating cycle is inextricably linked to the management of cash and the notion of liquidity.

Liquidity is the ability of a company to convert its current assets into cash, so that it can meet its current liabilities. In other words, do you have enough cash, or can you sell some of your assets quickly enough, to pay your immediate obligations?

If the answer is no, your business is at risk. Being illiquid means you have assets, but you just can't turn them into cash quickly enough.

By contrast, insolvency is when your liabilities exceed your assets, and you are technically bust.

Illiquidity can kill you even if you are a solvent asset-rich business. If a company runs out of cash in the short term, it does not matter that it is solvent in the long run. It will die before.

Silicon Valley Bank was illiquid. Northern Rock PLC was illiquid. All PE funds are illiquid by definition and have a problem. They can't pay their investors who maybe think it's time to get out.

Here is how Mohamed El-Erian reacted when Blackstone decided to limit withdrawals from their property fund as too many investors were looking to exit:

"One of the consequences of the prolonged period of very cheap money and abundant liquidity was to encourage some asset managers to offer relatively liquid products that invest in relatively illiquid assets – in both private and public markets. These products can behave very differently in a world of more patchy liquidity."

Never invest in long term assets with short term debt. That always creates a dangerous liquidity mismatch.

To avoid illiquidity, it is critical to always keep cash at hand. You need a cash buffer. But that is not easy, especially when others pressure you to not do that. Some shareholders do not like when too much cash is *"sleeping"*. They will attack you for your prudence.

"Greed-is-Good" types.

What these investors do is they attack companies that they think are poorly managed, and then buy enough shares to be able to influence the way it is run. They are typically private equity firms or hedge funds. Very often it ends up in a proxy battle where activist investors will try to replace current board members with people of their choice. Always know your *"cap table"*.

Activist shareholders push companies to avoid excess cash *"not working"* in the bank. They ask for share buy backs to boost the share price or for the company to pay dividends. This is what happened with Apple in 2013 when Carl Icahn, a Gordon Gekko type raider, bought a 1% stake in the company. His goal was to improve shareholder returns by making better use of cash. At the time Apple had $130bn in cash. Enough to overcome almost any crisis. But Icahn claimed some of that cash should return to shareholders, and eventually managed to convince Tim Cook to undertake buybacks. As well as this, Apple paid its first ever dividend in 2013.Naturally, this massively pushed up the share price. Icahn netted around $2bn.

The management of your cash reserves is key in corporate finance. This is especially true in companies with high operating leverage.

Not to be confused with debt leverage, operating leverage is a metric of your company's cost structure.

OPERATING LEVERAGE AND SCALING

In the Silicon Valley Playbook, all this is now described in terminology like *"unit economics"*, and *"scalability"* but the concept is anything but new. Those old management accountants have always been working with a strategy on operating leverage: the higher the fixed costs (in proportion to total costs), the greater the operating leverage.

A sports sponsorship agency, with basically salaries as their fixed cost base, is very highly levered operationally. It is what I call, exaggerating to make the point, the *"monkey-on-the-back"* management style. If they are lucky, these businesses will turn a profit in months 11 and 12 each year. Before that, they are on the desperate hunt for revenues, to cover a relentless cost base. And because of this, they will take on some business, some revenue, that isn't making so much profit.

This absolutely is one source of the useless revenues of the Pareto Principle: too many businesses with high operating-leverage find themselves taking on revenue that isn't giving margin.

Operating leverage = (Sales - variable operating costs) / EBIT

Let's imagine a company with the following figures:
- $200k in sales
- $190k in total costs
- $150k of variable costs
- $40k of fixed costs

From this information we can calculate operating profits (EBIT): 200-150+40 = $10k.

As a result, operating leverage in this case is (200-150)/10= 5. A fairly average number, as shown in the next page.

OPERATING LEVERAGES

So, 5, in this case, means that a 1% increase in sales will lead to a 5% increase in operating profit. But also vice versa. Leverage always works both ways. In difficult times, if the company struggles, a high degree of operating leverage will negatively impact earnings in the same ratio; an operating leverage of 5 also means that a 1% decrease in sales will lead to a 5% fall in earnings.

In turbulent times, high operating leverage is not a good thing. Much better to have lower fixed costs, and flexibility as to how and when you bring extra variable cost into the business.

Understanding operating leverage is important.

Scalability and unit economics has been the Holy Grail in VC mentality. Build a platform and then scale aggressively with positive unit economics. This is why up until very recently VC has solely focussed on top line growth. Now VCs are all asking their companies to cut fixed costs, reduce operating leverage and focus on profitability. That's a tough ask.

This all leads to capital budgeting, the necessary planning and forecasting of the business in the near future.

A BUDGET ISN'T ABOUT NUMBERS

The best budgeting is entirely strategic. In all my career, the best example of this was in EMI PLC. The process was split into two. Strategy and Numbers.

The strategy discussions were where the individual music labels would define and articulate their mission and vision as a creative business. How they would manage the talent, artists and staff, how they would find that balance between art and bubblegum, Hollywood and Arthouse, credibility and profits. This forced each label to really think about what it was trying to achieve, and explain it to head office. I found this truly illuminating as an exercise when I saw it.

Only when all that was agreed, were we, the CFOs, told to go away, work up the numbers and see if the business that we envisaged financially stood up. As a model, as operating leverage, as working capital, and liquidity. Often it didn't, and you had to go back to the drawing board.

This approach is the complete opposite of so many companies who ask a score-keeping accountant to *"take last year's budget and add a bit on to revenues and costs."*

Good capital budgeting will translate the overall strategy of the firm to create alignment and be more efficient, making sure the organisation has budgeted enough cash to operate on a daily basis, cover its immediate liabilities, and survive in case of economic downtimes.

The industry of sport should be a very efficient business model. Very often, especially in Europe, it is not. Almost always illiquid, often insolvent.

Why?

Players, players, players...

Sports cannot operate without hard salary caps, and that means *"knowing when to say no"*.

Chapter Twenty

KNOWING WHEN TO SAY NO

The profession of corporate finance is mainly about allocating capital.

"I like concentrated bets, I like fat pitches, and then swinging big at fat pitches. And if a fat pitch doesn't come along, I just like to let it go past, and say no."
Stanley Druckenmiller, one of the all-time great investors

If the CFO has done his/her job well, capital at this point will have already been raised in the right structure, from the right people, aligning all the risk appetites in harmony. And the overall cost of capital will be known.

So how do you allocate capital correctly, to what, and on what basis? And what do you say no to?

"Over time, the skill with which a company's manager allocates capital has an enormous impact on the enterprise value".
Warren Buffet

Simply, you need to identify what is going to create the most value for the business and especially for the shareholders.

Thus, what this chapter is really about is how does one create value when investing?

Real value, not nominal, and not accounting value.

For example.

"Where should I invest? In which part of my business? Should I renovate the stadium or invest in the squad?

Should I invest now or wait and think about it next year? Should I wait and see if the club gets promoted?

When is the right time to replace existing assets? When is the right time to get rid of a player?

How much should I invest? The trade-off of excess capacity vs the opportunity cost of shortage? What is the cost of owning assets that are not currently being used? And how much am I missing out if I don't have the capacity to satisfy the demand?

How long should I be investing for? The choice between long-term and short-term assets? Should you go for cheaper assets even if it means they will not last very long?"

The objective is to invest in assets and projects that generate a return on capital higher than the cost of that same capital. If the company's cost of capital (WACC) is calculated at 8%, then a project that returns 9% is creating value, and vice versa. That is why the cost of capital is also considered as the hurdle rate. Any investment should guarantee a return at least equal to its cost of capital. Otherwise, you should not invest. This is a simple yet profound lesson, and was articulated in its purest form by Joel Stern, and called Economic Value Added (EVA).

EVA = (Return on capital - cost of capital) x capital invested

EVA is for me the Holy Grail. It is really understood by few, who often prefer simpler, more intuitive metrics like revenues or profit.Yet, it is absolutely critical to understand that you can make a profit while generating a negative EVA at the same time. A scenario that is destroying capital.

Let's illustrate this point with an example.

Take a sports club willing to invest £100m in a new stadium (a strategic & complex multi-year project). The CFO will develop a financial model, estimate the initial investment required and make assumptions about revenues generated by the venue each year, as well as the lifetime of the stadium. Let's say it makes annual profits, after direct running costs, of £8m over all 20 years. Since the initial investment is £100m, a £8m annual operating profit gives an 8% (8m/100m) return on capital per annum.

It seems like a nice profit and a decent return on investment. An 8% return on capital is not stellar for such an investment and risk, but it's not bad. Infrastructure investing is usually around that benchmark. But there is a missing piece here if we want to assess this investment properly, and that is the cost of capital. What if the stadium was financed with a corporate bond costing 10% per annum? That means capital costs 10% and gives a return of 8%, therefore:

EVA = (8% - 10%) x 100m = (2)m.

This means this project would actually burn capital and destroy £2m in value each year. And yet it is EBIT profitable!

To make sure we take on *"good"* projects, serious corporate finance works from cash flow and cost of capital. And for good reason.

Revenue is vanity, profit is sanity, cash is reality.

It is very common in the venture capital world to hear the question: *"When do you go cash positive?"* Businesses have cash coming in and out constantly. Whether it is through paying suppliers, charging customers, paying salaries, or investing, business operations generate either a cash inflow or outflow. The cash flow simply is the net balance between money coming in and out over the course of one year.

To be very clear, being cash positive is not the same as being profitable. If a business makes one dollar of profit, it does not mean it will get one dollar credited on its bank account. It can be confusing, and counterintuitive but that's the reality of accounting. First of all, revenues and expenses are recognised in financial statements when they are earned, not when they are paid. In accounting, a sale does not always mean cash coming in immediately.

Just remember cash flow never lies, whereas profits can be manipulated.

"Earnings are an opinion; cash flow is a fact".
Alfred Rappaport Economist

Another one of my hiring techniques, after the questions on Beta, diversification, and appropriate discount rates, is to throw candidates some set of accounts and ask them for an immediate reaction as to the health of the company. What do they look at first? The girl or boy that flips through immediately to get to the cash flow statement is the person I want to hire. Conversely, you'll often see in business the passenger non-executive director (NED) who simply compliments a rise in revenues and pockets his/her fee.

Value is created when your cash flow streams are sufficient to beat the cost of the capital used in generating them. This is EVA, and if we use it to assess if projects are creating value, beating the cost of capital, is it the cost of capital of the entire company, or the individual project, that we should use?

This is a perennial debate in corporate finance. Is the discount rate the actual cost of the money you sourced, or a number that fully compensates risk!

Many projects are financed in isolation, perhaps like a stadium. The cost and discount rate of the project is not necessarily equal to the overall WACC of the firm. This is fundamental to consider.

Although most companies use their WACC as a proxy for the discount rate of a particular project, it's not really correct. In most situations, the investment opportunity of a new project will be riskier than the company's established core business. Similarly, large projects often require to raise new capital, meaning they will have their own capital structure and cost, likely different to the overall company's.

Let's take an example from the master of all this, Warren Buffet. His magnificent conglomerate Berkshire Hathaway is as solid as they come. Prudence and rigour mean they sit as the most stable of companies across many diversified industries. Buffet has made Berkshire as risk-less as possible. As such, his cost of capital for the whole group will be low. Say 6%.

Now let's assume that Buffet wanted to get into sports. He wanted to use all that excess cash on his balance sheet in a play to make the MLS the dominant football/soccer league in the world.

Actually, he could do this very easily; he is a big shareholder in Apple.

What discount rate should be used? The cost of capital of Berkshire Hathaway? 6%? Most certainly not. The riskiness of the MLS project is way higher than the level of risk in Berkshire Hathaway as a whole, so I believe that there is zero chance that Buffet would allow his CFO to assess the MLS vision using the low cost of capital of the overall firm.

Each project should work with a hurdle rate of return to compensate for specific risk.

This leads us into the nuanced and potentially confusing world of *"project finance"*.

This is a term used to describe projects where the capital used to finance the project is sourced separately. These investment projects are considered almost as separate ventures, in isolation from the rest of the company.

Let's say Buffet likes the MLS idea, and also has managed to finance it with outside debt he secures from, let's say, Goldman Sachs. Let's assume that the debt conditions have no parent company guarantee and are thus ringfenced. Let's assume that Goldman, without those parent company guarantees, misprices the risk and asks for a low interest rate on the debt. They charge too little, say 7%. Buffett can finance his project totally separately.

What discount rate should Buffett's CFO use in the model? The entire project is financed externally by debt at 7%. The riskiness of the project should demand a hurdle rate much higher than 7%, but that risk in practice now lies with Goldman, not Buffett. Berkshire Hathaway has actually transferred the fully priced risk of the project to Goldman Sachs.

So, can Berkshire now use 7% as the discount rate?

For the MLS deal, the very best CFO could comment:

"Mr Buffett, you are not pricing in reputational risk. If this fails, that will cost Berkshire intangibly."

Reputation is fundamental for someone like Buffet who understands that it takes years to be built, but can disappear overnight, causing his overall future cost of capital to increase above the 6% of today.

"Lose money for the firm, and I will be understanding. Lose a shred of reputation for the firm, and I will be ruthless."
Warren Buffet

For such a risky MLS project I believe you should be using VC discount rates of 25%.

Finance we can see is more philosophy than science, and the art is in the choice of the discount rate. And why, like in so many things, it's not even the final destination that is important, but the journey to get there. A great corporate financier will see the road and think hard.

Another way, similar in concept to EVA, to assess if companies are creating value, beating their hurdle rate is to do a NPV (net present value) calculation based on DCF (discounted cash flow). Others do the same kind of modelling and call it finding the Internal Rate of Return (IRR).

This different terminology is, frankly, all unnecessarily confusing, because it's all about basically the same thing. Taking future cash flows to see if they create a positive value, once discounted for the approximate cost of capital.

This book has hopefully explained sufficiently at this point how we arrive at a discount rate, the time-value of money, the risk-free rate (rf) and premia for risk in debt and equity capital.

When using DCFs, or IRR, the modelling isn't hard. Most spreadsheet software now has all this functionality baked in; and AI will automate all of this grunt work so much more. Knowing these maths formulae won't be enough to get you a job, and what is really hard is deciding on the right discount rate and forecasting well the future cash inflows. Because a slight change in your assumptions will greatly affect the final valuations.

Cashflows and earnings aren't easy to forecast. In finance there is a phrase of crucial importance: *"Quality of Earnings"*. A company's quality of earnings is revealed by dismissing any anomalies, accounting tricks, or one-time events that may skew the real bottom-line numbers on performance. Once these are removed, the reliable ongoing earnings and cashflows can be seen clearly.

"Forecasts usually tell us more of the forecaster than of the future".
Warren Buffett

Assessing what the future revenues will be is particularly difficult in the business of sport.

Our product is all about unscripted one-time events: a successful year qualifying for the Champions League, the sale of a player for enormous profit, a bull-market moment for a category of sponsor (crypto and NFT) and of course, promotion and relegation. Plans likely won't hold.

"Everyone has a plan until they get punched in the mouth."
Mike Tyson

There is something even more subjective in DCFs. To value a business, we should consider all cash flows that will be generated *"during its remaining life".*

Defining the *"remaining life"* part is where it gets really hard. No one knows how long we will live. Neither does a business. This is exactly where, once again, corporate finance enters the realm of EQ, pragmatism and judgement, and needs to deal with an extremely subjective variable in the world of *"valuation".*

Understanding Terminal Value in business, in valuation, is an elite corporate finance technique.

This is perhaps the most controversial topic to conceptually understand, especially for the non-finance person.

How long will a football club last? How long will the sport of tennis last? How long will Google's ad model survive AI and ChatGPT?

Many top businesspeople will say that beyond 7 years out, they can't really have any accurate idea of where the business will be, especially with the current rate of change and innovation.

They are right. But equally, it would be very unfair and misleading to assess a long-term project over just 7 years. The EPL is going to be around a lot longer than that, isn't it? Chelsea FC are even signing a lot of players on contracts longer than that.

So we are obliged to try and put a value on the *"remaining life",* to estimate how the annual cash flows will grow or recede, into perpetuity, from year 7 onward.

Pragmatically, any project is therefore typically broken down into two parts:
- the DCF of the first 7 years of the project (It does not have to be strictly 7 years);
- the Terminal Value of the investment, as a proxy for the perpetual value generated beyond year 7.

Gordon and Shapiro gave us the formula to calculate Terminal Value (TV).

TV = [CashFlow in year 7 (1 + growth rate)] / (Discount rate - growth rate)

Once again, this formula looks daunting. It isn't really.

The key variable that jumps out is the number you need to put on the *"growth rate"* of the business into the distance. For example, what is the growth rate of the broadcast rights of French Ligue1 starting from 2030?

Rather challenging to estimate one could suggest.

Once you have some estimate of your number for growth, you can calculate the Terminal Value of the business seven years hence. You then need to discount it back to today's present value.

Discounted Terminal Value = Terminal Value / (1+discount rate)^(n+1)
With n being the year where the last expected cash flow is to be received. In this case, the terminal value needs to be discounted as if generated at the end of year 8.

In the past, in the Brealey and Myers textbook, this focus on maths and formulae was exceptionally intimidating. But arguably it wasn't even the real point of the learning. It was *"form"* over *"substance"*. Hopefully this book is different.

In reality, depending on my estimates of growth, (which are absolutely a finger in the air, if you think of those French football rights)...I can make the calculation of Terminal Value whatever I want it to be. And given that Terminal Value can deliver a very significant difference to the final overall DCF, how meaningful is all this theory really? How meaningful is DCF itself? It is full of assumptions of cashflow, growth rates; it is extremely sensitive to the discount rate you apply.

Be very wary of the person trying to sell you something based on these models. At best, they are only a basic indication of worth, as we shall discuss in the next chapter on the Truth about Valuation. At worst, it's a form of gaslighting. One thing however is not subjective in all this modelling.

If interest rates go up, valuations arithmetically all come down, as your discount rate rises automatically, and savagely affects future DCF and Terminal Valuations.

"Interest rates are to asset value what gravity is to matter".
Warren Buffet

The importance of interest rates cannot be overstated and they dictate the capital markets. Any financier worth his/her salt will reflect on all the deals signed off on these kinds of models to 2023, when interest rates were very low, and Terminal Values were high.

And they will go white. Because they know that the rise in interest rates has now driven a horse and cart through those numbers.

Let's try to illustrate all this with an example of an NPV model for a new stadium:
- initial cost $100m
- 20 years of positive cash flows of $8m
- assumed discount rate 5%

As an example this is how we would calculate the present value (PV) of the cash to be received in year 20:

Present value of cash flow in year 20 = CF of year 20 / (1+ discount rate)^20
$$= 8/(1,05)^{20}$$
$$= 3.02 \quad \textit{(See this figure in the table below)}$$

So doing the same for every year, we will have the NPV of the whole project, and we will be able to make a decision on whether or not we should move forward with the investment.

As you can see here, the sum of all discounted cash flows over the course of 20 years gives $99.7m.

YEAR	1	2	4	...	20	TOTAL
ANNUAL CASH FLOW	8	8	8	...	8	160
DISCOUNT FACTOR	0.95238	0.90703	0.86384	...	0.37689	
DISCOUNT CASH FLOW	7.62	7.62	6.91	...	3.02	99.7

It kind of washes its face, after investing $100m of capital, over 20 years at a 5% cost of capital. But we still need to add in some kind of Terminal value!

In this example, we have to consider the case of an asset with limited lifetime. Therefore, what really matters here is the salvage value of the stadium. To simplify, let's assume here the land is worth $25m, which means the terminal value is $25m.

But as we said, the terminal value is received at the end of the project (20 years), and therefore, it needs to be discounted as well.

Discounted terminal value = 25 / (1,05)^20 = 9.4
Hence, (at a 5% discount rate), receiving $25m in 20 years is only worth $9.4m today.

We can pull all this together.

Overall NPV of project = - Initial investment + Discounted Cash-flows + Terminal Value = (100)
+ 99.7 + 9.4 = $9.1m

Thus, in this case the club should in theory move forward with the construction of a new stadium because that would represent a positive NPV of $9.1m.

At a 5% cost of capital. Any higher, and the project is very marginal. Talking about the journey more than the destination, lets note the critical importance of the Terminal Value in this example. It's what moves it from loss into profit.

"The first rule is not to lose your money. The second rule is not to forget the first rule."
Warren Buffet

This is why Terminal Value is so critical, so controversial. It is very often the deciding factor which can make or break a project. But let's forget the accountancy and talk finance.

Would you, the reader, have invested $100m upfront for a project that after 20 years, and with a low 5% discount rate, only breaks even, and needs Terminal Value to make the figures turn black?

There is no correct answer, but hopefully the questions to be asked are clearer!

The honest truth is that a good corporate financier can make the final NPV/DCF valuation be whatever he/she wants it to be. They can choose a growth and discount rate to give the final valuation people want to see. We need to justify a big valuation? Use a small discount rate and say the project isn't that risky. You want to negotiate the price down? Assume low growth and apply a big discount rate in the modelling. Back it up by saying the asset is full of risk; apparent and not.

Eg if I were bidding for an Italian football club, or Serie A rights, and wanted to build a case for a low valuation, I start talking about all kinds of risk in Italy. Country risk, macro finance instability, unsustainable debt burdens, a media sector under real pressure with piracy, Italian unpredictability in general and how all these would affect the value of a club.

It is all like Geri Halliwell, who when asked at a Spice Girls audition what age she was, allegedly replied:

"What age would you prefer me to be?"
Ginger Spice

This is the art of finance. A skilled and confident operator can make a case for a wide spectrum of valuations; all of which will look credible.

Young finance students should always be asking:

"What assumptions on growth and discount rate should I be using in this model, and for what reason?".

If they aren't asking that, be worried about them. And if they are too sure, be worried about them even more.

The realpolitik of business and corporate finance is right here. Buffet himself is very humble and lucid about all this. He believes it is essential to understand the underlying business and its potential risks if you want to evaluate the discount rate accurately. Below a certain threshold of understanding, Buffet does not even bother trying to assess the discount rate:

"That's just playing games with numbers. It may look mathematical but it is mathematical gibberish".

Whenever you invest in something, it also means you likely decided not to invest in something else. To run a business, opportunities will need to be prioritised. This is called capital rationing.

Fans of Olympique Lyonnais and Arsenal will be very familiar with capital rationing as they heard for years the justification for lower spending on players was because of the need to invest the capital in a new stadium.

So when there are multiple investment opportunities offering that very positive DCF or EVA, how do you select one? Other criteria come into it.

THE PAYBACK PERIOD

If the last chapter talks about how cash is king, there is always going to be a premium on projects paying for themselves as quickly as possible. The payback period is the time required to recover the initial investment cash in a project. It is a good indicator of a project's liquidity.

Depending on the context, you might want to prioritise projects paying back quicker even if their profitability or NPV is lower.

BANG FOR BUCK

"For $41m you built a playoff team. You won the exact same number of games as the Yankees but the Yankees paid $1.4 million dollars per win and you paid two-hundred and sixty thousand" John Henry to Billy Beane (MoneyBall)

This is about understanding how much value is generated from 1$ invested?

It can be calculated very easily, it is the DCF of the project divided by the capital initially invested:

Profitability = DCF/Capital invested

Going back to the example of a club's stadium, let's assume that instead of building a new stadium, the club could decide to renovate and slightly increase the capacity of the existing stadium. The initial investment is lower ($20m) but so are the additional revenues generated ($3m). The figures of both projects are summarised in the below table:

	BUILDING NEW STADIUM	RENOVATING STADIUM
INITIAL INVESTMENT	$100M	$20M
NPV OF PROJECT	$9.1M	$3M
PROFITABILITY	9.1/100= 9.1%	3/20=15%

The NPV resulting from building a new stadium is higher than the renovation, but the bang-for-buck of the investment is much higher in the case of renovating the stadium.

Here we have a project with a clearly higher NPV, but it is tying up so much more of your precious capital. $80m more in fact.

If that is being provided by others, in project finance, no real problem. But rarely does taking on outside capital (normally debt) come without terms and conditions (covenants), and in some way, you will always be restricting your room for manoeuvre, or your flexibility to act.

If instead you have to find and use that capital yourself, it inevitably will be at the loss of possibilities in other areas. Some predictable (if I do the stadium, I can't buy those players), some less so.

So the opportunity cost of capital is also strategic, and about leadership vision and adaptability. You can't take advantage of events if you have pushed the limits of your corporate finance strategy. There is real value in keeping powder dry, especially in a fast-moving sector. Since there are so many unpredictable/uncontrollable *"events"*, we must try to keep our options open as much as possible. The desirability of an investment increases with its inherent flexibility, because flexibility allows you to adjust your plan when new pieces of information become available. Risk management is always fluid and in real-time. This is where what are called *"real options"* are useful.

Essentially, real options are about breaking down projects into multiple phases, observing what happens in each stage and using that new information to determine whether the project is still worth pursuing. Real options are particularly common in CAPEX-heavy industries like pharmaceuticals, oil & gas or mining. All these sectors require gigantic upfront investments, and their success is uncertain. Imagine having the possibility to delay the main decision on investment to a later time, once you have more information about the way things may evolve.

This is called the *"option to defer"* (or delay) the investment. In some cases, you cannot delay the investment. You have no other choice but to invest today, to maintain, say, first-mover advantage. Yet, you might still have the possibility to adapt your behaviour during the project. Even abandon the project. Sometimes it is the right thing to do when new data on risk and reward is available. You would do better to stop the bleeding.

Knowing you'll be able to walk away if things go wrong is extremely valuable, and the *"option to abandon"* allows a company to quantify this advantage (while the classic NPV approach doesn't).

REAL OPTIONS IN SPORT

Imagine an English Rugby Club currently in the 1st division with a very old stadium. The club would like to attract more people to increase ticketing revenues. To do so, it's considering the construction of a new stadium.

This is a risky investment as the club is "yo-yo", going up and down multiple times in the recent years.

More importantly, there are rumours the league will adopt a closed league model in 2 years, that means there is a chance the club would be stuck forever in 2nd division. Investing in a new venue clearly would only be profitable if the club stays in the top division. We wouldn't need a model to work that out!

Let's imagine the overall investment is £100m: £10m to buy the land and £90m to build the venue. To simplify, we will assume the construction will take 2 years and the stadium will be used for 16 years. That means the stadium will start being used in year 3 and the overall project lasts 18 years.

The investment will be staged the following way:
- club must pay £40m today (£10m for the land + £30m of construction costs);
- then the club will pay further £30m (construction costs) end of year 1;
- and the remaining £30m (construction costs) at the end of year 2.

In addition:
- the discount rate for this project is estimated to be 10%;
- the annual cash flow generated from year 3 onward is forecasted to be £18m if the club is in 1st division, but only £9m if the club goes down.

	TODAY	YEAR 1	YEAR 2	YEAR 3 To 18	SUM OF DCF
CLUB AVOIDS RELEGATION (50% CHANCE)	$-40M	$-30M	$-30M	$+18M	$+24M
CLUB IS RELEGATED (50% CHANCE)	$-40M	$-30M	$-30M	$+9M	$-34M

For the first years, the figures are the same, the difference comes in year 3 onward, whether the clubs manages to stay in the closed 1st division or not. We can see that if the club stays in the 1st division, the project returns a positive NPV of £24m. Otherwise, this project returns a negative NPV of £(34m). Since each scenario is equally likely to happen with a 50% chance, the NPV of the whole project is:

50% x 24 + 50% x (-34) = (- £5m)

That is a negative NPV of £(5m) for the overall project, and the club should not invest. Now imagine we have a new piece of information. Say the local football club would like to commit to repurchase the stadium for £80m if the rugby club is relegated.

That is a completely different story, and is a *"real option"*.

Let's see how this affects the desirability (NPV) of the project:

	TODAY	YEAR 1	YEAR 2	YEAR 3 TO 18	SUM OF DCF
PROMOTION (50% CHANCE)	$ -40M	$-30M	$-30M	$+18M	$+24M
NO PROMOTION (50% CHANCE)	$ -40M	$-30M	$+50M*	0**	$-17M

*£50m = - cost of construction + sale of the stadium= -30 + 80
** The stadium would be sold at the end of year 2 in this scenario. So there would be no more revenue for the rugby club.

So if we factor this new information in, the NPV of the project is affected. If the club stays in 1st division, the NPV remains +£24m. However, if the club goes down, the NPV is now £(17m). Thus, the overall NPV of the project is now:

50% x 24 + 50% x (-17) = + £3.5m

So taking the option to abandon into account, a project which initially returned a negative NPV is now worth pursuing.

Too often, businesspeople tend to be stubborn with investments because they estimate they got to a point where they have already paid too much to give up. That is the *"sunk-cost fallacy"*.

People are reluctant to abandon a strategy or course of action because they have heavily invested in it, even when it is clear that abandonment would be more beneficial. Humans often struggle with this for two reasons:
- abandoning means realising a sure loss. It feels like wasted money;
- you need to admit you were wrong. That's hard.

But the reality is, you should always assess an investment looking forward and ignore what you have already spent, and sunk, as cost.

Finally, in some instances, companies may even consciously take investments returning a negative NPV. Investing in a project today may open up other valuable projects in the future. Hence, the project is worth pursuing if the option associated (to take other projects in the future) generates enough value to largely offset the loss of the initial project. This is the *"option to expand."*

In reality, it is a version of a call option. And the cost of the first project is the option cost.

When David Beckham joined LA Galaxy, taking a 70% pay-cut, that decision needed to be taken considering the full *"option to expand"*:

- David Beckham would get a percentage of all team revenue. Therefore, even though his immediate earnings weren't significant of themselves, they could potentially skyrocket in the following years. Beckham in fact earned over $250 million during his five year with LA Galaxy, which actually made him one of the highest paid footballers at the time;
- Beckham also bought himself a call option on an MLS team for a strike price of $25m when he retired. Beckham exercised his option and became the owner of Inter Miami CF which is now valued at $585m+. An incredible return on the $25m expansion fee. And now that Lionel Messi has joined Inter Miami, this was a *"real option to expand"* of value.

Finding a process to assess when to say no, when to allocate capital, with full optionality, built in, is for sure a very elite skill.

The real take-way I would suggest is this. Forget the maths and the modelling. Your capital has a cost. Work it out with intelligence. Then have it in the front and centre of your mind that projects need to better that cost of capital. The models and formulae you use to achieve that are important but are a commodity skill. Use your IQ and EQ to feel the music. That's why they will be paying you the big bucks.

Chapter Twenty One

THE TRUTH ABOUT VALUATION

No serious investor or corporate financier falls in love with assets. The skill and technique of the best operators is in coldly looking to buy that which the market has undervalued and to sell that which has been overvalued. To do this, one needs to have a firm grasp of the hard principles and techniques of valuation, and then to understand very clearly the reason for the difference between the value of something, compared to its current market price.

There are traditional methods to arrive at an estimate of the actual intrinsic value of an asset or company and there are factors explaining why the market pricing may be significantly different. I believe that, for the various macro-economic and geopolitical reasons we have discussed, the market forces of efficient price discovery are now very out of kilter, certainly distorted, compared to the true value of assets. And that includes sport.

In theory, markets are efficient, and companies should always be priced correctly, because market participants are rational and have the same access to any new piece of information. But market efficiency is just a theory. In practice, the market's ability to price assets correctly is questionable. *As Walter Schloss says:*

"the market is an emotional place that appeals to fear and greed."

The last 40 years have seen a dramatic increase in asset values from house prices to company values and, of course, sports assets. By many metrics, assets have never been more highly priced than they are today.

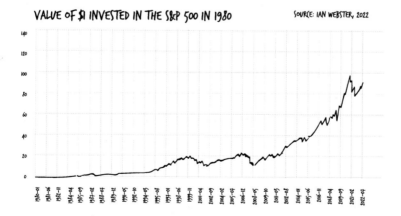

VALUE OF $1 INVESTED IN THE S&P 500 IN 1980   SOURCE: IAN WEBSTER, 2022

Companies are usually valued as a multiple of their annual profits or cash flow. This is called the Price Earnings Ratio, or PE, for short. A well-known, standard means of valuation, something Ben Graham would recognise, values companies at circa 10 times annual profits or cash flow. And 1-5 times revenues, depending on profits margins.

BEN GRAHAM, THE INTELLIGENT INVESTOR

In Graham's era-defining book of the same name, investing with a margin of safety means always buying an asset at a significant discount to its intrinsic value. That way not only does this set up investors for higher returns, but it also minimises the downside risk if things don't go as planned.

Buy companies intrinsically worth $100 for $70. That is the foundation of his *"intelligent investor".* Such set-ups are rare these days.

A company with revenues of £100m and good profits margins of 15% is likely to be valued in the £120-200m range. Any debate from there is about growth. A company can obviously command higher multiples if people expect revenues and profits to be increasing. The multiples may go say to 20x profits or 10 times revenues. Or more. In July 2023, Apple Inc, a company everybody knows, was valued at near 30 times earnings. In anyone's language this is high, but for a company whose growth seems to be stalling, it is very high. The mean historical PE ratio of Apple over the last ten years is 19.32. The current 29.18 PE ratio is 51% above the historical average. This a good datapoint, but it isn't, on its own, the explanation for Apple's overvaluation.

Over the years, many people have developed various sophisticated evaluation tools around this idea of valuing companies as a multiple of profits. Here is one below showing that stock markets are currently valued exceptionally highly.

We are in territory even beyond the dot.com bubble of 2000.

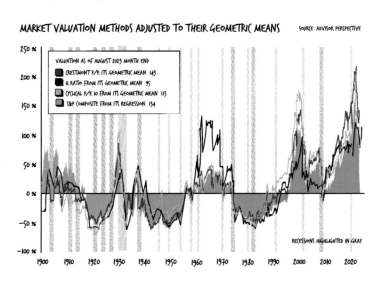

MARKET VALUATION METHODS ADJUSTED TO THEIR GEOMETRIC MEANS   SOURCE: ADVISOR PERSPECTIVE

VALUATION AS OF AUGUST 2023 MONTH END
- CRESTMONT P/E ITS GEOMETRIC MEAN 143
- Q RATIO FROM ITS GEOMETRIC MEAN 95
- CYCLICAL P/E 10 FROM ITS GEOMETRIC MEAN 113
- S&P COMPOSITE FROM ITS REGRESSION 154

RECESSIONS HIGHLIGHTED IN GRAY

Equally, there will be other people who don't think this, and will use their version of data and graphs to argue for undervaluation. Company pricing on stock markets are a function of people's expectations of growth and their optimism in general. In bull markets, PE multiples rise; in bear markets, they fall. By definition, a market and its prices is the meeting of buyers' and sellers' optimism and opinions.

So the truth about valuation is that there are no absolutes and no truth. Valuation is not about right and wrong.

But if stock markets and their companies in 2023 look to be rather fully valued on many historical metrics, they are not alone. One of the major themes of this millennium is the increasing unaffordability of houses and housing.

AVERAGE UK HOUSE PRICE, £ THOUSANDS
SOURCE: REFINITIV, NATIONWIDE, 2022.

"With the average British home now costing about nine times the mid-range income, and average monthly rents in the capital and outside London having hit record levels in the first quarter of the 2023, millions of Britons are living in areas where they can afford neither to buy a mid-priced property, nor to rent a home without spending a disproportionate part of their income."
Guardian, June 2023

A McKinsey report in May 2023 described the effects of years of QE, excessive debt and the murky world of finance, equally bluntly:

"The past two decades have generated $160 trillion in paper wealth but sluggish growth and rising inequality."

The valuation of all assets, from houses, stock markets, art, classic cars and fine wines have gone through the roof, especially compared to average earnings. You just can't pump up an economy with so much debt and money printing and not have the affects seen in asset prices.

All of this suggests that the rise in valuations in these years is more of a bubble created by the abundance of cheap capital, than the result of strong asset performances and intrinsic valuation. Valuations have far outgrown their underlying economics.

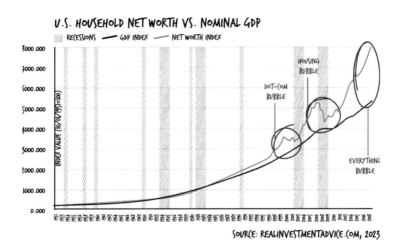

SOURCE: REALINVESTMENTADVICE.COM, 2023

Many of my investor colleagues are feeling rather worried at the Everything Bubble.

"Pessimists got that way by financing optimists".

All this obviously applies also to sports assets.

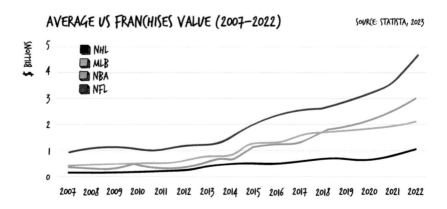

Chelsea FC, which was bought for $233m in 2003, was sold to Todd Boehly for $3.16bn in 2022. Similarly, Manchester United's owners, who acquired the club for little less than

£800bn in 2005, are today exploring options to sell the club, reportedly in the range of $3-6bn. But $3bn is not $6bn. Why such a wide spectrum of price?

That is because there are multiple ways to perceive and value an asset or business, each returning different figures.

In the old Brealey and Myers textbook, the calculation of *"valuation"* is an arithmetic and technical exercise, based on formulae. Of course, none of that can be ignored, and still forms the building blocks of the corporate financier. But 40 years later, in 2023, I don't think it's the truth about valuation. It's like trying to explain the greatness of Ayrton Senna by describing how his car worked.

The ultimate goal is to understand, as best you can, an asset's intrinsic value, so that it can be compared to today's market price, and you can assess the opportunity and the possibility of return on capital.

In corporate finance, there are many methodologies to calculate the intrinsic value of a company, or assets throwing off a stream of income (called yield).

Let's look at 5 ways to try and calculate intrinsic value.

BOOK VALUE OF ASSETS

The most obvious starting point is to look at a company's Balance Sheet to determine the book value of a business. That is to say the accounting value of equity, of what belongs to shareholders. The book value of any company is simply equal to the firm's assets minus total liabilities.

Company Value = Book value of Equity = Total Assets -Total Liabilities

Assets will include Fixed Assets, like land, buildings, machinery; and Current Assets like money owed from clients, stock inventory and cash in the bank. On the other side of the Balance Sheet, liabilities include debts owed, whether it is to bondholders, to banks, to the taxman or to suppliers, and essentially it is the value on your Balance Sheet that belongs to a third party and not to the company.

The accounting and auditing professions have a choice in reporting all these in the financial statements. Do they subjectively try to show what assets and liabilities are really worth today (known as *"mark-to-market accounting"*), or do they follow a more objective approach and simply record everything in the books at their cost, when they were paid for.

Valuing assets at their market value is subjective, and hence open to interpretation, whereas actual cost is easier to verify; there is a contract and a payment. For right or wrong, Balance Sheets and accounting principles follow the more objective, more prudent, cost approach. They will only mark-to-market on the downside, but never on the upside. As such, Balance Sheets are relatively limited in their utility. It's more what they don't tell you that is interesting.

Interpreting a Balance Sheet is a skill. The best don't read a Balance Sheet, they just *"see"* it, between the lines, in a flash. Here are some of the obvious questions good accountants and auditors will always ask:

- what is the true value of fixed assets at market value? Lore has it that when Sir Martin Sorrell finally took over JWT in the mid 80s, with a lot of debt, it was touch and go on the numbers and solvency. All until Sir Martin realised that he had actually captured a golden windfall of $200m hidden in the value of the Tokyo office, more valuable than the Balance Sheet had shown;
- is the inventory stock in the Balance Sheet old and superseded? Have better products come out? Has it been lying too long? You'd be amazed how many companies are carrying values of stock that are basically worthless;
- is the money owed from your clients (called sales ledger or debtors) actually going to be paid? Companies have an obligation to make provision for bad or dubious debtors balances, but, once again, you'd be surprised what gets reported as "money good";
- is the cash in the bank of the Balance Sheet real? Or is it being moved around to show more than there is? One of the major questions around the travails of crypto exchanges like FTX, Binance and Tether, is: do they actually have the cash their Balance Sheet says they have?
- are there hidden liabilities not shown in the Balance Sheet? One example from the world of football is the classic *"hidden agents commissions"*. Anyone who has worked in football will know this dynamic: agents commissions on transfers deals are often not recorded or paid in full. Agents allow this because the quid pro quo is that the club will continue to use those agents for new players or getting rid of existing ones. This kind of liability - future obligation, restraint of trade - is not shown in the Balance Sheet;

FOOTBALL CLUBS ARE FULL OF HIDDEN LIABILITY

When I spent some time in 2014/15 helping Erick Thohir, the one-time Indonesian owner of Inter Milan, many gentlemen's agreements with the old owner, Moratti, surfaced. This should be one of the first questions on due diligence when buying a football club. Are all liabilities declared in here, or do you have debts (actual or moral) off the books?

- what level of contingent liabilities do you have? Legal cases you may lose? Patent battles? Key personnel or clients you know are about to jump ship;
- what is the unrecorded value of intangible assets? Think about a brand for example: how much is it worth? Should it be amortised? If so, what's the lifetime of a brand? More than ever, we live in a world of intangibles, especially in sport. An experienced operator will look hard at the assets side of the Balance Sheet for *"intangibles"*, like goodwill, patents, research and development capitalised. Especially if the numbers are significant. These assets are subjective, and any total book value principally composed of these elements is always a red flag. Not because they don't represent "value", but because they are subjective and deserve a deeper analysis. You can't take "subjective" to the bank. As Albert Einstein said: *"not everything that counts can be counted and not everything that can be counted counts".*

IT IS A WORLD OF "INTANGIBLES"

There are two particular intangibles in sport: the value of playing talent and the value of brand.

In sport, in Europe, the biggest asset purchases are players, and the accounting treatment of that is well established. If you buy a player for £100m, that goes into the asset side of the Balance Sheet. You then need to depreciate (amortise) that value over the length of that player's contract. If it's a 5-year contract, you need to charge a notional amortisation charge of £20m per year. At the end of year 1, the net asset value is £80m with 4 years still on his/ her contract. Simple and clear enough, but open to uncertainty. Is this player injured, are they happy, has their value in the market deteriorated due to poor form?

The accounting asset value can thus only be a guide to assess true value.

The scandal at Juventus football club in 2022/23 shows the scope for creative accounting. Players get traded and transferred every 6 months. If the player above, valued at £80m is then sold, say for £60m, that is a hard accounting loss of £20m. If sold for £90m, that's profit of £10m. Juventus decided to *"game"* the accountants with swap deals. Selling one player for another player, often as a barter. If I swap my £80m player for another club's player, in a no-cash trade, the two clubs can assign whatever nominal value they decide to these players. In the case of Juventus and Barcelona, they assigned both players with valuations well in excess of book value. Generating profits on the trade, but no cash. These profits, totally notional and fake, allowed both clubs to record profits to help them stay within UEFA salary Financial Fair Play parameters. Neither player was worth the nominal transfer fee, but both clubs made a profit, and now have in their Balance Sheet players at a book value well exceeding true value.

The other intangible asset that renders book value analysis difficult is the *"brand"*. Sport is the ultimate community business and the biggest clubs have also become global brands with millions of loyal fans. This is extremely valuable for a club and can make a significant difference in the final value of a franchise.

The NY Jets and the NY Giants are the two NFL franchises in New York City. They play in the same league and even in the same stadium. Yet the Jets franchise is valued at $4.8bn while the Giants are valued at $5.75bn. Why such a difference? The Giants are just a stronger legacy brand (the franchise was created in 1925, 35 years before the New York Jets). The Giants brand is more distinctive, winning, and with a larger and more loyal fan base.

It is here that accounting falls short. Brand isn't bought with a cost you can record, it is built over many years. It is difficult to put a hard value on a brand, but there is now an entire profession using formulae to put a number on brand equity, with league tables each year around the most valuable. It's a calculation using several variables. Broadly speaking, we could summarise brand equity like this:

Brand Equity = brand awareness x brand reputation

As a sceptic of all these formulae, I am reminded of the movie Dead Poets' Society, where Robin Williams (Keating), asks the students to rip out as meaningless what they have just read as the golden formula to calculate the value of poems and poetry.

"If the poem's score for perfection is plotted along the horizontal of a graph, and its importance is plotted on the vertical, then calculating the total area of the poem yields the measure of its greatness. A sonnet by Byron may score high on the vertical, but only average on the horizontal. A Shakespearean sonnet, on the other hand, would score high both horizontally and vertically, yielding a massive total area, thereby revealing the poem to be truly great."

I, like Keating, believe that there is no way for finance to reliably calculate brand, or other intangibles like patents, IP and so on. There are limits to data and its use. Anyone who tries to tell me that there is will again represent a massive red flag for me in assessing them and their Balance Sheet.

In sport, similar formulae have been finding traction and favour, assessing the value of sporting events based on subjective criteria like *"quality"*, *"jeopardy"* and *"connection"*. I find this totally meaningless.

It is now hopefully clear that *"book value"* has major limitations in our quest for intrinsic value, and is only useful as a backstop, an underpinning. There is a common put-down directed at my accounting profession:

"they know the cost of everything, book value, but the value of nothing."

And it is true. An asset's true value is around its yield; what it will generate in profits, cash or dividends in the future. You do not own machinery or patents for themselves, but for the cash they will generate. The real value of a stadium is its ability to generate future match-day revenues.

Imagine you have a hot dog business outside a stadium. It is a small shop where you have all the equipment needed to sell hot dogs. The total value of assets (the value of the real estate + the value of all kitchen equipment) is $600k. You still owe $150k to the bank as part of a loan you took out a few years ago to start the business. Thus, according to the asset-based method, the book value of your business is therefore:

600-150= $450k.

So if someone offers $550K for your business, it may seem like a pretty good deal, and you might want to accept. But that would be a mistake and undervaluing your asset. It ignores how much cash your business generates now and in the future.

In sport, valuations are not based on book value of bricks and mortar, or even players, but are a bet on the future direction of sports media rights. Look at the NBA franchises value, and you will notice a dramatic increase in value from 2014 onward.

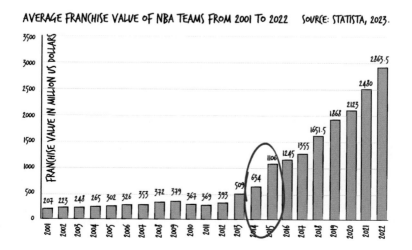

AVERAGE FRANCHISE VALUE OF NBA TEAMS FROM 2001 TO 2022   SOURCE: STATISTA, 2023.

2014 is when the NBA signed a new nine-year deal media rights deal with ESPN and TNT. The new deal was worth $24bn, nearly three times as much as the previous one. Good corporate finance needs to assess these cash flows and yields with what are called the Discounted Cash Flow (DCF) and/or the Dividend Discount Model (DDM) method of valuation.

DCF

In the previous chapter we discussed at length the mechanics and concept of DCF, NPV and indeed EVA. This kind of modelling is by far the most common method to put an intrinsic value on a business or project. It needs to be done, even with all its inherent weaknesses around subjective assumptions regarding growth and discount rate. It will give you at least another idea of value.

THE DIVIDEND DISCOUNT MODEL (DDM)

If a bond is valued on its interest yield, an equity share is valued on its dividend yield. As people say, dividends don't lie.

To make it simple, and because it is hard to know what the future dividends will be, investors make an assumption of the growth in dividends in perpetuity.

Valuation = Dividend Y1 / (Discount rate - Dividend growth rate)

Assume an MLB franchise paid a dividend of $1.50 per share this year and expects them to grow in perpetuity at 5% per year. Let's say the company's cost of equity capital is 8%.

The dividend for the coming year would be $1.50 plus 5% = 1.575 The calculation of the value of each share of the MLB franchise would be:

Dividend Y1 / (discount rate - growth rate) = $1.575 / (8% - 5%) = $52.50

Multiply the numbers of outstanding shares by $52,50. If there are 100,000 shares, the company value is $5,250,000.

This approach was particularly popular back in the days when Ben Graham was still an active investor (in the 1930's). At that time people were still traumatised by the Great Depression of 1929, and a big emphasise was put on cold, hard dividends. Investors were more risk-averse and more interested in securities paying safe, steady cash flows through yield. Consequently, to attract investors, companies had to pay money to shareholders in the form of dividends. Over the last 40 years, things have changed. Sentiments have changed. Many companies have decided to no longer pay dividends at all, mainly with the justification that the company was growing so fast, with so many needs for new investment, that it preferred to keep profits retained in the business. The dividend basis for valuation has fallen out of favour (for now).

This book, with a specific chapter on Yield, believes this is about to reverse.

FINDING VALUATION VIA COMPARABLES

Another method for arriving at valuation is merely to look at similar companies and assets sold recently. This is called benchmarking or comparables.

This has grown in popularity, fuelled by the rise of M&A transactions. It has become prevalent because easy to use. It's an exercise in *"what are other companies like me valued at?"*

You just need to follow these 4 steps:
- identify a peer group: a group of companies that have been traded recently and can be compared to the one we are trying to value. This means companies within the same industry with similar size, maturity, business model, growth perspective and so on. You usually need 5 to 10 comparable companies;
- pick a relevant financial metric that will be used to compare the target company against its peers. There are various metrics possible but most commonly analysts use EBITDA or Revenues (Sales). Once again, we need to read between the lines with EBITDA. Many experienced investors, like Charlie Munger, call it *"bullshit earnings"*. For them, EBITDA is fundamentally flawed and very easy to manipulate. To some extent, revenues are more reliable. First, they are less volatile and harder to manipulate than earnings. The popularity of revenues can also be explained by the fact that, in today's world, a lot of companies are just not profitable.;
- calculate the ratios (Value/ EBITDA) or (Value/Sales) for the peer group. That will give you a multiple you can then apply to your target company. As an example, let's imagine we use a peer group composed of 4 companies. The information is summarised in the below table:

COMPANY	FIRM VALUE	EBITDA	SALES	VALUE/EBITDA	VALUE/SALES
A	$170M	$13M	$47M	13X	3.6X
B	$150M	$14.2M	$56M	10.5X	2.67X
C	$200M	$17M M	$64M	11.7X	3.12X
D	$95M	$6M	$20M	15.8X	4.75
AVERAGE	–	–	–	12.75X	3.54X

- apply the multiple given by the peer group to your target company. If, on average, the peer group is valued at X times its earnings, you multiply the earnings of the target firm by X to get its valuation. In the example above, the companies should be valued at 12.75 times EBITDA and 3.54 times Revenues.

As we can see, this method is much easier to use and therefore more convenient. No need to go through the complex calculation of the cost of capital, nor to forecast cash flows for the coming 10 years. However, it does have some significant drawbacks that need to be highlighted.

Firstly, the choice of the peer group changes everything. Depending on the companies used as a benchmark, the valuation will vary significantly. Multiples in the Media & Entertainment industry will typically be around 15-20 times profits, whereas it is often less than 10 times in the industrial and manufacturing sectors.

We can perceive immediately the importance of the narrative and its influence on the peer group. Take Tesla as an example: should it be compared to car manufacturers or tech companies? It is a key question because the growth perspectives, and therefore multiples applied, are much higher in Tech/Software. It's therefore no surprise that Elon Musk is eager to position Tesla as a tech company in people's minds and speak about how innovative and disruptive the company is. At the beginning of 2021, Tesla's valuation was twice as much as General Motors, Ford, Volkswagen and Nissan combined, whereas it obviously sold a lot fewer cars. Narrative plays a crucial role in valuation.

TESLA'S STOCK PERFORMANCE IN 2020 (COMPARED TO THE S&P 500 (AS OF DECEMBER 21)

SOURCE: STATISTA, 2020.

Secondly, we could argue that the simple fact of using a peer group is fundamentally wrong. No two companies are the same. Any attempt to get a fair representation of a company's value should be much more granular than simply looking at previous transactions. There will be obvious reasons why companies from the same peer group should still trade at

different multiples:
* the volatility of their earnings;
* qualitative parameters like the calibre of management;
* recent news in the market that was not available when previous transactions happened (innovation, new regulation, interest rates etc.).

Would it be fair to value the excellent Brighton FC on the same comparable metrics as Leeds United? Absolutely not.

Thirdly, since the comparables rely heavily on previous transactions, if those are flawed, the next one will be too.

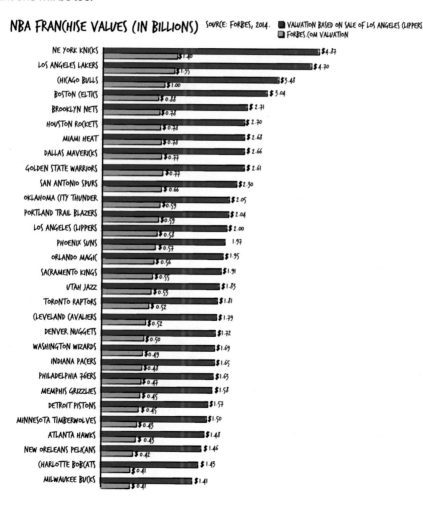

NBA FRANCHISE VALUES (IN BILLIONS) SOURCE: FORBES, 2014. ■ VALUATION BASED ON SALE OF LOS ANGELES CLIPPERS ■ FORBES.COM VALUATION

The graph in the previous page compares Forbes Valuations of the NBA franchises (in 2014) with the value, based on the price paid by Steve Ballmer to acquire the LA Clippers the same year. The discrepancies speak for themselves.

Instead of $1.4bn, the New York Knicks are suddenly worth almost $5bn.That is how bubbles are created. If my neighbour values something like this, it must be right.

This fallacy is the core thesis of the incredible book by Charles Mackay called *"Extraordinary Popular Delusions and The Madness of Crowds."*

Comparables do not really measure the intrinsic value we seek. It is actually better described as a benchmark of current market price, not *"value".*

PER USER UNIT ECONOMIC VALUATIONS

This has been very much the Silicon Valley Playbook in the last 15 years. Each user/customer of a business has a lifetime value (LTV) to you (how much profit you will make from them over a lifetime). This figure will be extrapolated from past results and big data modelling on assumptions.

You then need to calculate how many more such customers a business can realistically expect to capture, compared to its Total Addressable Market (TAM) and competition. And what the marketing cost of getting them, called cost of customer acquisition (CoCA), will be.

This is well suited to high operating leverage businesses like software platforms, that, once built, do not have many more on-costs for extra customers and sales. The more units sold, the higher the margin. This has been the way so many of this generation's companies have been valued: Uber, Snapchat, Peloton, Netflix, WeWork.

Since 2021, this whole philosophy has been looked on less bullishly, as the VC industry has retrenched. But it is exceptionally important to consider. In sport, much of the thesis for valuing franchises and clubs more highly has been around this phrase:

"We have 1b fans. Loyal fans. If those were valued the way a user is valued in Pininterest or Snap..."

• • •

Every one of these above valuation methodologies has limitations. They are all based on significant but volatile assumptions. So good investors will always use multiple methodologies, and the calculation of the intrinsic value of an asset or company is more a spectrum than a precise figure. That is why we have a range between $3-6bn for Manchester United.

Market price on the other hand is fiercely independent of intrinsic value.

Price is what you pay, and value is what you get"
Warren Buffet

This is probably the most famous quote from Buffet. Investors and empire builders always make money by knowing the difference between the current market price of something and its intrinsic value.

The price of something, like beauty, is in the eye of the beholder. Two people looking at the same assets will potentially attribute two different prices to them. And even the same person could attribute two different prices to the same asset depending on when asked. The price of a bottle of water is different the day you are in the Sahara than when you are strolling around Glasgow in November.

Market price is simply the amount of money someone is willing to pay to acquire an asset today, if matched by what the seller is willing to accept. It is fundamentally objective and practical, not in any way theoretical, and a function of various things.

First of all, it's ancient supply and demand.

In economics, one of the first things they teach you is that, in any market, the price of anything is dictated by supply and demand.

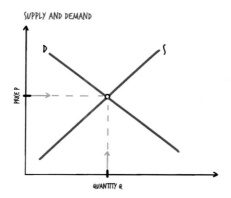

This classic graph shows that when supply and/or demand moves, the equilibrium price adjusts accordingly.

If an asset is scarce (low supply) and sought after (high demand), the market price will reflect that. Be that top location houses, the best IT developers, or sports assets.

The best traders don't try to calculate intrinsic value. They make their trades around how they think people will cherish an asset in the near future. The rise in the valuation of AI stocks in 2023 is not based in any way on their intrinsic value. Nvidia is not valued correctly at $1 trillion. It is priced at this level because traders believe that this is an asset class that will attract more and more capital.

Real world pricing in markets is therefore often built on the sentiment of an exciting new investment theme. Investors will rush into a particular company or sector simply because it is popular, a trend.

Sports assets, clubs and franchises, are scarce and what's scarce is expensive. The supply of sports assets is relatively fixed. It's not easy to create more supply of a Manchester United or Chicago Bulls. The last tickets held by the tout/scalper will go for more money than his first sell of the day.

When you also have excess demand, from investment funds full of cheap capital, from sovereign wealth desperate to own sport, from the usual trophy hunters, prices are going to increase, regardless of what your DCF model tells you.

On average there is only one NFL franchise for sale every 4 years, whilst there has been a huge growth in the number of people wanting this type of asset. The number of billionaires in the world has gone from 470 to 2700 in the 40 months to 2023. The acquisition of the Denver Broncos in 2022 illustrates the growing appetite of investors for NFL franchises. The Broncos sold at a price approximately equal to 9x revenue, whereas The Carolina Panthers (which was the previous record deal), sold in 2018 at a 6x revenue multiple.

9x revenues is by Ben Graham standards a very chunky valuation, but this is the wall-of-money reality of valuation.

Forget all the theory and formulae, it's all as simple as the Marrakech Grand Bazar. Supply and demand, scarcity or abundance. Price is more the result of a negotiation, which means it is all about bargaining power.

In any transaction where there is a clear imbalance between supply and demand, one side is *"price-maker"* while the other is *"price-taker"*.

It's the same in auctions for sports rights. If you only have one bidder, as my case in 2002, no model about theoretical intrinsic value, like Mr Oliver's, is worth the paper it's written on.

Thankfully, in the sports sector there has been no recent scarcity of demand. The limited number of premium sport properties, combined with the fierce competition between multiple broadcasters, has pushed the price of sports rights higher. With sophisticated auction techniques facilitating endless rounds of higher bidding, the winner has often overpaid for what they consider must-have sport. Your business needs to have it, and you need to make sure your competitor doesn't.

It happens all the time. The more popular the league, the fiercer the competition. Looking at the Premier League, we can see how Sky consistently outbid other broadcasters to win.

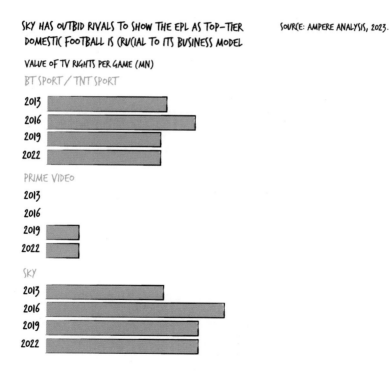

SKY HAS OUTBID RIVALS TO SHOW THE EPL AS TOP-TIER DOMESTIC FOOTBALL IS CRUCIAL TO ITS BUSINESS MODEL

SOURCE: AMPERE ANALYSIS, 2023.

VALUE OF TV RIGHTS PER GAME (MN)

This dynamic started in 2012, when the rights for the 2013-2016 seasons were auctioned. That is when, BT, an unexpected candidate coming from nowhere, looked to acquire two of the seven packages available.

From that moment, Sky decided they would offer a premium to make sure they would secure the most valuable packages. That is how important the Premier League was/is to the Sky offering.

Sky Sports paid £4.1bn while BT Sport spent just over £1bn for the 2016-2019 cycle. The value of media rights went from £3,018bn up to a combined £5,136bn; a 71% increase in the value of the EPL media rights (a rise never seen before or since).

Mediapro buying Ligue 1 French football is another striking example. The Spanish broadcaster offered to pay €1bn to acquire the rights of the French domestic league, and, at that price, all other bidders walked away wondering how they would be profitable. Unsurprisingly, Mediapro never turned a profit and ultimately left. Winner's Remorse.

The dynamic between supply and demand will be constantly changing, meaning that prices will vary.

Great investors and corporate financiers will make an assessment on the level of continued *"demand"* for sports assets from broadcasters, investors and the Middle East. How long will the trend of sports assets, as a theme, stay hot?

It is so crucial to understand that this demand will always be a function of intangible and emotional inputs.

One of these is what is called *"strategic value".*

In business, there can always be strategic benefits to acquiring and *"integrating"* a business. The value of an asset isn't always merely about what it brings of itself, but what it adds to what you already have.

We need to understand the strategic value of acquisitions.

Vertical integration describes a situation where a company acquires businesses either below (suppliers) or above (distributors) them in the value chain, to create synergies and reach sufficient scale.

Horizontal integration is when a company buys its competitors, to increase market share. Facebook acquiring Instagram for $1bn in 2012 is an example. At that time, it seemed like a lot of money for a company generating no revenue, but essentially Zuckerberg bought a competing product that could have become a big rival in the future (or worse, it could have been acquired by Google). Disney buying Pixar or Google buying Youtube are deals based on the same strategic thinking.

The common rationales behind strategic purchases are the following:

"We need to buy it, so our competitor doesn't get their hands on such an asset or technology."

"We could build this ourselves, but (over)paying for it now saves us crucial time-to-market, and we know this is a vertical where first mover will dominate."

"We are missing this geographical market and this company immediately makes us relevant there."

"Fills out of product/market offering immediately".

Sport has examples of this: broadcasters like Comcast buying BSkyB. Penn buying Barstool. Fanatics buying PWCC.

Strategic value can also be created by attempting to increase control over a particular industry or sector. This is probably the consolidation strategy that CVC is pursuing in rugby. They have now invested in several professional leagues of the northern hemisphere as well as in the 6 Nations. By investing in multiple leagues, the private equity firm will potentially be able to align interests of the various governing bodies to maximise revenues.

Commercial strategy is the reason Amazon acquired the rights for the NFL, as sport is a great way to get more traffic on their platform and sell more. Amazon know that a Prime member will buy 3 or 4 times more than other consumers and they need to convert casual customers to Prime. For this reason, they paid $715m for just one season of the Lord of the Rings. As Jeff Bezos (Amazon CEO) said:

"when we win a Golden Globe, it helps us sell more shoes".

Sport is often just an asset that is a loss-leader for a bigger strategy.

The huge investments from the Middle East into sport are all *"strategic"*, part of a geopolitical plan of economic growth, power and influence. Sportswashing, if that is a fair representation, is totally strategic in thinking.

Similarly, when Silvio Berlusconi chose to invest serious capital to make AC Milan one of the greatest clubs in Europe, the objective was not to get financial return. The return was in brand power, narrative and reputation.

Influence is valuable because it allows sports owners to unlock other business opportunities, *"options to expand"*, like maybe having leverage over local authorities to undertake real estate projects.

Overall, strategic value is where the corporate finance juice is. But it is also too often the siren song that tempts the foolish or egotistical. Often it is the convenient excuse used to *"overpay"* for something.

In sport, there are clear examples of clubs overpaying to prevent a player signing with the rival, of broadcasters overpaying for rights to make sure the competition does not get them. These things are hard to translate into numbers to be modelled. In June 2023, Draftkings, a US betting company, made a $195m offer to acquire Australian based bookmaker PointBet, outbidding Fanatics by $45m. DraftKings probably felt obliged to offer more money in order to defend its 25% share in the US betting market against Fanatics. Others would say DraftKings just wanted to take revenge over Fanatics after they suddenly walked away from a potential merger in 2021.

How many value destruction sins have been committed in the name of *"strategy"*? How many deals done in high profile industries are based simply on testosterone and ego but justified as *"strategic"*.

The cold reality is that emotion is a major driver of the differences between intrinsic value and market price, especially in sport.

"I have only been the owner of a football club for a short time, but so far, I have found it to be very time-consuming, emotionally exhausting, financially idiotic and utterly addictive".
Ryan Reynolds

Sport is unique and some people want to live the ultimate experience of owning a club.

Rocco Commisso, the billionaire owner of the Mediacom cable TV provider, bought Serie A club Fiorentina after a failed effort to take over AC Milan. I myself had tried to get him a minority stake at Juventus. He said it was the best way to reconnect with his Italian roots.

Similarly, a year before he bought the LA Clippers, Steve Ballmer failed to acquire the Sacramento Kings (his strategy to relocate the team to Seattle was not well received). It seems that Ballmer was so eager to get himself an NBA franchise that he was willing to pay a premium.

Investors are emotional humans and often act as such. They start running when others run;

sell when other people sell; invest when others invest. This herd mentality affects market sentiment and distorts prices. Ultimately, we have to realise that we live in a world where momentum and sentiment overwhelm the fundamentals in the capital markets.

The price of anything is not the hard value coming from future cashflows, but whatever the next person is willing to pay for it. In bull markets, this is called The Greater Fool Theory. No matter how silly you are, you will be fine as there will always been a bigger fool willing to pay more.

To succeed in corporate finance, to be an excellent investor or CFO, to be able to see opportunities and know when to pay a strategic premium, you need to have some view as to what the real value is. In theory, if you are convinced a business is overvalued, you shouldn't be buying. Good deals will be made when assets trade at a price significantly detached from what seems value.

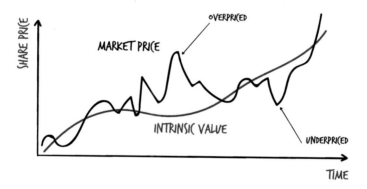

Buy the fear and sell the greed.

Bear markets in particular are a great opportunity for long term value investors, as these selloffs generate unique buying opportunities. Fear tends to manifest itself much quicker than optimism in financial markets. Due to this emotional asymmetry of investors, markets are much more volatile to the downside.

The real task is to identify when the markets bottom. Is it cheap or is it just less expensive?

This is where the *"art"* comes into corporate finance. Can you read the *"sentiment"* before anyone else? Can you take advantage of it? Can you see when it's going to turn?

There is no maths or science in that.

It's Eddie Murphy in *"Trading Places"* explaining why the price of pork belly futures is sure to go down:

"Christmas is around the corner and I ain't gonna have money to buy my son the GI Joe with the kung-fu grip. My wife ain't gonna f*** me if I got no money. So they're panicking right now screaming SELL SELL to get out before the price collapses."

As in any marketplace, the reality is that some very smart operators will see this as an opportunity to make money by exploiting these inefficiencies. This is called *"arbitrage"*. Arbitrage only exists as a consequence of market inefficiencies. Ironically, arbitrage resolves those same inefficiencies, by trading them away.

Imagine a situation where the train ticket cost £60 but the fine if you don't have a ticket is only £50. People will not buy a ticket and pay the fine. And they will choose to do so until the railway company realises the flaw and raises the fine well above the ticket price of £60.

Arbitrage opportunities are very hard to find but they can be extremely profitable. In fact, it is a risk-free way to make money. But they will be short lived. Traders will buy in the market with the lower price and then sell in the market with the higher price, which eliminates, usually very quickly, the discrepancy and rebalances the prices.

We've seen some examples of arbitrage in Sport, with a particularly famous example in Baseball. From the 1990s, statistical analysis became prevalent, as described in Michael Lewis's famous book Moneyball. The book talks about how Billy Beane, at that time manager of the Oakland A's, started to use analytics to identify and sign players that were undervalued by the market. The Californian franchise had one of the lowest budgets, and so they had to spend money wisely to maximise every dollar.

"If we try to play like the Yankees in here, we will lose to the Yankees out there."
Billy Beane in Moneyball

Oakland had to do things differently. Beane and his team realized that the ability to get on base, which is critical in baseball, was not priced in correctly. It was undervalued, since most teams preferred to focus on other players' attributes. Consequently, Oakland bought *"cheap"* players who were not necessarily considered *"good"* but were in fact excellent at getting on base. That way, he managed to assemble a team which performed much better than expected given the franchise's budget.

Baseball suits this approach because it provides more data than almost any other sport. Each team plays at least 162 games per season. The more data, the more accurate the model.

But, as with anomalies in financial markets that are doomed to disappear, this could not last forever. As other teams realised how powerful and effective Billy Beane's scouting strategy was, they started to do the same. The Boston Red Sox applied the same model (with a much more significant budget) and won the World Series in 2004 (86 years since their last title). The direct consequence of other teams copying the Oakland A's was that the arbitrage opportunity vanished. Those players who were really good at getting on base became highly sought-after. They weren't under-priced anymore.

• • •

So, there is no truth in valuation. There are only arbitrage opportunities when the market price gets too far away from what we calculate as intrinsic value.

Our industry still talks comfortably about the value of rights and franchises at the premium end always going up. Funds and banks are investing in, and lending money to, sport, on this basis.

The bull case around sport as an asset class is around a re-rating as a B2C business but only time will tell if that is true, and if clubs can really crack the D2C code.

In sports rights, my own view, that the intrinsic value is much lower than market prices, has not been consensus. This is the bear case.

Investors, like me, who always fall back on intrinsic value, and have been appalled at how high all market prices have gotten, have all done incredibly badly in the last 10 years, shouting out loud that markets were too high, that Tesla or Nvidia was absurdly highly priced, that there was an *"Everything Bubble"*.

We may have been right that market pricing was wrong, and well ahead of value.

But as J.M. Keynes said:

"markets can be irrational longer than you can remain solvent".

Part Four:
Sport Is Adrift At Sea

Chapter Twenty Two

SPORT'S PERFECT STORM

Sport has got itself into a mess and there is no guarantee that it will make it to port. Is this industry ready to confront its Perfect Storm? In business, change happens through both internal and external forces, and if we can anticipate them, we have a better chance. But if instead we insist that all is fine, take comfort in 150-year traditions, and dismiss new trends as passing fads, we will all surely be washed away in waves of disruption.

"The first step in solving a problem is recognising there is one"
Will McAvoy from the Aaron Sorkin's Newsroom TV show.

History and business have always been best understood through the lens of the three macro themes: money, demographics and geopolitics (including religion). Each of them brings its own threats and challenges, but, together, bleeding into one another, they make for significantly increased volatility and risk. This is obviously true also for sport.

MONEY

This book has explained how the various rivers of money flow into the industry of sport from four main sources: fans, sponsors, the media sector and the providers of capital. All four of these revenues streams now look to be uncertain and unreliable, and represent existential threats to the viability of sport; or at least to how the industry has operated to date, its mentality, its business model, its relationship with athletes.

FANS

Even if the sports fan is exceptionally loyal, the industry, like many others, is now facing a cost-of-living crisis. Its customer, that fan, often a normal working person of modest means, will see his or her budget of disposable income come under severe pressure, through rising inflation, higher mortgage payments, and redundancies, supercharged by the arrival of AI capabilities. See graph on next page.

We lose more than we create. With less, if anything, to spend, fans will be forced to make choices; perhaps give up that season ticket, not buy the latest merchandise, not gamble on sportsbooks, not *"invest"* in digital goods. And maybe not even pay for to all those fragmented subscription services they need to follow their passion.

Even if the fan dollar, and its purchasing power, remains sticky and resilient (low Beta) sport needs to ask itself where and to whom that dollar will go? More and more to the premium end of the market? Or worse still, to the pirates?

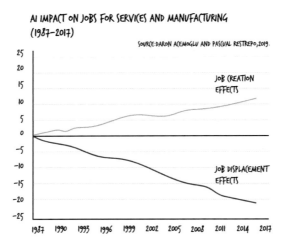

AI IMPACT ON JOBS FOR SERVICES AND MANUFACTURING (1987–2017)

SOURCE: DARON ACEMOGLU AND PASCUAL RESTREPO, 2019.

SPONSORS

The industry has got very confused about the role of sponsorship, even when the evidence is right in front of its eyes.

The middle-class sports of rugby, golf, tennis, and cricket often attract good sponsors, interested in the brand awareness and value-association. Rolex would be a good example. These sponsors are however pretty rare at the blue-collar end of the sector. Sports like football attract sponsors who aren't so interested in association with those intangible values, and see their sponsorship simply as a proxy tactic for acquiring new customers at low cost, principally for betting and crypto providers.

Sponsorship at its core is a function and sub-section of a marketing strategy and budget, which correlates well to the growth, health and spending power in an economy. It is high Beta. A deep recession would be a real problem even for the Rolexes of this world, as a marketing budget is one of the first to get cut when grizzly CFOs ask for cost savings, and value-for-money reporting. Here sport is vulnerable, as it can't give modern sponsors what they actually want, which is a direct qualified right of conversation with a sports fan.

Sponsors want sport to give them fan data, make an intro, and let them get on with marketing to them. The richer the data the better. Why should Mercedes be a sponsor of Manchester United when most of that club's fans can't afford their product? If the club could instead provide Mercedes with the exact details of the fans that did have that spending ability, this would be hugely valuable. If you also knew how long they have owned their current car, triple the value again. If AC Milan could tell potential sponsor, Pampers, the details of those fans married within the last 2 years and facilitate a dialogue, that has immense value to someone selling nappies/diapers. Yet, sport doesn't know its fans and still thinks sponsors like to just hang around the events and see their logos besides our heroes. That may have been true in the old days, but it isn't enough today. It is easy to talk about aspiring to act like a consumer business, knowing your customers and their rich data, building a direct relationship with them; but doing it is far from banal.

This is an industry which has not in any way monetised the passion and loyalty of its customers. It hasn't had to. It is desperately late and behind on customer relationship management (CRM) and segmented marketing. The commercial departments of most sport entities are ill-equipped to have a modern conversation with today's breed of sponsor, and there is a real risk that, at some point, the serious sponsorship market will lose patience with sport, and spend their budgets elsewhere. If we are entering tougher times, this deficiency in a core skill set will bite hard. There will be an urgent need for the re-skilling of an entire industry, which sadly will likely resist it. A recession will force that on them, removing their complacency and inertia, with alacrity.

THE MEDIA SECTOR

For 30 years, Big Media has driven the industry of sport and pushed up its revenues and valuations. The broadcast sector has been florid and rich; a fantastic business with great margins, based around a wonderful, bundled product called Pay/Cable TV, offering very juicy 38% margins. Beautifully highlighted below, a graph worth study for all industries.

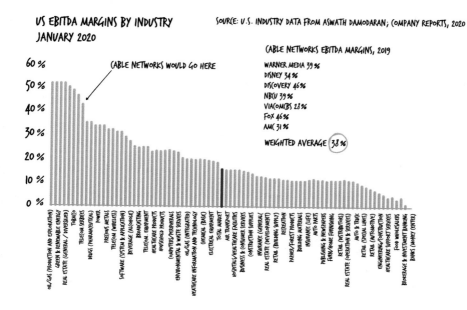

US EBITDA MARGINS BY INDUSTRY JANUARY 2020

SOURCE: U.S. INDUSTRY DATA FROM ASWATH DAMODARAN; (OMPANY REPORTS, 2020

CABLE NETWORKS EBITDA MARGINS, 2019
WARNER MEDIA 39%
DISNEY 34%
DISCOVERY 46%
NBCU 39%
VIACOMCBS 28%
FOX 46%
AMC 31%

WEIGHTED AVERAGE 38%

CABLE NETWORKS WOULD GO HERE

At the same time, old TV in America has always invested heavily in sport, as the last great aggregator of a live audience of eyeballs to sell to advertisers.

Sport for broadcasters was the must-have content, with a loyal built-in audience, and proven appeal. It is less risky than making a film or TV series or launching a new band that may or may work.

But now the industry should look at what is happening in Big Media and ask itself if the broadcasters will still be able to pay, and, if so, for which games.

The portents aren't good, and we have seen how the bond vigilantes have already started sniffing around the large media companies. The flash-boy traders always know.

For our little boat, this is the big wave.

The old media model is finished, and the entire sector is now struggling with trying to pivot its own product/market fit, and revenue model, for new tastes and demands. The cash cow of a PayTV/Cable bundle is decaying at pace, with people switching off and cutting the cord.

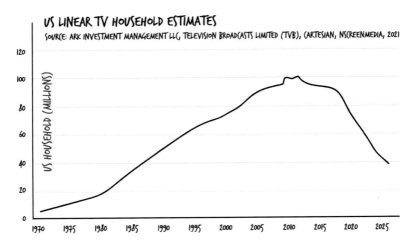

This *"cord-cutting"*, started a few years ago, and it is estimated that by 2026, only 42.4% of all US households will have PayTV subscriptions, down from 52.4% in 2022 (source: Insider Intelligence).

Ten percentage points in the next three years!

People are leaving traditional cable TV because they want different forms of content, and want it delivered differently. They are switching to streaming and video-on-demand (VOD).

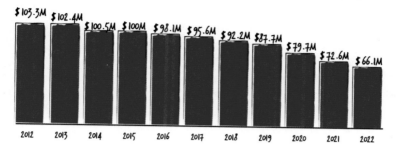

CABLE SUBRSCRIPTION   QI DATA IS USED FOR EACH YEAR / SOURCE: LEV AKABAS, 2023.

IN THE PAST THREE YEARS, THE CABLE BUNDLE HAS LOST A QUARTER OF ITS SUBSCRIBER BASE

$103.3M $102.4M $100.5M $100M $98.1M $95.6M $92.2M $87.7M $79.7M $72.6M $66.1M

2012 2013 2014 2015 2016 2017 2018 2019 2020 2021 2022

In 2022, streaming represented a bigger share of the market (34.8%) than Cable (34.4%) and Broadcast TV (21.6%) for the first time ever. Netflix alone was responsible for 15% of Global Internet Traffic in 2022.

The demographics theme bleeds openly into this. Myriad reports in recent years show us that kids today don't watch TV in anything like the volumes of the past.

MOST AMERICANS WATCH SPORTS ON TV, BUT YOUNGER AMERICANS ARE MORE LIKELY TO TURN ON STREAMING SERVICES

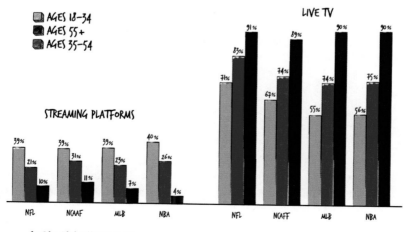

AGES 18–34
AGES 55+
AGES 35–54

LIVE TV

STREAMING PLATFORMS

	AGES 18–34	AGES 35–54	AGES 55+
NFL	39%	21%	10%
NCAAF	39%	31%	11%
MLB	39%	23%	7%
NBA	40%	26%	4%

LIVE TV

	AGES 18–34	AGES 35–54	AGES 55+
NFL	71%	83%	91%
NCAFF	67%	74%	89%
MLB	55%	74%	90%
NBA	56%	75%	90%

SOURCE: IPSOS JANUARY 13–15.

This dramatically changes the revenues and costs of the whole industry.

The entire media sector, and consequently sport, has taken much comfort from the fact that the *"cut the cord"* trend would be more than compensated by new streaming platforms picking up the slack at sport's tenders. Much capital in the last decade has been invested in new media and content companies like Buzzfeed, Vice, Roko and FuboTV. In their drive for penetration, these wannabe Netflix "+" businesses, like DAZN, ESPN+, Disney+, have dramatically changed the value chain of the entire ecosystem.

This frenzy of disruption has felt like we were back to the early 90s, with waves of fresh money betting on huge new markets and equity growth.

But broadcast via streaming is just a much less profitable business model; and now that immediate profits, not growth, are demanded, there isn't so much capital today that is willing to finance penetration and scale just for the sake of it.

The *"Streaming Wars"* maybe won't, as hoped, generate a substantial new and additional "bid" under sports rights.

It is a lower margin business because fundamentally it is the exact opposite of what made PayTV such a fantastic model for so long. The Pay/Cable TV bundle has always implicitly been about making people pay for products they were not really consuming, as with the old music LP. When that is removed, this inevitably leaves streaming businesses with reduced margins, far from the 38% average enjoyed by Cable TV businesses. Technical and marketing structures are also not insignificant.

Add in consumer subscription fatigue, and the reduction in COVID-era viewing habits, and we now see a media sector having its core product, Pay/Cable TV, losing customers and the substitute direct-to-consumer (DTC) streaming platforms starting to struggle.

There may be more ways than ever to consume media and sport, but if few of them are making any money, and Big Finance has lost its appetite to fund losses, we have an industry at risk.

The hoped-for new entrants in Big Tech, (Facebook, Google, Apple, Netflix and Amazon) have to date been rather picky in what they buy from sport. And when they do, it is very much on their terms, and in the formats they need. Apple has clearly stated that it won't bid for sport on a territory-by-territory basis. Netflix prefers shoulder content and docu-series, to live sport, Amazon wants to cherry-pick around major retail moments that work for its e-commerce.

And still our reading of the Perfect Storm hasn't included perhaps the biggest threat of all. Piracy is just very easy in a digital world. It destroyed the business model of the music industry and now has sport in its sights. The estimated cost of global piracy is $28bn a year. For far too long, senior executives at Big Media just haven't seen this coming. They are the direct descendants of those I saw in the music business in 2001.

All these media companies will therefore actively seek to change their relationship with sport, especially non-Hollywood, non-premium, sport. Broadcasters will be less optimistic and generous, more back-ended and performance-dependent. Digital technologies and rich data analytics shine a sharp and clinical light on opaque bundles of sports rights to reveal exactly where value is generated, and we will see that very few pieces of content can today reach the critical mass required to make money in the old media model. When content is abundant, and a lot of it is replaceable, very little is a must-watch for consumers, and therefore a must-buy for broadcasters. Media companies will be asking themselves what content they really need to make a sustainable business model, and they will select what sport has to offer. They will have less patience for sports rights and formats that don't clearly drive audiences and revenues. A stronger focus will be put on the financial return of each piece of individual content, to see what materially moves the needle of ad dollars, increasing subscribers or reducing churn. KPI focused; more cold, less romantic.

The broadcast sector in reality is hunkering down now and will want more bang for its buck. They will inevitably demand a risk-sharing approach with their rights-holder partners. This has already started to happen with very public statements on future strategy from the C-Suite of everyone from Discovery/Warner to IMG Media.

DAZN, for example, drastically needs to reduce its annual $2bn losses. It owns the rights of Serie A, football in Italy, where the decline in subscribers has been dramatic. The numbers of Pay-TV subscribers paying to watch Serie A in Italy went from 4.3m in 2015 down to 1.9m in 2023. It's difficult to see a scenario in which Italian football's broadcast monies are not going down significantly.

Some probably anticipated these changes, to the business relationship between media and sport, better than others. Those who saw the big opportunity 30 years ago were maybe the first to see the reverse now. In 2018, Rupert Murdoch decided to sell the majority of Fox's assets for more than $70 billion to Comcast and Disney. Other observers would say that we reached the peak of subscription valuations when the Athletic was sold to the New York Times for a reported $550m. Maybe these deals were indeed the last choppers out of Saigon. There will be less media companies, and few of them will be *"in funds".* This will take the froth out of the *"Streaming Wars".* There will be fewer bidders for live sports rights, each with a much lower *"walk-away"* number in tenders. The lower budgets will be spent in a much more prudent and risk-adverse manner. That means a propensity for well-established big brand sports, and perhaps less appetite for the 2nd, 3rd, 4th tier of sports rights. Some of these will probably be going *"no-bid"*. There will be even more polarisation in sport: those that work for their broadcast client and those that don't.

"At DAZN, we tried secondary sports and tertiary sports…None of that stuff works. What works is top of the pyramid rights that people have to see."
Jon Skipper (former executive chairman of DAZN).

Clear. The much-loved sport bundle upon which the entire ecosystem is built is going to be ripped apart.

We can squeal all we want, but it's inevitable. The people who finance Big Media, like Len Blavatnik of Dazn, will now demand finance-led cherry-picking, and sport will receive a bid for its various rights accordingly. Versions of:

- *"I'd like to buy only the 4 Celtic and Rangers Old Firm derby matches please."*
- *"Men's tennis at Wimbledon is longer and works better for my audience; can you take out the women's game from the tender? I don't want that; it's not enough content hours and has little appeal."* (Equal pay as a problem for sport may seem rather quaint).
- *"Would the MLB and even NBA consider just selling me the playoffs? Or even just the 4th quarters or 8th and 9th innings?"*
- *"I really have no interest in the group stages of the Europa league, I'd just like to take the quarter finals onwards."*
- *"I only want the Sunday back 9 of your golf tournament, and I want the option to pay less if the leaderboard has no big names."*

We can see exactly this happening at EMI PLC or Universal Studios. Less and less capital is being allocated to niche artists and films, with budgets instead evermore weighted to blockbuster, low-risk output like the Marvel Universe and what are ironically called movie *"franchises"* of recognised IP and actors. For sport, this will be the same, substituting Black Panther and the Rock, for the Cowboys v Packers, Liverpool v Manchester United, LeBron and Messi. One of the first victims of this was arguably the women's football World Cup in 2023. To put this into context, it was the first time FIFA auctioned the Women's World Cup separately from the Men's. Until then, the rights of both competitions were bundled and sold together to broadcasters. When unbundled and sold separately, no one seemed to be that interested in acquiring the rights of the women's tournament. Or at least, not willing to pay the price asked by FIFA. For instance, in England the BBC and ITV made a joint offer of around €9m, which is only about 8% of what was paid for the previous men's World Cup. While Infantino lamented this as *"a slap in the face"* for female players and women worldwide, broadcasters justified their position by saying it would be extremely difficult to get a decent return if they were to pay a higher price. Finance doesn't do virtue-signaling, especially when capital is scarce and costly.

In the Financial Times in April 2023, Ivan Gazidis, ex CEO of Arsenal and AC Milan analysed all of this very well:

"If the rich continue to get richer and we see more and more unsustainable investment in player salaries, agents fees, transfer fees and so on, we might end up in a few years time at another rupture point, and that's what I'm afraid of... this is not healthy for the game. Now, even billionaires struggle to compete. We see the massive investments that are coming from the Middle East in particular, but elsewhere as well. And for any club that is looking to be sustainably managed, that's a very, very difficult environment to compete in. Fans, of course, demand that their teams are competitive. But there's a direct line between those types of pressures and that instability. What I'd love to see is tighter financial regulation, not with the expectation that football clubs will be normal businesses. I don't believe that they are, I believe they're social-cultural institutions. But what I would like to protect football clubs against is the absolute demand that they make huge losses every year."

Few sports, and their leaders, are ready for this. They have become addicted to routinely putting out a paint-by-numbers tender for rights and just sitting back. Seeing this oncoming wave in its full horror will be a shock, and they will panic. They will have to realise that their value and salvation, their asset, is in their hard-core community, big or small, of passionate fans.

This is a catalyst for a change to a B2C business model where sport curates its own community, creates and markets its own storytelling, knows its fans and participants directly and deeply, and changes how it does business. But it is painful for any business or sector to change its DNA, mentality, business model and way of operating.

History shows that very few elephants learn to dance. *"Who Says Elephants Can't Dance?"* by *Lou Gerstener* (CEO of IBM from 1993-2002) explains IBM's historic turnaround from the brink of bankruptcy and product obscurity, as an obsolete mainframe supplier, to the forefront of the technology business. The book articulates how to manage change.

IBM is rare, as it difficult to change your model when you have structured your cost base, in sport's case, the salaries of the sporting talent, as fixed multi-year costs.

If Big Media insists that sport needs to be more risk-sharing, and thus more uncertain about its revenues, how can it sign and respect those player contracts? There is nothing worse in business than having lumpy and unavoidable fixed costs, that you hope you can cover with variable revenues. That is a cardinal sin of running any type of business, a recipe for *"not making payroll"*.

Remuneration structures with sports' talent was already changing a bit, as Leo Messi's revenue-sharing deal with the MLS and Apple shows, but it is going to have to get much more radical.

A totally new social contract is needed with players.

I'm not optimistic. Every industry that has had to do this has struggled to communicate the need for change to unions. People are resistant to taking a step back on remuneration, benefits, flexibility and security in their workplace, even in the face of simple arithmetic. This is a lesson I learned from my own father, a car-worker on the line at Chrysler in Scotland. Unions didn't want to and couldn't change. The result: no cars are made in Scotland today. It won't be easy to persuade athletes to take lower and more risky remuneration, especially when players and their unions are evermore recognising their leverage, drawing power and value. The new generation of fans is much more loyal to players than to clubs. Athletes like Messi, Ronaldo or Mbappé are true superstars with their own audience. They are the big brands now.

When Ronaldo joined Juventus, Real Madrid (his previous club) lost 1m Twitter followers within 24 hours, and Juventus saw a 25% increase in its Instagram followers. When Ronaldo joined Al-Nassr, the club went from 860k followers up to 9.6m (more than any premier league club outside of *"The Big Six"*). The same happened for Inter Miami after they signed Messi. The club has now more Instagram followers than the other 28 MLS clubs combined, which is also more than any NFL, NHL or MLB franchise. We wait to see what his signing does for subscriptions to AppleTV.

The direction of travel is clear, like the Supreme-Court enforced introduction of name, image and likeness (NIL) rights for college athletes in the US. Once again, sport didn't manage that change itself, but was forced to accept it, which is its constant and suicidal trait. More such challenges are just over the horizon, like the ownership of player data and health records.

Big Media and its providers of capital will now really shine a light on sport's hole in the hull.

Today we know it is organised and sold in bundles, called leagues and tours, where there is de facto an underlying cross-subsidy between brand-name clubs and stars, and the average athlete, community franchises and clubs.

There is a proverb in Italian, *"la coperta e' corta"*, *"the blanket is too small"*, which refers to having insufficient resources to meet all your conflicting objectives. If I use the blanket to cover up to my neck, my feet are exposed and vice versa. Sport can't satisfy everyone, and market forces will just end up doing it for them. They will coldly seek out and exploit the cross-subsidies of sport's bundles via what finance calls *"arbitrage"*.

Arbitrage is a relentless force for realignment of value and has been the engine of the recent attempts to create breakaway leagues and formats. Sport and its bundles will always be vulnerable to financial arbitrage, where undervalued athletes and teams will be tempted by the offer to earn the actual market value they create, without having to subsidise other players or teams.

Here is where sport's blanket is always going to be short. Solving polarisation and arbitrage is mutually exclusive! When you realise that, you wont look at our industry the same again.

The more you try and reward those big brand clubs and athletes for what they have created in value, the more you polarise the problem. You make the rich richer, and the gap to the poor wider. If you try and balance out, you are actually making the market inefficient, and creating space for the arbitrageur's whisper:

"We can see from the data that people tune in to see you guys. You are the ones to bring the eyeballs and the sponsors. Why do you accept receiving so much less than that, in distribution of monies? Would you be interested if I could remedy that?"

Both media broadcasters and corporate financiers, those who made sport rich in the last 30 years, now want a polarised product. And if sport doesn't agree, the market forces of arbitrage will do it for them. With brutality.

PROVIDERS OF CAPITAL

The capital markets that have offered the sport and media industries years of cheap capital, leveraged even higher by debt, are now over. The 40-year bull market on Wall Street and Silicon Valley, that has pumped optimism and valuations, is showing clear signs of reversing. We look to be at a Fourth Turning in our society, the end of the current 80-year cycle of growth, maturation, entropy, and now rebirth. There will be a reduction of the flows of easy money, from Wall Street and Palo Alto, into sport and media, and those reduced funds will be concentrated in fewer and fewer destinations, at lower valuations.

The banks and PE funds that have been so willing to invest and lend against future sport rights value at club and league level will become less generous, if they provide capital at all.

And when they are still there, their money will come at a heavier price.

Some consider our times mature for a Minsky Moment.

Named after economist Hyman Minsky, this refers to the onset of a market collapse brought on by the *"blow-off"* speculative activity that defines an unsustainable bullish period. It's the point in time when a sudden decline in market sentiment leads to a reset. How this reset plays out, in dealing with hugely excessive levels of debt, will create extreme uncertainty and volatility. Whatever the size and ferocity of this Big Finance storm, the COVID period clearly marked a *"top"* in so many valuations in sport.

All this comes at a time when sport badly needs fresh capital. Much of the industry, like many European football and rugby clubs, and Olympic sports, haven't got two brass farthings to rub together. They are maybe not yet insolvent, but they are certainly illiquid.

We should be warned that Big Finance, even in a Minsky Moment and a bear market, does not disappear. It just morphs more into a more deadly vulture mode.

"The time to buy is when there's blood in the streets."
Baron Rothschild

The treasure chests of predator capitalism will still be potent. They will fund both challenger governing bodies, leagues and club/franchises.They will seek to reorder the old-style vertical pyramid of sports into smaller more homogenous categories of product/market fit. They will lend capital all across the Balance Sheet, with structured deals that reward and protect them. They will accelerate the trends of polarisation, arbitrage and new formats. They will empower the market forces.

So far, both polarisation and arbitrage, which are already present in sport, have been relatively limited, as times have been good all around. A rising tide was indeed raising all boats. Not anymore, capitalism in hard times is cold and callous, especially to people who need money.

DEMOGRAPHICS

Economic growth, money and prosperity comes from a simple equation: population x productivity per head.

"Demographics are destiny."
French philosopher Auguste Comte

Sport is dealing with the realities of a generational conflict. The Boomer generation has done rather well financially, accrued generous pensions, made housing unaffordable for young people, and abused the planet and the climate. Boomers have allowed themselves a quality of life they couldn't afford, by mortgaging the future with debt that will now sit on the shoulders of their grandchildren.

Human nature is such that our generation of boomers like this world just the way it is, and don't really want to see it change.

Younger people know this and are angry. They have little time for all that, and now want real change, in some cases revolution.

Sport is not going to be immune from this.

In terms of demographic population, Europe, in particular, is falling off a cliff, and aging dramatically. In the cultural home of sport, the legacy fanbase is dying off.

Europe today represents less than 5% of the planet's population, the USA likewise. Yet so much of the West's thinking, sport included, seems to find a way to ignore the other 90%. My sector uses derogatory terms like "tourist" fans from Asia, when they really should be asking themselves serious questions about the ongoing centrality and hegemony of fandom in Europe.

Comte's demographics and its destiny isn't just geographical. It's also around changing values, tastes and behaviours.

1 IN 3 GEN ZERS DON'T WATCH LIVE SPORTS SOURCE: MORNING CONSULT, 2022.

RESPONDENTS WERE ASKED HOW THEY MOST OFTEN WATCH LIVE SPORTING EVENTS WHEN NOT IN PERSON

■ BROADCAST OR CABLE TV ■ UNAUTHORIZED STREAMING ■ I DO NOT WATCH LIVE SPORTING EVENTS
■ STREAMING VIA A LICENSED STREAMING SERVICE ■ ANOTHER WAY

Sport is facing the threat of a meaningful shift in young people's leisure and entertainment habits. New audiences have dramatically different needs, in terms of the content they want, how they want to consume it, and where they want it delivered. In fact, it is unclear whether they want to consume (live) sport content at all.

More fundamentally, it is unclear whether they are even willing to pay for it.

"No, GenZ will not fucking pay for your OTT subscription".
Dan Porter, Founder of Overtime

It is yet to be proven what, if any, appetite the new generations will have for paid-for content even as a concept. To date, their Spotify and Netflix subscriptions have been debited to parents' credit cards, and when they are not, GenZ has shown how it effortlessly turns to piracy. It's a generation that has never learned that the creation of content has to be paid for. They have grown up with the idea of user-generated Instagram and TikTok that is without cost.

So this is a difficult customer base to monetise, as they have muscle-memory on *"free"*.

Capitalism is about choice and innovation. Where once there wasn't much entertainment alternative to sport, as offered in its traditional form, today those choices are endless. Gen Z (born between late 90's and 2010) and Alpha (after 2010) have little connection and fit with how sport currently presents and offers itself, and our industry will have to ask itself if the product it offers is still attractive to these customers, and if its traditional model can still work in this digital age. But it isn't all doom and gloom with this demographic. They do spend money on digital goods in gaming and metaverses. According to a study from Razorfish, in 2022, Gen Z spend 15% of their *"leisure budget"* in the metaverse. In 2027, it will be 20%.

Likewise, 69% of GenZ gamers spent money on games. Roblox revenue was $2.2bn in 2022, with a $51.29 average booking per daily active user (ABPDAU), which is how the company monitors what players spend on accessories to upgrade their experience on the platform. But more importantly, half of Roblox's players are under 16, and they are paying for all kinds of virtual goods and digital props, often in micro-payment form. This is a large market to be captured.

Kids will indeed spend on entertainment, if delivered correctly and in the right product/ market fit. But sport needs to change its thinking immediately, or it will lose the war for these new demographics.

"You have to make them a fan by 18, or you'll lose them forever."
Tim Ellis, Chief Marketing Officer, NFL

As the arrival of Elvis and Little Richard spelt the end of the jazz and crooner era of music entertainment, so new forms of sports and adjacent content will arise, appearing equally disrespectful and uncouth to our traditions.

Sport must now be prepared to kill some of its sacred cows, as formats and content drift much more to the influencer and celebrity world. Whilst the Boomer audience currently pays the bills, the reality of a different offering for the young creates a classic innovator's dilemma for the industry.

Traditional sport organisations need to realise that what got them here won't get them to tomorrow. Their model really hasn't been fit for purpose since the invention of digitalisation and the mass-popularity of the internet two decades ago.

Transitioning, and changing modus operandi, is particularly difficult when political governance is a problem, when the people at the top don't understand the coming challenges, and don't know how to adapt.

GEOPOLITICS

The history of sport has given us structures, hierarchy and power based on hard geographical lines.

To use the example of the globe's biggest sport, football, each nation state has a local all-powerful Lord, called their Football Association (FA). They are the autocratic governing body of the entire sport within their borders. They rule supreme. These feudal lords then represent their nations at the political Congress of their peers from other countries on international bodies like UEFA (for Europe) or FIFA (the world). Same at the IOC.

The best way to visualize this is to think of the Senate in Star Wars. And like that Senate, its dysfunctionality generates and even guarantees leaders like Palpatine. These organisations live a daily death-match around geopolitics, and have done so since the 1970s.

In 1974, the old English head of FIFA, Sir Stanley Rous, Corinthian in his mentality, representing the traditional roots of the English Game, stood for re-election as FIFA president. He was defeated by the vigorous canvassing of João Havelange and by the resentment felt by African and Asian countries at the European domination of FIFA.

Big Sport is utterly geopolitical, and has, in finance terms, a fault line that one day will cause an earthquake. The bulk of football's money for example comes from Europe, but FIFA's immense power and control comes from the game's emerging markets. That just doesn't work.

It is difficult to see any alternative outcome to this than the people still investing in sport being forced to take the old governing bodies out of the equation. The IMG Endeavor group, on buying the World Wrestling Entertainment (WWE) group, said it best:

"We are the owner and commissioner and have autonomy to make all commercial, operational and competition decisions."

Conflicted governance and vicious politics are the biggest risk when trying to keep the sports that we love in some way still relevant. The industry has too many stakeholders, all with very different agendas. From the IOC and FIFA to the PGA, it is nothing less than high politics, full of compromises, horse-trading and *"pork"*. The protagonists make a priority of keeping their own positions of power, rather than actually trying to improve things.

The business of sport is an inelegant chaos of compromise, but it is really nothing compared to the great geopolitical chessboard of our age.

We have lived 30 years with a certain expectation of increasing *"globalisation"* under the hegemony of Uncle Sam as policeman. Where the supply of the West's energy needs had been secured by a Henry Kissinger oil deal with Saudi Arabia in the 1970s. For the guarantee of the supply of energy, the USA protected Saudi, and tolerated their regime. There was one condition; all oil had to be traded globally in $. This cemented the US dollar as the world's reserve currency, meant all trade was in the greenback, and all countries needed to hold dollars in their wallet, creating demand for the American coin, and allowing the US to run huge deficits financed by those foreigners.

This is where the *"Murky World of Finance"* is so germane to this book. When Henry Kissinger did the deal with the Saudis half a century ago, around the same time they came off the gold standard, the hegemony of the USA was secured, and Saudi was to the world untouchable, a *"made man"* if you will.

Now all that certainty is in doubt, with the world going multipolar, as competing powers maneuver for ascendancy, and the nation state is again on the rise. Thucydides Trap is a phrase ever more common in today's world, describing a tendency towards war when an emerging power threatens to displace an existing superpower as a regional or international hegemony. It is used in the 21st century to describe a potential conflict between the United States and the People's Republic of China.

The biggest geopolitical issue of our time is Saudi Arabia perhaps distancing itself from that old deal with the USA and getting very close to Americans' rival in the Thucydides Trap, China. The Chinese are now offering the Saudis a bargain that appears to be exactly modelled on the U.S-Saudi deal of 50 years ago. Arms, tech and protection, in exchange for oil, denominated in yuan. If this happens, everything we've known for years is up for grabs. If the dollar's reserve status is threatened, a whole load of very big dominoes will start to fall.

Indeed, geopolitics itself is now in its own Fourth Turning and the relatively risk-free stability of the last 80 years of Pax Americana is being threatened.

Saudi Arabia, with its human-rights issues and non-inclusive values, with which sport seemingly has so many issues, is right at the very centre. So it can't be anything but very unfortunate, in terms of extra volatility, that the Kingdom of Saud has decided that our industry will be the central plank of its strategy to diversify its entire economy away from reliance on oil.

Sport will be the main weapon of their soft power and diplomacy; and the geopolitics and money of the Middle East, and especially Saudi Arabia, is now totally altering the balance of the sports industry. They are throwing what seems like unlimited capital into owning sport and bringing it to its local destinations of Neom and Qiddiya.

All this is most apparent in them buying the PGA golf tour, or their clubs attracting the biggest football players in the world. They are relentless sponsors of sports like F1 and boxing. They are now coming after mixed-martial-arts and the UFC. Their capital also underpins the LPs of many of the PE and VC funds investing in sport.

Saudi Arabia is absolutely serious in its plans to buy sport. The principles of polarisation and arbitrage will be applied by them without pity, and the Middle East is the one place today where capital isn't under pressure and still abundant.

The Arab world is also Muslim. If this is all happening at the same time as many editorials discuss what they call the angst around the Islamification of Europe, via mass immigration, and it represents extra risk and volatility for this sector.

All of these currents will inevitably force sport to change and reinvent itself, just to survive.

Newton's first law:

"Every object will remain at rest or in uniform motion in a straight line unless compelled to change its state by the action of an external force"

Chapter Twenty Three

FINDING THE LIFEBOATS

Writing a book with a serious editor has been educational for me.

I've been incredibly fortunate to have worked in these chapters with a world-class author, who actually knows what he is doing. Tobias Jones is a true football fan, Evertonian, and with his own best-selling publications, like Ultras, has displayed how much he feels this subject matter of sport.

More than all that, he has shown an amateur scribbler like me what works and doesn't work in trying to deliver a book like this. His advice has been invaluable, and, even at 59, a journey of humble learning for me. Every day is a school day.

His main writing counsel to me in this journey was to take out the "chatty chumminess" that has become my style, in both my podcasts and Sunday Column blogs, especially for a book that in many ways aspires to be some kind of finance textbook.

It hasn't been easy seeing his edits come back with multiple red lines through the fluff of what I thought was colour and personality, with a professionally cold side-comment "doesn't add anything".

At the start of the process, I will admit that I, silently, didn't take this well at all, but over the months, I have learnt he was right, and I think I am improved as a communicator, and the book is the better for it.

But then you look around, at this world in which we live, this sector we inhabit, and you notice what is working. Today, the world of content, influence and narrative is dominated less and less by facts, and is evermore driven by personality and opinion. You don't seem to need any more to be factually correct or surgically insightful, with solid verification to back you up; you just need to be popular and entertaining. Joe Rogan, the combat fighter turned podcaster and sports commentator, is the most popular opinionist around, consistently attracting huge audiences to his 3-hour long podcasts. He is a true star in today's world of content creation and media, with a dedicated and loyal fan base, despite often taking the road less travelled on the accepted consensus wisdom of the day; from Covid, to Trump, to Mike Tyson.

It seems that, at the end of the day, the audiences of this era reward personality and connection over iron-clad didactic education and information.

And this for me undoubtedly also informs the future editorial line of the media sector, and the industry of sport.

For these reasons, in this last chapter, trying to provide an idea of what we need to do to save sport, I see no option but to offer a personal hard opinion, even a chatty one!

But there is no bombast that my views are either correct or complete. They are a suggestion for a new direction of travel, in an industry adrift.

Hopefully it does "add something" and is always entertaining. If it rambles too much, and is not tight, this isn't the fault of Mr Jones, who I genuinely thank profoundly.

• • •

Many of the protagonists in the sports industry, in a shower of dropping pennies, are now gripped by some level of fear. The future of the sportsbiz, and their own, is uncertain.

The disruption in the media and finance sectors, the radical shift in the sentiment of the providers of capital, the distortions driven by price-insensitive Gulf money, and the changes in audience tastes amongst younger generations, are simultaneous shocks to the system.

There are still some optimists, like on the Titanic, convincing themselves that it will all be OK. Every time we get glorious, unscripted moments of drama on the field of play, these romantics fall back into dismissing all the issues, comforted by how *"special"* sport is.

This is the biggest risk to the industry: it is so powerful, and so beautiful, that it seduces all of us into thinking there's no problem.

That's an error.

In business and finance, to prevent this, to focus reality, you will often be asked to analyse a situation with the use of a tool called a SWOT analysis (Strengths, Weaknesses, Opportunities and Threats).

The previous chapter would in this way be the Weaknesses and Threats facing the industry of sport.

This chapter as a mechanism aspires to be a proxy for the S and the O.

Glory lies with the optimist.

What are the Strengths of Sport?

Sport matters in ways nothing else does. It can engage and enrage, turning normal, balanced people into screaming dervishes in the space of an hour. Nothing else can do this with such passion; neither politics nor music, neither art nor Fortnite. It is objectively the golden product.

Lord Sebastian Coe, in opening the London Olympics in 2012, put it best.

"There is a truth to sport, a purity, a drama, an intensity, a spirit that makes it irresistible... In every Olympic sport there is all that matters in life. Humans stretched to the limit of their abilities, inspired by what they can achieve, driven by their talent to work harder than they can believe possible, living for the moment but making an indelible mark upon history."

We all know this to be true. It has something extra and unique as a differentiator from modern entertainment content, and the crushing forces of the market.

Glory obtained with classic sporting values is something few other entertainment categories can deliver. Glory is beyond success, popularity and audience. It's historic.

"Get up, Prince of Troy, get up! I won't let a stone take my glory."
Achilles to Hector, Troy

Sporting glory is compelling to all, beyond any cold economics. Gestures of purity, to your opponent or fans, in a world evermore searching for meaning or purpose, are without price.

Gen Z absolutely loves meaning and purpose; they may not find time for a 5-hour clay court war of attrition at Roland Garros, but they, and we, will always be suckers for things like Derek Redmond's father rushing onto the track in an Olympic 400m final, to carry his son over the line after a hamstring rip.

This incredible and unique value, to date, has largely been untapped, as sport itself has no real in-house marketing and branding skills to fully monetise these moments. Today, sport's glory and drama are recorded by fans in real time memes on social media. Linear long-form TV, no matter how splendid the commentator may be, is yesterday's way of recording instant history.

Sport and its arenas are cherished experiential places of sacred memory. If music albums are the soundtrack of our lives, sport every week produces *"where were you?"* moments, none of which are snackable or transient. They are too important to the timeline of all our lives.

Games are a key fabric of society, a social asset. For physical health, educational values, community, diversity, and inclusion, playing sport is unrivalled. A dressing room is truly a gymnasium for life, and sporting activity is the antithesis of the plague of young people, hunched over a small mobile screen, evermore in their echo-chamber bedrooms. A path to a better society.

Our industry has serious asset value, possessing both the strongest brands and IP, but also tangible equity in real estate and customer databases. The left-hand side of the Balance Sheet is very solid.

Sport is now the only mass audience aggregator left for the media sector. It is the last place, in a world of video on demand (VOD), for broadcasters to generate a sizeable live audience. You cannot run a modern media business, especially on linear TV, without a strategy for live sports content. American networks would have existential questions asked about them if their output were not anchored around top live rights. This gives premium sport enormous negotiating leverage, as we see every day in the big leagues in the USA. In an increasingly digital world, authentic physical experiences will become more valuable. Ironically, digital abundance will perhaps create physical scarcity.

Fan loyalty is unmatched in any product in the world, and this should make for stable and regular income streams, in theory, the last element of discretionary spending to go. In finance terms this is low volatility, lower risk, higher value. Sports assets in this way are considered by many as uncorrelated, which means they offer a natural hedge in a balanced investment portfolio. Sport thus should always be a desired asset class.

In addition, sport still has a strong investor bid:
- investment funds have raised capital that is as yet unused, needing to be deployed;
- sovereign states want to own the industry of sport for reasons of geopolitical soft power, and to diversify their economies away from over-reliance on fossil fuel industries;
- there have never been so many bored ultra-rich billionaires.

The S in the SWOT is very strong.

This is not an inevitable sunset industry, whose time has come, where we manage decline with as much elegance and dignity as possible. This cause isn't hopeless. Doves will be seen after the floods. There will be land after the storms.

We all have a duty to sort this.

But it won't happen by itself, no matter how much wishful thinking there is in the sector (after a thrilling Wimbledon or a great World Cup final).

Because none of these amazing strengths of the sector have saved sport from getting itself into a hellish mess of the last 30 years, confused as to what it is and what it should be. Complacency has left the industry vulnerable to the storm. It's neither fish nor fowl, neither business nor Corinthian.

Where are the opportunities? The "O"?

For the best of us, every problem has always been an opportunity.

• • •

Of all the weaknesses and threats that we have articulated in this book, there is one overarching sack of ballast that prevents sport from keeping its head above water.

Any ship, but especially one off-course, needs a captain. A leader with a hand on the tiller, knowing where he/she is going.

All of us have seen Captain James T Kirk in Star Trek. Whilst he listens to a crew he loves and trusts, is kind and generous, it is only he, at the end of the day, who decides, with urgency, bravery, altruism and vision. He is a very capable and benevolent dictator.

"Democratic governments border on anarchy; monarchy on despotism. Anarchy is powerless; despotism can do great things."
Napoleon Bonaparte

Perhaps unpalatable, but with age and experience you realise that Napoleon was right. In times of crisis you need a very strong dictator, with quality, clear and decisive leadership. In my own experience, of 40 years, exceptional people will solve most problems, and grasp most opportunities. Find your captain.

And yet, sadly, this thinking is almost the complete opposite of the governance of sport today. In the last 30 years, this industry has, with some obvious exceptions, totally failed, especially in Europe. That failure has come about through a lack of proactive leadership, the inevitable paralysis of democratic compromise, and an under-skilled industry.

The greatest opportunity for the business and product of sport is in trading-up to leadership and C-Suite *"excellence"*. Because the underlying value in the sector is there. It just needs much better management.

The best CEOs come from the most banal and commodity of industries. Those with low barriers to entry, and no Unique Selling Proposition (USP). These leaders have no natural advantage and therefore can only succeed by superior strategy, marketing, execution and people skills. They need to earn their living, and a future, every single day, by looking at competitors, innovation, disruption and what could hurt them tomorrow. Paranoid from the moment they wake up.

Mediocre people instead naturally get lazy and comfortable, especially if they have the in-built protection of a monopoly, as most of sport is.

A special and unique product, organised as a monopoly, is the worst recipe for a strategic vision. Any person, or organisation, not being challenged to improve, will always tend to fuzziness, with woolly ideas of their worth. They get flabby and defensive. The BBC in the UK is exactly like this. Complacency, the opposite of paranoia, has in this way cost sport dearly.

Being a sport CEO, president or top dog is arguably the best and one of the most highly paid jobs in the world. These are not-for-profit organisations, with no real accountability on costs, that, on the international stage, make their revenues using other people's efforts and assets. To be specific, international football and rugby gets to organise monopoly sporting jamborees like World Cups, calling up, basically gratis, the playing talent employed by someone else, the clubs. They keep the resulting billions in revenues, less their own abundant cost base.

What other business is like this? There is no cost of sales, and you are a monopoly.

Sport, like the old music industry, is today run by a pretty consistent demographic; of 50+ mainly white males, who have grown up with a clear idea of what their sport should be. They were fans themselves, and most are actually decent people. They have had the luck to preside over a rising tide in the value of sports' broadcast rights which has made them and their companies rich and successful. Blossoming media revenues has deceived these people, convincing them that a bull market was actually their own brilliance, and has distracted them from the change that was absolutely needed for a new digital world.

Today's leaders of sport, with some clear exceptions, are absolutely the last people who have the will or energy to confront the coming storm. Indeed, in many cases, their thinking is unabashedly selfish; to hold on until retirement with the status quo. They are nearly there after all.

There is no incentive, especially financial, for these incumbent leaders in sport to change.

Upton Sinclair, the American writer and political activist, worth a second mention in the book, said it best:

"It is difficult to get a man to understand something when his salary depends upon him not understanding it."

Jay Monahan, and his handling of the arrival of LIV Golf, is the perfect example. The PGA Tour was a monopoly, incredibly resistant to change, and criticised by many of its own players for exactly that. The leadership however saw no reason to evolve. Their reaction towards a challenger to this monopoly was unbudging resistance, even using xenophobia around the Saudi backers of LIV, and dismissing all ideas of format innovation. In the middle of 2023, after this period of war, the PGA merged with the Saudi PIF fund, who basically became its owner.

This is the future of all of sport if it doesn't recognise the problem. It will be the EastmanKodak for the new millennium. That company saw the changes coming, they even had the solution with digital camera technology they invented. But they didn't have the mindset, or will, to do anything about it. They no longer exist.

The huge upside opportunity to be grasped by this industry is in just fixing bad structures, bad governance, delivering bad leaders. It's useless to invest in the current institutions in the hopes of marginal gains. This Fool's Errand is what has failed spectacularly with the PE firm CVC and its investments in rugby.

So be radical. Knock it down and start again. You can't put lipstick on a pig.

What does that all mean? How actually can sport now get Captain Kirk on the bridge of the USS Enterprise of Sport? The gap between saying, and actually doing, in business, in finance, is significant.

The good news should be that the Pied Piper, any provider of new money and capital, normally calls the tune, and gets to appoint the captain they want. Why does Big Finance and sovereign wealth not just get the best? Like Elliot Capital did with Gazidis, like Abu Dhabi did with Man City (taking the top people from Barcelona).

In sport, this is not as easy as it may appear, especially at the all-dominant governing-body level.

The best won't come!

When PE funds take over a poorly run business with good assets (like sport), they hire a turnaround CEO, a change-agent. And they give this person huge personal financial incentives to make all the necessary changes and all the inevitable culling. These turn-around CEOs are serious people and have one simple request:

"Let me get on with it. Don't second guess me. Don't make me work through committees who slow me down. If I'm failing just sack me, but don't make me walk through treacle."

The best people won't put up with a constitution and governance that doesn't allow them to do their job. The best people need to be fully empowered, or they walk.

When one thinks about how institutional sport is structured and governed today, it is so easy to see how big a problem this is. FIFA, UEFA, IOC, the FAs and leagues like Serie A are formally set up as businesses, but they are better described as NGOs, trade associations or even quangos.

There is no clear line of sight on decision-making and change-management power.

To return to Bonaparte, it's a democracy that is in reality a powerless anarchy. It just will not be able to change. Providers of fresh capital, ultimately the change catalyst here, will, going forward, need to be very considered about only investing in the sports and structures that are ripe, and prepared, for change, either through desire or desperation.

For example, what is the easiest path for Saudi Arabia in its drive for influence in football? To grind through the politics of the FAs, Confederations, and FIFA, or just use their capital to bring the playing talent to them? And then negotiate with UEFA and FIFA from a position of power?

Similarly, take women's football, and women's sport in general. As a potential product/market fit, with a huge total addressable market (TAM), female sport is one of major opportunities for our industry.

But, today, for example, female football is basically a bolt-on to the traditional men's game and governed by those same structures and demographic of leader. Specifically, FIFA, UEFA, and the local national federations. So, to me it seems highly unlikely that this will succeed, not because of the product, but because of the leadership and governance.

Would it not be better to recognise that these old structures are no longer fit for purpose, and dispassionately conclude that they are de facto unmanageable in a traditional business sense? To continue the Star Trek analogy, they are the Kobayashi Maru Test. There is no possible win.

What an opportunity there is to create new and nimble governing bodies, with fresh capital from enlightened investors, and hire the right CEOs. As SailGP and the Professional Triathlon Organisation have done with two Olympic sports that were dying on the vine, and failing their athletes.

Where do we find the Captain Kirks to lead these new structures? How can we attract them? How do we assess them?

When I was asked to advise the fledgling Israeli Professional Football league 10 years ago, they wanted me to meet the new proposed CEO, a respected outsider from the car industry who was seen as a rising star of the Israeli business community. At dinner that first night, one-to-one, I asked him:

"What kind of sport's leader do you want to be Oren?"

He looked perplexed; he came from a world of *"normal"* business, of growth, market shares, budgets, profits and year-end bonuses. Hitting targets or moving on.

"Why have you taken this job?" I asked him.

"To make a difference, to get things done? Or to do what most do, and enjoy one of the best jobs in the world, in a monopoly, in a not-for-profit, with a lovely expense account, watching some of the best occasions in life? Because to really get things done in sport, you will need to rock the boat, annoy many people, old athletes and media, challenge their cosy status quo, and strive for change."

People of talent on a fast-track career, with options, will always answer as Oren did:

"If I'm going to use my time to do this, Roger, it needs to be to rock the boat".

I worked with Oren in Tel Aviv for 4 years, an entire rights cycle. He rocked boats, broke eggs and made magnificent omelettes in Israeli football. He's one of the most talented executives I have ever seen. Brave, sensitive, yet cold when needed, he took no prisoners, and moved C+ performers to A- as they followed him.

He is very rare in my experience. Many may even start off like him, as ambitious purists and ideologists, but they often get ground down, or even seduced, by the old governance of sport. But for new modern fresh structures and governance this talent will come.

Sport needs people with gravitas and EQ who can win hearts and minds. It should seek the people who can speak to fans, players and media as orators.

Perhaps even create content. As Cicero, told us so beautifully 2000 years ago:

"Docere Delectare Movere." "Teach, Delight, Move."

We are in the era of the charismatic celebrity leader in business. Sport needs to find them. Attracting the top top people is a big opportunity for sport. If you get the governance right, get the personal incentives right, then the product is so sexy and important, that the best will come. And they will lead and inspire us back to shore.

American sport, where structures are much simpler, the Adam Silvers of the NBA, the Roger Goodells of the NFL, are top operators, and perhaps prove this point exactly.

To get to this place, old governance needs to be pulled down. I believe there to be no alternative. It has put us right in the middle of this storm.

Great visionaries often can turn apparent adversity to their advantage. If 2023 is the year when the weight of Saudi Arabian money has shown its intent to utterly disrupt sport, with little respect for all structures and leaders, perhaps they can be a positive catalyst to start over.

Because of exactly that, it is sad to see so many people who should know better, from Jay Monahan down, resisting Saudi capital into sport, when their money is already everywhere in our economies. At best it is naivety of the highest order, at worst, rank hypocrisy. In Monahan's case, selling out to LIV Golf after months of the most appalling vitriol, it is the latter. He is not alone.

In a future free from the IOCs and FIFAs of the world, sport still has to find a future as a sustainable business model.

It's not on dry-land yet.

● ● ●

The business model of sport is fundamentally flawed. It's analogue in a digital world. We've said that it is also utterly chained down by Innovator's Dilemma, which in simple terms describes how difficult it is for an existing organisation, making decent money and serving an established customer base, to address the disruption of the future, and attract new customers.

The old model monies, whilst decaying, are still there, and difficult to leave behind, especially for an industry that has always needed to be risk-averse and short-termist. To be very fair, it's not easy to look strategically into the future.

The operations of sport and sports teams require certainty around how much money it can pay for athletes and players. The cost of talent in sport is not a flexible variable cost today. It is instead a fixed and lumpy multi-year commitment.

You need safe and certain money up front, and for this reason, sport does not willingly get into the B2C game of building its own media business, selling subscriptions and advertising. Same with its licensing efforts and merchandise contracts. All of these could and should be more remunerative for the industry, but this approach is by definition uncertain, volatile and risky. And when you have to pay athletes, come what way, that uncertainty is not something it is set up to handle.

So, our sector has allowed others to build tremendous businesses on-top of its IP and fan loyalty. Newspapers, media companies, social media companies, shoe manufacturers and so on. In their dash for the minimum guarantee, the safe money up front, the sportsbiz has left too much to others. Sky built a serious business and asset equity value on buying sports rights, and they are only the most obvious example.

"The untapped future for sports is in monetising the lifetime value of their loyal customers, beyond selling tickets and merchandise and maybe a subscription to Sunday ticket."
George Pyne, Founder Bruin Capital

Normally then, these incumbent media companies would have no incentive to change the status quo. But the opportunity for sport is in timing.

Broadcasters, and the streaming platforms, are all now looking for a new commercial relationship with sports, as they simply cannot afford to pay the current prices of rights. DAZN and BT Sports for example are making very significant losses, and as the general sentiment in the capital markets has now changed from growth to sustainability, they now themselves need to make material cost savings. They are looking for a risk-alignment model. Less money up front; more revenue-sharing.

This is therefore a golden opportunity for the sport industry to perhaps have the best of both worlds and accept a lower minimum guarantee rights fee from broadcasters, in exchange for more of the financial upside, and sharing of data on customers. Maybe also joint-ventures (JV) for the league-owned-and-operated media hub. They have a common interest to fight piracy. A true partnership.

The benefits of this B2C mindset and partnership with broadcasters are not only in better back-end revenues and customer data. It is also in what is called in finance as a sector *"rerating"*. The capital markets and investors put labels on things, and value them accordingly.

B2B businesses are almost always valued on a much stingier basis than B2C. Per-user valuations are given to B2C, whereas low multiples of revenues and cashflow are awarded to B2B companies.

The label, or the perception of the label, is thus fundamentally important to an asset class.

So much of what is going to happen now in sport, disruption, polarisation, unbundling, financial arbitrage, is around this gear-crunching change from B2B to B2C. The pivot to George Pyne's world of lifetime value per customer, cost of acquisition, ARPU tactics, and churn management.

So, if sport can organise itself to be considered as a B2C business, it would be re-rated as such, the same way tech companies are in Silicon Valley. This is a not insignificant opportunity for sport and its equity valuations.

To grasp this opportunity, sport cannot avoid a serious discussion with its athletes, convincing them to take more of their remuneration on the back end.

• • •

Following the lead from venture capital and PE, where so much of the remuneration of the main actors, the founders, change agents, experts in execution, is in the incentives, be that bonuses, revenue share, or even equity, sport has an opportunity now to convince the elite stars that they will be financially better off playing it *"long"*, by taking less secure money up front, but more in total. If sport can in this way shift more of its talent cost to variable and backend, it can then, only then, afford to say *"no"* to all these B2B minimum guarantee deals.

Remember the shoe deal that Michael Jordan did with Nike, and how that has been a dripping roast for him every year? Or Sir Alec Guinness negotiating a part of the box office takings of Star Wars? Obe-Wan and his vision was well rewarded.

This year Messi has moved to the MLS, accepting a share of the AppleTV subscriptions generated.

So, there is a credible pitch to be delivered, hopefully with success.

As every great company or start-up knows, any incentive plan is delicate. It requires a clear understanding as to who in your human resources really moves the needle, and who is commodity. Good practice tells us that you shouldn't use too much of your option pool on average commodity staff. It would be the same in sport. Who is box-office, and needs incentives, and who should be grateful just to be in the room?

Sport has an opportunity to recognise and embrace an inconvenient truth. We were not all created equal. Remunerations and incentives need to be precise, cold and value-driven.

This kind of ruthlessness is often seen as brutal, and even immoral. But this is a hard finance book, talking about the business of sport, an industry adrift, in need of radical solutions. And Charlie Munger is right; show me the incentives, and I'll tell you the outcomes.

So, yes, the biggest potential win for the industry of sport is in controlling the cost of athlete talent, making it results-based variable. Like in America, work to a system of hard salary caps; find your true stars, reward them accordingly, also perhaps with equity in their employing clubs. The new social contract.

The really harsh reality is that if sport for whatever reason prefers to ignore this truth, the market forces will just do it for them, via the financial wrecking machines of polarisation and arbitrage. That process is already in front of our eyes.

So, the order of action is likely this:
- work out which athletes move the needle;
- try and convince them to take more of their remuneration at the backend;
- be ruthless with commodity talent; and if they hold out for too-high fixed-cost pay, just replace them. It is a huge global market for commodity sporting talent;
- use workable salary caps;
- hopefully in this way, you have reduced your need for excessively high and certain up-front money;
- that allows you to move significantly towards a B2C model and knowing your customers;
- leave behind the constant quest for more minimum guarantees;
- get a valuation rerating on a per-user IP business.

A new model and mentality starts to take shape. Lower fixed costs, lower operating leverage, allowing for more flexibility for informed decision-making, and cash/capital management. The price-insensitive remunerations offered by the new Saudi League will be a significant headwind to negotiating with playing talent in this way. But that is a separate and bigger discussion.

Asking your 10th man or woman for black-swan scenarios may turn up this.

CAPITAL FROM THE MIDDLE EAST

Sport is now dominated by the endless capital coming from the Middle East. This is causing significant turbulence as it unbalances the status quo in structures and traditional hierarchies. At the same time, in Italy, France, Spain and Eastern Europe, there is evermore angst around the *"migrants"* from different cultures. The summer of 2023 saw Paris ablaze, and Lampedusa overwhelmed. It is very possible that all of these countries become more right-wing, protectionist and populist. There will undoubtedly be votes in anti-Islamism. Jay Monahan has shown how easy an option it is.

This could lead to a political rejection of Arabian capital *"buying up traditional working-class sport."* There is an *"event"* scenario that European football could be, at worst, nationalised and, at best, heavily regulated under the propaganda that it is a social asset of national significance.

It is not a zero-probability outcome that someone will propose to formally classify football as the social and community asset it is. Football is a monopoly and, as such, it could be argued that it should be regulated as a *"utility"*, with a governing body that determines the reasonable *"return"* the owners should earn. The water, electricity, telecoms, rail industries are social assets, where market forces are controlled, and have to be. All monopolies have anti-trust parameters for a reason, with a regulator capping their returns. This type of work is formula based, well established, and isn't radical as a concept.

Take the UK as the working example where the EPL is the leading league.

English football (EPL/EFL/FA) revenues are £5bn a year. More or less. Today they are paying all that away in player costs of £5bn. And then some. With a really serious wage cap, you reduce that to £3bn and that, at this point, becomes the risk capital deployed each year in football in England. You allow clubs to make an agreed, regulated 10% return on capital. That's £300m (and £300m profit more than they make today!). Doing this, the industry of football is creating excess annual profit of £1.7bn (5bn-3.3bn) a year.

One sole governing body, the merged leagues and FA, now have serious serious money to invest in what is the national game, and its communities. To take our game back to where it came from, the working-class communities. Money for stadia, academies, facilities, community coaching, an elite performance institute, schools and women's football.

That £1.7bn would facilitate football to get away from its fatal short-termism; to make those changes to its model to B2C; to develop its own direct relationships with its fans. Maybe even stop giving all its margin to other businesses. If this was attempted across all of the EU and UK, it would keep competitive balance between European leagues. This would be potentially a massive vote-winner for any populist politician.

Our industry needs to be scenario-planning all the black swans.

• • •

The collective noun for sport and the fan is dead. If today, sport has many different customer audience needs, perhaps we should deal with this problem by putting people in separate lifeboats, where there is at least some kind of idea of rowing in the same direction to safety. This is called strategic marketing.

Strategic marketing is about laser-focus in matching product to audiences, working out true individual USP and appeal, through deep research, customer knowledge, A/B testing, informed product development and commercial promotion. It's a very skilled and sophisticated business practice.

Whilst the Volkswagen group owns various car brands, like Audi, Bentley, Cupra, Jetta, Lamborghini, Porsche, SEAT, Škoda and Volkswagen, and motorcycles under the Ducati name, they are all marketed separately, to very different customer bases.

LVMH is a luxury conglomerate operating over 75 different House brands, from Louis Vuitton to Christian Dior, from Moet to Givenchy, from Tiffany to Bulgari. All of these products and brands have their own audience and their own positioning. Again, they are managed separately.

So why does sport think it doesn't need to do that, when its audiences are now patently so very diverse? What discount rate and cost of capital should be used?

This is an industry endlessly trying to attract new audiences around the edges, with additional gimmicks and content presentation, whilst at the same time trying to not lose the legacy fan. I think this is a battle of Charge of the Light Brigade insanity. VW doesn't try to compromise on a one-size-fits-all product, to keep all of its audiences and customers happy. It goes the other way: it segments, with gusto.

Segmentation and positioning are a key part of strategic marketing. And it links to pricing. If sport is now getting too expensive for much of its core working-class market, the answer must be in better definition of the product/market fit. Otherwise, customers will be forever lost. Again, the luxury market is a good benchmark; they have products for all budgets, and implicitly make moving up the price bracket aspirational. Mercedes has entry-level options for their brand.

The opportunity for sport is to embrace this strategic marketing mindset completely. There is no future for sport in trying to find a compromise offering; it needs to embrace polarisation, differentiation and niche.

The most obvious product segment to define is what is premium sport, and what is the remaining long tail.

The world of Big Media and entertainment is going premium. These companies will only want a product that makes a return for them, at the lowest possible risk. They are no longer in growth mode; they are in cold profit or loss mode. They are in the game of making money, and they know what works, and what really doesn't. Taking a guesstimate on the success of non-premium sports rights, with that risk, will just not be in their playbook anymore.

Investors wanting to own sport for wider reasons, like Saudi Arabia, will end up in the same place tactically. They get more bang for their buck at the top end of the market, as image and soft power by definition comes from assets that really matter.

Younger generations, and the people investing in that audience, want the big names too.

All of this leads to the same final resting place. The famous stars and brands will polarise from the rest of sport, leaving the industry likely structured with a premium product, and a long tail of niche offerings.

Our industry needs to just accept that. And manage it proactively, without moaning about the past.

How this is achieved is the industry's biggest challenge, especially in Europe where there is a history and tradition of fluid social mobility and meritocracy, that will always reject this type of approach. Something like this isn't in the *"spirit of the game"*. But sometimes you have to kill your darlings, amputate a leg, in order to survive. I believe we all need to get our heads around this.

The sacred cow of promotion and relegation, the poster child of this debate, needs a serious discussion.

American sports, and others with closed leagues and talent rebalancing, have a far greater chance of holding their product together in the face of all this polarisation and financial arbitrage. But even they are not entirely safe, as the PGA/LIV saga demonstrated. So, open, European leagues, with relegation and promotion have, in my opinion, absolutely no chance of resisting the inevitable market forces.

The evidence is already clear. Even without the recent flows of money from Wall Street and the Gulf, the experience of the EPL is more than enough evidence. They broke away as a structure 30 years ago, and their success since then has generated a virtuous circle of global media money attracting better talent, improving quality, attracting more media and so on. They have fully polarised from the rest of English football (the EFL) and indeed the rest of European football; and this is absolutely the source of the Super League attempts from Real Madrid, Barcelona and Juventus. These great clubs have no option to just accept marginalisation and lack of competitiveness with lesser brands like Chelsea and even Brighton. They owe it to their fans to find a solution.

Polarisation has already mortally wounded the torso of European football, and it is bleeding out. The petrodollars from Saudi Arabia will do the rest in short order.

The status quo is not an option, and European football is at risk of imploding, and ceding its 150-year hegemony to the Middle East or America.

The opportunity is for sport to clear its head and not fight this; but set itself out to be successful all across the spectrum, by segmenting and defining its product/market fit. The derby between the football clubs of Sheffield doesn't need to take place on the global stage of the EPL to have meaning and value. It just needs to know its audience really well, and market to them successfully. That is a niche business, but there's nothing wrong with niche if you're honest that's what it is. If the globalisation of the 90s, that coincided with the professionalisation of the sport business, is on the wane, and we are reverting back to local and national economies, is this not an opportunity for a humbler and more sustainable version of sport?

Just as there is a growing and profitable business in niche cinemas showing arthouse movies to a well-defined audience, surely that is a possible vision for sport? A similar example, in a resurgence of vinyl records, also points to an optimistic vision for *"niche"*.

Relegated sports teams don't lose all their fans. Often being in a lower division has no real effect on the vast majority of community sports clubs. Sometimes it even increases attendance.

Perhaps the health and sustainability of our industry does not depend on always having to aspire to be getting promoted or winning. The appeal is perhaps in something bigger than that. In fact, there is now a whole market segment of football fans who are aggressively rejecting the success derived from what they call the *"financial doping"* at, say, Manchester City. They consider it inauthentic, and not *"proper"*, driving them back with passion into their communities and local teams.

There is significant evidence of people turning away from this top end of the game, creating an audience for a purer, more simple version of sport. This is an opportunity for our industry.

The top end of sport, the Hollywood product of mass global appeal, just needs to be well-defined, as does what is absolutely not in this category. The painful civil war in golf has made all this very clear. The Majors are different and will always be a separate sporting and entertainment product.

Whilst this is easily identifiable in individual sports like tennis and golf, it is less apparent in teams sports like football, cricket and rugby. International team sports, which are unfamiliar to American fans and investors, is a conundrum that needs to be solved. As this is what funds and permits the old, bloated governance and antiquated leadership.

Elite test match cricket, touring rugby teams like the British Lions, and of course international football, struggle for space in the sporting calendar, fighting for player availability in club-versus-country jealousies. The root problem is financial, and not sporting: who is paying for the players and who gets to make the money from them?

International governing bodies, if they still need to exist, have to end their mindset around it being their right to use the athlete employees of clubs, at will. Calendars need to be negotiated, certainly with full windows for the classic events, but with the cost of the players allocated fairly and intelligently, also with the athletes themselves.

International sport needs to start paying its way or die. Once it is structured like this, fairly, so many of the excesses and largesse of places like FIFA will dissipate.

A major opportunity, for sport, although difficult and complex, is to sit down and work out a model to define, structure, and protect the blue-ribbon premium product of each sport, to allocate costs and revenues correctly.

One could suggest that the answer to all this is in *"less is more"*. Sadly, the reason for expanding World Cups and European championship is not commercial or sporting. The chance of these extra smaller teams actually being a valuable protagonist in the competitive event is more than two standard deviations away from likely. It is all political; a vote winner tool at the FIFA conference.

Fresh strategic marketing thinking is needed. We are currently going in the wrong direction with over-supply.

For example: the Football World Cup is dominated by a dozen consistently elite teams. Which luckily match up quite well with the major commercial media markets. They should be the seeds who are always participating. A short and sharp tournament of 16 teams (adding 4 earned wildcard places) is arguably the correct product/market fit. There is no real reason to be taking time with Northern Ireland versus Kosovo. It is merely *"filler"*. Qualifying rounds to be one of the four is an interesting product, but it's very niche, and very local. Manage it as such.

Premium sport, if defined correctly, will be a stable and immensely valuable product. It remains the only place to generate live audiences of scale, and it has a major opportunity to also negotiate better terms with broadcasters around data, storytelling, user experience, personalisation and distribution, as well as adopting classic audience crossover tactics to grow their sport. There are many major music and movie stars, for example, who are avid table tennis players, or golfers. Premium sport is only limited by its ambition, its vision and its skills to capture as much of the value chain as it can.

The remaining long tail of sport, like any niche business, needs to have a Business Plan if it wants to attract capital and survive. The major block to this is the dependency culture of so many of these sports, utterly addicted to hand-outs and subsidies from the bundle.

The IOC is the worst possible solution for sports who need to live more than once every 4 years. Being drip-fed a bit of money won't save them, but it's enough to stop them actually going and making an independent plan with strategic marketing.

Niche sport in fact isn't going to be easy; but it has many more advantages as a product than most think. And, there is generational change in the wind that could fill their sails. Gen Z and Alpha have no knowledge of, and don't care about, the IOC and all those quangos. They are either sucked in by the product, or they aren't. My own daughter, aged 19, has been drawn into the influencer world of the Paul brothers and celebrity boxing. She drinks Prime. Women's football has not touched the sides of her interest. This is the opposite of what we would expect. She came to sport through cross-over from influencers.

These new generations are not easy, but this is an opportunity. There are not easy for any marketeer, not just sport, and the prize of that TAM is actually unprotected, in the open. Up for grabs. Note how many celebrities have developed new alcohol brands, all taking significant market share.

Specifically for Gen Z, where the ongoing appeal of traditional sport is most under threat, the opportunity is to treat the offering, premium and niche, as a distinct product with completely different brand values. Bring in the people and techniques that know and operate with this demographic. Embrace the worlds of influencers, Web3, blockchain, gaming and new products without regret or embarrassment. Work out, as in any FMCG business, what newer customers are prepared to pay for and why. Try and capture for sport a part of their very significant expenditure on virtual goods

and digital props, in gaming and metaverses.

• • •

Less is More.

Sport's product/market fit today is losing focus simply through careless oversupply of product. There are too many games and events offered, to try and generate more revenues for all the various governing bodies and stakeholders. What is not apparent is that the average value of each of those games is often dropping, through excess supply. The principle of scarcity in business, and life, tells us that people and customers want more and more of what is rare. It is no coincidence that the NFL is so successful. Their actual events are very limited in number, and they keep attention in the sport high with ancillary interest from the transfer market, the combine and the draft.

Value goes up significantly with rarity, and this is an opportunity for sport, especially in an era where every top athlete on the planet is complaining about overplaying. If this is not proactively managed in time, the toy will break.

• • •

There are 8 billion people on this planet; most of them feel the same way about our circuses as we do. And yet today the industry seriously addresses only a fraction of them, servicing a demographic of those who are now 50-year-old men, mainly in the USA and Europe.

Women have been largely ignored, and the populous Asian market has been seen as relatively marginal and too poor, financially, to move the needle.

A projection of demographic trends tells us that this will not be the case in 20 years time.

"I skate to where the puck is going to be, not where it has been."
Wayne Gretzky

American sports, like baseball, who actually call the local tournament, the World Series, need to drop old and insular thinking. No other FMCG business thinks like this. Apple doesn't think like this. Neither does Spotify.

Once again, tragically, the major block to this vision of a global market is in sport's governance. That is organised around impregnable geographical borders and is how the analogue world thinks.

Capturing the full potential of sport's universal global appeal, its demography, its immense TAM, has enormous upside for sports.

• • •

KYC, know your customer. You can't do segmented strategic marketing without data, and deep knowledge, on who consumes your product.

One of the most comical characteristics of the sports industry in the last 15 years has been watching incumbent advertising and promotion agencies in sport denying the benefits of serious investment into knowing and understanding the fan. Laughably, people who know only about media values and brand awareness told the industry that rich data did not matter. Thanks to them, sport missed what every other consumer industry has been doing for two generations: customer relationship management (CRM), and targeted data-led marketing.

The industry however now has a big opportunity to skip a technology cycle and fully embrace the possibilities of data, through AI.

AI, linked to quantum computing, will devastate every industry, at the same time empowering those that use it to do amazing things around efficient personalisation of product and delivery.

If B2C and segmentation does become a central plank of how the sports industry organises itself, AI gives the skilled user a superpower in delivering the right content to the right person, on the right channel, at the right time.

It also promises massive financial opportunity in cost savings around content creation, around commercial processes like ticketing and merchandising, around talent recruitment and retention (both on and off the field).

Once, the production of sports content was a top-down, one-way, lean-back offering. But we have seen on social media the power of user-generated content. AI will turbo-charge all of this. If sports fandom used to be directly related to actually playing the sport as children; today the same correlation applies to content creation. If they are creating memes, they are likely to be long-term fans.

The two biggest sports in the world, the NFL and the EPL, owe a great deal of their current appeal to fantasy sports. People actively involved in researching and choosing their teams, watching the games and then trash-talking their friends when their players have been benched or blank.

Understanding the dynamics of fantasy is the fast-track to success in finding a sustainable model for sports. The two main protagonists FanDuel and Draft Kings, in this way, were perfectly positioned to take advantage of one of this industry's biggest opportunities.

• • •

Fantasy leads to betting. Whether we like it or not and whether moral or not, the world loves a bet and sports fans really love a bet.

Two significant opportunities for the business of sport arise out of new ways of dealing with the bookmaking industry. The first one is the opening up of a very large new betting market in the USA, state-by-state. Secondly, to date, sport has taken the money from betting under the old guise of risk-less money up front. The odd affiliate deal, selling media exposure through players' jerseys, stadium billboards and game data. The fans of sport are much more valuable than that, and bookmakers know this, even if sport hasn't seemed too bothered to care.

The betting industry has 2 two key metrics. The lifetime losses of the punter (LTV), and the cost of acquiring (CoCA) that customer.

Sport has sold its fans to bookmakers way too cheaply for CoCA.

It has also sold its game data, to the likes of Genius Sports and Sportradar, to create betting events, for too little.

There is nothing to stop sports brands vertically integrating and capturing more of the betting value chain for themselves. British football owns all its game data via a company called Football Dataco. This company could sell directly to bookmakers, and capture the margin currently taken by the intermediaries.

The best leaders in sport will recognise that the whole area of data ownership is going to get very complex and will manage the change before the courts force it upon them, as happened with NCAA athletes.

• • •

Take the intermediary's margin.

"I put two children through Harvard by trading options. Unfortunately, they were my broker's children"

Jason Zweig, Wall street journal columnist

The intermediary in sport doesn't just apply to the betting sector. Sport has loved the luxury of not having to work too hard to commercialise its value, and the sector is awash with all kinds of brokers, agencies, in rights, sponsorship, licensing, data. They all take a juicy margin that exits the ecosystem.

Vertical integration is a major opportunity for sport. Many of the PE investments in sports leagues have identified that this intermediary margin is there for the taking, if sports can vertically integrate better.

Good CEOs will look at their businesses and one of the first things they will do is assess what real added-value is being offered by broking intermediaries to justify their cut.

• • •

Reducing *"leakage".*

A couple of years ago, at a sport's conference in New York, I nearly fell off my seat listening to senior media executives, one from ESPN, refer to the losses from piracy, as inconsequential *"leakage"*. If ESPN had been an independent listed company, I would have shorted the stock, for this appalling complacency alone. My regret from not extrapolating that trading impulse into their parent company, Disney, burns to this day. Their stock has lost 50% of its value since that conference.

The threat of piracy to sport has been clear to all for at least a handful of years. It's been a clear and present danger. And yet it seems still to be underestimated risk in the C-Suite of sport. The fans and consumers have known how to pirate very well for a good while. Watching this play out in sport, exactly like some kind of Groundhog Day from what I saw in music 20 years ago, is chilling. The same complacency abounds.

If piracy is costing the content industries $28bn a year, it doesn't take much improvement on this metric to represent a major financial win and opportunity for sport.

History shows that trying to combat piracy through the courts, with legal deterrents, doesn't work. It is a silly whack-a-mole strategy that failed the music industry completely. And yet this is what sport is doing. It seems to think that it can stop it by convicting the odd small fish in the distribution chain. That didn't, and doesn't work, anywhere. The organised crime of the illegal drug industry surely tells us this?

The opportunity lies in changing the product.

A simple video feed will always be prey to the pirates, and those lost revenues will change the attitudes of broadcasters, especially in a bear market. This ultimately will kill sport's business model, be in no doubt. The problem and threat is much bigger that our industry appreciates. It's existential.

What is much harder to pirate is a platform of integrated activity; where the video feed itself is merely the sun, around which the planets of *"doing not viewing"* spin.

Planets of e-commerce, watch parties, betting, fantasy, social feeds and memes, digital goods purchases, all offered with micro-payments.

For the last 15 years, our industry has talked endlessly about 2nd, 3rd, and 4th screen consumption of sport.

The opportunity lies is going back to one integrated screen.

This type of platform cannot be pirated so easily, if at all.

• • •

Know how to be attractive to the guy with the money.

Sport has no right to think it is owed an existence, it needs to earn a living. And show it generates a financial yield or return.

It needs to convince providers of capital of this, be they Big Media or Big Finance, by knowing how they think, what they are looking for, to set out their stall to make a match.

This is what every start-up in the world does to attract capital. It's what independent music does, what arthouse movies do, what games publishers do. It's what every bigger company does with its bankers, and or Wall Street earnings-calls.

People often say I'm a Cassandra, wailing about the imminent doom facing sports. And it's true that I am pessimistic about the financial and fan sustainability of traditional set-ups. But I'm also excited because sport is evergreen. It can't be boxed in by committees, quangos, lawmakers and monarchs.

Sport is central to the human experience: it's about play, about leaving behind the grime of the daily toil. People will always be drawn to it: participating, supporting, investing, inventing.

Games never stand still. Football became rugby, which became rugby football and rugby league. Rounders bled into baseball. Tennis and squash became padel.

The evolution of sport is constant and, for those who are hard-headed and realistic, there will always be an opportunity to get in at the ground floor, to invest early and become, perhaps, the majority shareholder of a whole new ball game. Opportunities in sport for investors will be plentiful. Everywhere.

This bubble in sports valuations will burst and, as usual, over-correct in the other direction. Assets will be arguably a cheap bargain.

There will be a cemetery of good sportech companies, with established clients and traction, that will have been mothballed as the capital dries up. Knowing where those companies are, how to assess them, how to strategically integrate them, is going to be a once-in-a-generation opportunity for excellent return on VC equity capital. Build-and-buy roll-up plays across various themes and visions for product/market mix. Every investor should allocate a part of their portfolio to a vulture sports fund.

I also believe lending to the asset-rich industry of sport for yield is always going to be a smart play. Providing debt capital, with the strongest covenants, high interest coverage ratios and early preferences on liquidation. This is true for a $1bn and $10k investment: it's a low risk, relatively low return. But if you understand credit control and risk, you could be content with a 10% yield on lending to the sports industry. Doubly so in a bear market.

"if you are living in a no-growth economy, and somebody can give you 12, 13% with almost no prospect of loss, that's about the best thing you can do"
Steve Schwarzman, Blackstone founder & chairman.

Operators will need many of the corporate finance techniques explained in this book; from managing working capital and cash prudently, finding the right investors, with the optimal and affordable levels of debt leverage. They will need to identify and price the levels of risk correctly and convince people that the return of any project or investment will more than compensate them. If sport does this correctly, there will be more than enough eager capital ready to buy a vision, of different niche product, brands, IP and income statements.

A clear recommendation for the industry of sport is to drop the entitlement and expectation that broadcasters will always bid for their tender, and bid higher. That

new kids will always like what they have to offer the way my generation did, almost by default. Once you drop this lazy complacency, sport can start to sweat all those great strengths and assets for a sustainable future. What an opportunity.

This is all about mindset and the search of excellence, even internally. The bull market is over, and we all in this industry need to raise our game.

• • •

The Perfect Storm is coming.

This world of ours in some ways reminds me of the calm in the Magnificent Seven, as Chris and his men are preparing the villagers for the inevitable attack. Nervous smiles hiding real panic, philosophical conversations about meaning and destiny. How is everyone going to react when it hits?

Hilario: *"Did you have any luck?"*
Chris Adams: *"Found a man who would have been perfect. With gun or knife, couldn't ask for any better. But he wouldn't do it."*
Hilario: *"The money, it was not enough?"*
Chris: *"He doesn't give a hoot about money."*
Hilario: *"A man in this line of work who doesn't care about money?"*
Chris: *"Men in this line of work are not all alike. Some care about nothing but money. Others, for reasons of their own, enjoy only the danger."*
Vin: *"And the competition."*
Miguel: *"If he is the best with a gun and a knife, with whom does he compete?"*
Chris: *"Himself."*

All you can do, is compete with yourself to get better. Focus on quality in everything.

There will be opportunities in this sector everywhere, but things will need to change. Not everyone will get to a lifeboat.

This Fourth Turning of Sport will be a moment of generational opportunity.

EPILOGUE

When Roger asked me to write an epilogue for Sport's Perfect Storm, I was delighted and honoured to accept. Now, as I sit here trying to craft something of substance, something that Roger's work deserves, the task feels monumental.

Over the years of our friendship, Roger's prescience with regards to the direction of travel for sport is matched only by his unflinching willingness to speak truth to power.

As you've seen in the pages and chapters that precede my own meagre contribution to this extraordinary piece of work, those instincts remain razor-sharp and the delivery of his conclusions, straight-forward and clear.

Sport faces an existential threat, one whose genesis you have now seen clearly and beautifully articulated: the rising cost of capital and the deleterious effect that phenomenon has on the industry's inordinate debt-load, the constraints that the rising cost of capital places on the companies and, at some point, on the nations bankrolling sport, the plight of the media sector in the age of cord-cutting, the chaos and confusion present among sponsors, the ineptitude and hubris of governing bodies and the completely unsustainable wages paid to players and agents across the sporting universe.

But sport is and always has been about the fan and it is here, in my humble opinion, that the true existential nature of the threat facing sport is revealed.

"Sport matters, and always has."

These five simple words, from the opening chapter of this book, form the very foundation of the arguments presented thereafter.

But why does sport matter?

Many would say it doesn't, and they'd be absolutely correct. In the grander scheme of things, sport doesn't matter.

At the end of a game, a match, a round, a cup final or an entire season, the players remove their caps, exchange shirts, shake hands, exit the arena and are gone, leaving behind them thousands of fans in attendance, and millions watching around the world, to deal with the aftermath of the result.

In dressing rooms or hotel rooms, athletes pick apart their performances collectively, placing blame and praise where warranted, each dealing with very personal success and failure away from the spotlight, before moving on to the next game.

Meanwhile, in living rooms, pubs and in the streets, fans celebrate or mourn en masse, in public and in ways which, to anyone who wouldn't describe themselves as a sports fan, make no logical sense.

But to the sports fan?

To the sports fan, the glory, the agony, the pain and the elation are all so very real. The adrenaline rush of seeing your team score a winning goal in what has become known, officially, as 'time added on for stoppages,' mirrors that of the deflation suffered by the opposition fans. The supporters of one team go to work the next morning feeling on top of the world while those of the other wake to face a day of recrimination and introspection. The winners take as much pleasure from the misery suffered by the losers as they do their own victory.

It was ever thus.

And yet none of it matters.

Not really.

At the end of a relegation season, the emotions felt by the fans of a football club anywhere in the world are almost identical: the team should be dismantled, the manager sacked, the chairman kicked out, and the board strung up outside the stadium.

Barely a few months later, as the start of a new season approaches, those same fans, are filled with fevered excitement at the prospect of once again returning to the stadium to watch that same team, *"their"* team, take them on another emotional journey filled with highs and lows, joy and pain.

Such is the nature of being a fan. Victory and defeat. Feast and famine. The margins between the two are razor thin and the fluctuations constant.

But they are hard-wired.

Once you fall in love with a game or a team or, as Roger so astutely points out, in recent years, a player, that's it. There's no way out - or rather there hasn't been until now.

Technology has now upended every aspect of what was, until quite recently, the recognizable fan experience, rendering the watching of teams competing in the stadium, or on TV, obsolete.

In recent years, a new generation of sports fans has dictated how the industry should deliver its product to them.

TV coverage is becoming ever-more multi-faceted, with various options for fans as to how to enjoy the experience of watching a game: want to watch the whole game? Easy. Want to follow your favourite star player? We have a dedicated camera for that. Want to watch any game where something exciting is happening? Allow me to introduce NFL Red Zone.

There are completely new formats of established games, designed to appeal to the far shorter attention spans of a younger audience (T20).

Sport has been forced to adapt and, in most cases, has seemed to do so successfully, with a series of ever-escalating TV deals being struck, which offered the illusion that, underneath, all was well, and the growth of sports as an asset class would continue both predictably and indefinitely.

Not so.

As Roger points out in parts two and three of this remarkable book, the world of finance has changed dramatically and that change threatens to drown the sports industry as the tsunami pictured on the cover of Sport's Perfect Storm approaches - relentless, constantly swelling and threatening greater destruction with every 0.25% increase in interest rates by central banks.

In my native habitat of finance, there are many stupendously wise and acutely insightful practitioners who have lived and invested through the cycle and understand what happens next. One of them, the brilliant Howard Marks of Oaktree Capital, recently offered an explanation for the problems facing not just the world of sport, but the world that extends far beyond, so succinct and to the point that Roger himself would no doubt be impressed:

"Largely, thanks to highly accommodative monetary policy, we went through unusually easy times in a number of important regards over a prolonged period, but that time is over."

That's it, in a nutshell.

The environment to which all of us, and particularly those immersed in the world of sport, have become accustomed has ended and the world we face is very different in nature.

Roger has provided a comprehensive explanation of how we got here, the problems inherent in the status quo and a practical and realistic set of solutions.

Read chapters twenty-two and twenty-three again. Then read them again. They summarize perfectly where we are and what must be done to try solve the problems faced by the sporting industry. None of it will be easy, but resistance is futile.

We now have to face the world as it is, not the world as we wish it to be.

Debts will be defaulted upon, clubs with great pedigree and tradition will likely fold, media coverage will shrink, revenues likewise, and the fan experience will be simplified because none of what's been built is affordable in this new world.

Rising interest rates focus the corporate mind like nothing else. The return of the Bond Vigilantes, to a world which thought them extinct, means the rolling over of the hundreds of billions of dollars in corporate debt will be fraught with peril, and teams, leagues and, in fact, entire sports (whose inability to generate positive returns were masked by the availability of essentially free capital) will be forced to adapt or die.

The wounded, as Roger has so presciently suggested, will be bayoneted.

The silver lining, however, lies where it always did - with the fan.

Sport is going to have to adapt, once again, to the fan, but not necessarily with new formats or snazzy gimmicks, but with a far more practical approach - one that takes into account the effect that the change in monetary policy has on those who ultimately bankroll every major sports franchise on the planet.

The key will be to find a way to provide an equally compelling product, built on lower revenues, to a customer who has less disposable income.

But that 'customer' isn't just a "customer."

That customer is a fan, and that is the best chance sport has to survive the Perfect Storm described by Roger.

The hardcore sports fan, the fan for whom the game and their team have real meaning, will be there - rain or shine, victory or defeat - but can the same be said for the casual sports fan, the fan who has been attracted to a particular sport by the glitz and glamour that easy money provides in abundance, by celebrities and "unmissable" events, hyped relentlessly on social media?

This battle for the soul of sport will require a series of incredibly important decisions, as its leaders grapple with the gulf that lies between two generations of *"customers."*

The older generation of die-hard fans, whose love of their game and their team grew from seeds sown in far simpler times, in far more fertile soil, and when the competition for their attention was minimal, but who will, sadly, soon no longer be around to walk through the turnstiles or subscribe to cable TV, are *"stickier"* but dwindling.

The younger audience are far more peripatetic in their viewing habits and allegiances - a phenomenon which makes long-term decision-making impractical if not impossible.

I personally suspect the answer lies in catering to the archetypal, die-hard fan of a sport in the belief (or perhaps hope) that the younger generation, as they age and inevitably find the demands placed upon on their time by a deluge of content, too much, will settle into a love of something real, and that changing the game to suit the needs and tastes of this particular generation, at this particular time in their lives to be flawed.

I fear the time spent adjusting the game to the fan base - Roger's ubiquitous product/ market fit - may prove to ultimately present larger challenges than the solutions it offers. (though, over the course of our many conversations, Roger disagrees and, if I've learned anything during the course of my magical journey holding onto his coattails on the Are You Not Entertained? podcast, it's that he, rather than I, is far more consistently right about… well, all of it).

The speed with which the audience turned on the celebrity boxing phenomenon of the early 2020s was shocking to behold. One moment the sparring celebrities were the focal point of the sporting hype machine, a money-making juggernaut and touted as the future of the sport and suddenly, without warning, the critics' eyes turned away from the carefully-managed *"spectacle"* of these events and decided to focus on the substance instead. As soon as they did, they found there was nothing of any *"value"* there.

Nothing real.

Nothing with which true fans of sport could connect. Just influencers and *"personalities"* who, whilst they brought audiences numbering in the millions, brought no new, lasting fan base, only those for whom celebrity boxing was just another car crash at the side of the road - one they couldn't help but stare at as they drove by, but which quickly faded from their collective memories once the initial jolt of adrenaline wore off a mile or two down the road. Similarly, shiny documentary features created by various streaming services to pull non-sports fans into the gravity of a series of global sporting icons were, after a brief period of generally positive media coverage, roundly criticized.

The reason for both is identical: a lack of authenticity.

When the business cycle turns, *"real"* once again matters and, beneath all the show, the fireworks, the flames, the billion-dollar contracts and the (until now) seemingly bottomless well of money, lies the reality of the fan experience.

It's a deeply-felt connection to meaning, to substance, uniting cities, countries and families in an irrational love of something that, ultimately, doesn't matter at all.

Except it does. It really does.

GRANT WILLIAMS
Lake Como. September 2023

Made in the USA
Columbia, SC
03 October 2024

61022665-3ff7-4ecc-bd71-b2cf73d494c0R01